Who is the Adventist Jesus?

Elmer Wiebe

Copyright © 2006 by Elmer Wiebe

Who Is the Adventist Jesus?
By Elmer Wiebe

Printed in the United States of America.

ISBN 1-59781-328-1

All rights reserved solely by the author. No part of this book may be reproduced in any form without the permission of the author. The views expressed in this book are not necessarily those of the publisher.

Unless otherwise specified, the biblical references will be taken from the New King James Version (NKJV), © 1982 by Thomas Nelson, Inc.

www.xulonpress.com

FOREWORD
by Rev. Verle Streifling, Ph.D.

When one studies different religious sects that stress some unique doctrines as restored biblical truths, further investigation often reveals they also hold some unorthodox views on the person of our Saviour Jesus Christ. Yet they will often use the same words and terms as the orthodox church, albeit with their redefinitions of these carefully concealed in their literature.

Having been raised in Adventism, who now hold the deity of Christ and the Trinity in their statement of faith, I was most unsuspecting of any aberrations in our views of Christ, for the near thirty years I was with them. Only after Dr. Walter Rea spoke at the Adventist Forum in San Diego in 1982, did I first hear that some of the pioneers had been Arian, and only by 1896 Professor W. W. Prescott actually identified Jesus as the "I AM" of Exodus.

This alarmed me as I had studied the Arian views of the Jehovah's Witnesses for several years, and became well established on the deity of Christ and the Trinity, that SDA now held. But the nagging question Dr. Rea left us was in essence: "How could any deny Jesus' deity, when we as Adventists had been blessed with God's messenger, our prophet Ellen White, who was so decisive in settling the other doctrines our church held?" She had written 25,000,000 words on so many issues—even the most minor points; so wouldn't God have shown her, in at least one of her 2,000 visions, *the correct views of Jesus Christ?* Dr. Rea opened my eyes to the discovery of much ambiguity in some of White's writing about Jesus. She held both Arian views and His deity, yet called Him the Archangel Michael. While our church covered this adequately for a layman, yet deeper study showed their position superficial.

Then too, I found ambiguity concerning Jesus' human nature, for in her writings we read Jesus had a fallen sinful human nature, like Adam's after Adam fell, yet other places said he had a sinless nature as Adam before the fall. Both views were held at the same time, stating that without them we have no saviour.

I didn't have time to fully research these issues, but as I was no longer SDA, I addressed the Bible's view, leaving off a thorough analysis of their earlier years. But in AD 2000, a fellow Christian apologist, Elmer Wiebe, caught the ball with enthusiasm, having the time to carry out this necessary work.

He had invited me to speak at his counter-cult convention, where he too became alarmed on learning that early SDA didn't hold Jesus' deity and the Trinity as was so commonly understood. Prophet White had claimed a vision that all the prayers, professions, and exhortations of the churches were an abomination to God, bringing these orthodox beliefs into disrepute among early Adventists.

A *Christian News* article about the convention spawned a flurry of letters to the editor denying that SDA and Ellen held such views as had been quoted. Elmer and this writer got challenges by their pastors defending the very views that their laymen denied in the paper. At the same time there were strong encouragements from former Adventists who rejoiced that these false views were exposed. This added fuel to the fire that such an exposé of these hidden SDA views must be completed and made available to the church.

Elmer worked on this exposé for over four years, finding much duplicity in present Adventist views, and far more detail regarding their earlier official Arian positions. He has virtually left no stone unturned in his research, showing that even Adventist publications which admit some pioneers had these views, are entirely inadequate, trying to keep Prophet White free from these taints, when in fact they all had their hands in the cookie jar.

Without knowing this historical context in SDA fundamental beliefs, it is impossible to understand their aberrant doctrinal views today and where they are heading. They are now returning to their Arian roots to uphold Ellen White's teachings and what was taught by their leaders for the first seventy years. This return is being facilitated by their Clear Word Bible, with scores of additions, deletions, and changes to hold and infuse Prophet White's views into the text, instead of what the Bible said for 2,000 years.

This makes Elmer's book a *must read* for any being affected by Adventist outreach today, as well as those teaching or studying comparative religions. In the light of other Arian or anti-trinitarian sects that have grown out of Adventism over the past 160 years, no Christian apologist would want to put this book back on the shelf, but would rather commend it to any and all other Christian ministers, for the sake of the body of Christ.

To that end, this writer strongly implores the reader to become very well versed in this area, and in defence of Christ's true deity, as well as His sinless and unfallen humanity. Realize the *implications that these aberrant Adventist views* of Christ have: how they affect the gospel of Christ, the plan of salvation—even our assurance of salvation by His finished work for us. *The ramifications* of these views are horrendous, so we must alert the church at all costs.

ABOUT THE AUTHOR

Having been raised in a nominal so-called Christian home where we attended church regularly, I witnessed firsthand the bondage of religiosity without the power of Jesus Christ. I was twenty-six when I confessed Jesus Christ as my Lord and my God. As a young Christian, I had my first encounter with two Jehovah's Witnesses knocking at my door. As the late Dr. Walter Martin used to say, a Jehovah's Witness can turn the average Christian into a pretzel in less than thirty seconds. Being frustrated by my inability to provide sufficient evidence for my dearly held faith in Jesus Christ, God used this situation as a springboard to get me into the study of Christian apologetics. After years of dealing with people of various religious persuasions, I founded CULTure Shock Solution Ministries in 1999. Our mission and purpose is to equip Christians to more effectively communicate the gospel of the real Jesus Christ to those caught in the cults and to aid those who come out with a support system. I've completed a number of recognized trades as well as training in various educational fields such as electronics, computer troubleshooting, and of course, my passion, the Bible. I'm a researcher of all religions. Investigate our website and freely download files to equip yourself at http://www.CULTureShockSolution.org. I am presently pursuing a doctorate in apologetics and comparative religions. I have a wife, Janis, and two sons, Micah and Jared, who are a tremendous support in my calling from God. Our family's home is on beautiful Vancouver Island.

DEDICATED TO

This book is dedicated to those in evangelical circles who love the Holy Scriptures above the traditions of men. They may have had red flags about the teachings of Seventh-day Adventism and its possible incompatibility with historical Christianity. This book is also dedicated to those in the Seventh-day Adventist Church who have doubts and areas of concern with its teachings, but can't put their finger on it. This book is not a casual read, but rather a reference book with official quotes for the purposes of studying the chronological changes made within Seventh-day Adventism concerning the person of Jesus Christ. In all these changes, they never removed the idea that Jesus Christ is some type of an archangel.

This is not an attack on those who are Seventh-day Adventists; but rather, an examination of what the Seventh-day Adventist Church has taught from its inception to the present day. This book is designed for those who desire to seriously delve into the most critical difference between these two faiths. While the Seventh-day Adventist Church is considered to be just another denomination in most evangelical circles, this subject of the identity of Jesus Christ must be examined with intense scrutiny as the most critical matter of any religious faith. We'll examine both sides of the issue and how each respective group has addressed it. Jesus Christ is the author and head of the true Christian Church. Let's investigate!

I express my deep gratitude to my friend, Reverend Verle Streifling Ph.D., a former Seventh-day Adventist, for his tremendous support through numerous means to help me make this research a success.

I also express my sincere appreciation for a dear Christian sister, a former Seventh-day Adventist who desires to stay anonymous, for the numerous boxes of Seventh-day Adventist literature that she forwarded to me. It immensely helped me with this critical research.

TABLE OF CONTENTS

Foreword v
About the Author ix
Dedicated to xi

1) Introduction 21
2) Analysis of the Arian and Semi-Arian Heresies 27
    Arianism 27
    Semi-Arianism 32

3) The Nature of the Seventh-day Adventist's Christ in
    Question 35
        The Nature of Christ 35
        In the 19th Century 36
        Prescott's Sermons 40
        First Half of the 20th Century 44
        The Change in Bible Readings 48
        The Evangelical Conferences 50
        The Ministry Magazine Articles 54
        Questions on Doctrine 56
        Froom's Movement of Destiny 59
        Johnsson and the Review 62
        The 1983 Gulley Quarterly and Book 62

The Book, Seventh-day Adventists Believe...........64
The Critical Question..65
The Book, Issues..71
   a. SDA's Jesus' Fallen, Sinful Human
      Nature...76

4) Early Adventists As Arians................................83
   a. Concerning the Trinity 83
      William Miller 84
      Joseph Bates 84
      James White..86
      J. M. Stephenson..89
      D. W. Hull...90
      Uriah Smith 94
      Smith's Views of Christ.................................98
      J. N. Loughborough 103
      E. Goodrich...107
      S. B. Whitney..107
      D. M. Canwright...109
      Canwright's 1867 Article.............................110
      Canwright's 1878 Articles 110
      A. J. Dennis 112
      J. M. Hopkins 112
      J. E. Swift 113
      G. C. Tenney...113
      J. H. Waggoner 115
      G. W. Morse..118
      C. P. Bollman..119
      The 1889 Yearbook.......................................119
      E. J. Waggoner 120
      D. T. Bordeau..122
      T. R. Williamson 122
      Samuel T. Spears 123
      A. T. Jones 125
      M. C. Wilcox 127

```
A. T. Robinson ..................................... 127
J. S. Washburn ..................................... 128
Opposes Prescott's Sermon .................. 128
His View of Christ ............................... 128
He Contradicts Himself ....................... 129
R. F. Cottrell ........................................ 130
J. B. Frisbie ......................................... 133
A Questionable Conclusion ................. 133
Ellen G. White ..................................... 136
Austin P. Cooke ................................... 137
V. R. Christensen ................................ 138
Summary .............................................. 139
```

b. Concerning the Father 162
   James White 162
   J. N. Andrews 162
   D. M. Canwright 163
   A. T. Jones 166
   E. J. Waggoner 166

c. Concerning the Son 167
   James White 167
   J. N. Andrews 168
   C. W. Stone 169
   E. J. Waggoner 169
   W. W. Prescott 171
   A. T. Jones 171
   J. N. Stephenson 172
   R. F. Cottrell 178
   John Matteson 178
   Uriah Smith 178
   Joseph Bates 180
   D. W. Hull 180
   G. W. Amadon 181
   Ellen G. White 183

WHO Is The Adventist Jesus?

  d. Concerning the Holy Spirit 186
    J. N. Loughborough 186
    W. C. Wilcox..186
    E. J. Waggoner...189
    A. J. Morton..189
    Uriah Smith 190
    J. H. Waggoner 191
    James White..192
    The Holy Spirit Is the Breath of God 193
    The Holy Spirit Is the Life of Christ 193

  e. Ellen G. White's Arian Views 196

  f. Moving to the Deity of Christ and the Supposed Trinity..197

  g. The Questions on Doctrine Denial..................199

  h. The Present Position 201

5) Ellen G. White's Aberrant Views of Jesus and God ...209
  a. Jesus, as an Angel..217
  b. Arian and Semi-Arian Views of Jesus.............218
    Seventh-day Adventist Anti-Trinitarians 218
  c. Jesus' Sinful Fallen Human Nature..................221
  d. Who Is in the Fullness of Deity Bodily?..........222
    Was the Father Also Human? 222
  e. Are Ellen G. White and the Seventh-day-Adventists Guilty of the Heresy of Tritheism......224
    J. H. Waggoner 226

6) Is Jesus Michael the Archangel as the SDA Teach? ...231
  Dense Fog Covering the "Light" 231

7) Did Jesus Have a Sinful Fallen Human Nature?	245
Why Contradictory SDA Views?	249
8) Will the Real Jesus Please Stand Up?	253
Who Is Standing When?	255
9) Finally Brethren	257
Appendix	275
1) Jesus Christ as God in the Bible	277
O Theos—"God" by Identity	277
Theos—God by Nature	278
Equal with God	278
Creator	278
First and Last	278
Saviour and Redeemer	278
I AM (Absolutes—Ego Eimi Without Substantives)	279
I AM (Emphatic—Ego Eimi Without Substantives)	279
Stone of Stumbling	279
The King	279
Almighty God	279
Mighty God (El Gibbor)	279
Ha Adon (The Lord, for Lord Of Lords)	279
The Rock	279
Lord of Hosts	281
Shepherd	281
Beginning and Ending	281
Lives Forever	281
Kurios (Lord)	281
Our Strength	282
Always Present	282
The One Pierced	282

Rewarder 282
Judge 282
Light of Life 283
Coming with Saints 283
Believed in for Salvation 283
Sustains the Universe 283
Hope for Mankind 283
Founder of Universe 283
The Same Forever 284
Forgiver of Sins 284
Holy One 284
Light of the World 284
Lord of Glory 284
Our Hiding Place 285
Gives Living Water 285
Worshipped by Angels 285
Gives Sight 285
Coming with Rewards 285
His Witnesses 285
At God's Right Hand 286
Declares End from Beginning 286
O ZWN (The Living Being) 286
Lord over Sabbath 286

2) Jesus Christ Biblically Shown as God by Nature 287

3) The Person and Deity of the Holy Spirit 291

4) Biblical Evidence for the Triune (Trinity) God 303
    Only God 303
    The Father 303
    The Son 304
    The Holy Spirit 304
    Omnipresent 304
    Omniscient 304

      Omnipotent 305
      Eternal 305
      Creative 305
      Immutable 305

5) The Biblical View of Man's Nature 307
      Mind 309
      Will 309
      Emotions 309
      Communicates 310
      Shape Or Form 310
      Outward man—Inward Man 313
      Physical Life—Physical Death 313
      Answers to Antitheses 314

6) Conclusion 317

Index 319

1

INTRODUCTION

For decades, there has been a cloud of confusion as to the relationship that the Seventh-day Adventist Church has with the historical Christian church. Seventh-day Adventism is primarily based on the teachings of Ellen G. White. They are a religion that is works-righteousness orientated with strict dietary laws. There are two primary wings to this religion. The liberal wing claims that the Bible is fallible with contradictions and errors. They have an Open Theistic view of God who doesn't know the future and is mutable. The conservative wing clings to the original writings of Ellen G. White. Collectively, they are a 'lifestyle religion' of vegetarianism. Some see the Seventh-day Adventist Church as just another denomination of the many denominational Christian churches—with a few peculiar differences. Others consider the Seventh-day Adventist Church a cult. This was certainly the case until the mid-1950's when Drs. Walter Martin and Donald Barnhouse met with the Seventh-day Adventist Church General Conference leaders; in the process they removed the label of "cult" from the Seventh-day Adventist

Church on behalf of the evangelical community. While some agreed with the Martin and Barnhouse findings, others felt these two men had been deceived by the leaders of Seventh-day Adventist Church. With the label of a cult removed, the Seventh-day Adventist Church has flourished and made many inroads into the evangelical Christian community. The question that any religious organization has to answer—whether Seventh-day Adventist or any other religious affiliation—is with regard to the true identity of Jesus Christ. This is the true test of whether a group is a cult or not. Every cult distorts the true identity of Jesus Christ and makes Him someone other than who He truly is. As we'll see, Jesus probed His disciples with this question and He has continued to do this through the ages until the present day through the Holy Scriptures that reveal His true identity.

The disciples of Jesus were asked a pivotal question by Jesus: "Who do you say I am?" Why would Jesus ask such a question? What is its significance? There were many views of who Jesus Christ was in New Testament times, but there was only one correct answer. This same issue is true in today's religious world. No matter what religious persuasion a person comes from, one must answer the question of who is Jesus Christ. Was He a mere man, an archangel, or some other form of being? Was He God Almighty in the flesh? Can they all be right or does His identity play any role in whether we have a false or true salvation? Matthew warns us:

> Matthew 24:24: "For false Christs and false prophets will arise and will show great signs and wonders, so as to mislead, if possible, even the elect."

Mark elaborates on this warning:

> Mark 13:21-23: "And then if anyone says to you, 'Behold, here is the Christ'; or, 'Behold, He is

there!'; do not believe him; for false Christs and false prophets will arise, and will show signs and wonders, in order, if possible, to lead the elect astray. But take heed; behold, I have told you everything in advance."

As the above passages indicate, there will be false Christs who will try to imitate the genuine Jesus Christ. There was only one Jesus Christ who died on the cross of Calvary to pay for the sins of mankind by the shedding of His blood. The false Christs, outside of Christianity, never shed a drop of blood for anyone in their religious group, thus giving the group a false sense of security. Christianity is based on the person and ministry of the true Jesus Christ. People can have many different views of your identity, but that doesn't make them true: there is only one of you. The same principle applies to the identity of Jesus Christ. There is only one true Jesus Christ. All other imitations are false.

With all these differing views, what would we consider as an authoritative source to establish Jesus Christ's true identity once and for all? Most people would point to the Bible, the Holy Scriptures of God. Consider Christ's question, "Who do you say I am?" using the Holy Scriptures as our frame of reference.

> Matthew 16:13-17: Now when Jesus came into the district of Caesarea Philippi, He began asking His disciples, saying, "Who do people say that the Son of Man is?" And they said, "Some say John the Baptist; and others, Elijah; but still others, Jeremiah, or one of the prophets." He said to them, "But who do you say that I am?" And Simon Peter answered and said, "Thou art the Christ, the Son of the living God." And Jesus answered and said to him, "Blessed are

you, Simon Barjona, because flesh and blood did not reveal this to you, but My Father who is in heaven."

Mark 8:27-29: And Jesus went out, along with His disciples, to the villages of Caesarea Philippi; and on the way He questioned His disciples, saying to them, "Who do people say that I am?" And they told Him, saying, "John the Baptist; and others say Elijah; but others, one of the prophets." And He continued by questioning them, "But who do you say that I am?" Peter answered and said to Him, "Thou art the Christ."

Luke 9:18-20: And it came about that while He was praying alone, the disciples were with Him, and He questioned them, saying, "Who do the multitudes say that I am?" And they answered and said, "John the Baptist, and others say Elijah; but others, that one of the prophets of old has risen again." And He said to them, "But who do you say that I am?" And Peter answered and said, "The Christ of God."

When we consider these words, Jesus is identified as "the Christ." To get the intended definition of the writer, one must go to the original Greek. In reference to *Strong's Exhaustive Concordance* #5547 in the Greek, *Christ* means "*Christos* (khris-tos); from 5548: anointed, i.e. the Messiah, an epithet of Jesus."

John 8:24: "I said therefore to you, that you shall die in your sins; for *unless you believe that I am He, you shall die in your sins.*"

As we explore different references, let us keep the question of who we believe Jesus Christ really is at the forefront of our minds. His identity is essential because if we have a false view of who Jesus Christ is, we will die in our sins regardless of our spiritual experience with a false jesus. Is our idea of Jesus based on faith or presumption? True faith is based on established facts; whereas, all presumptions are based on subjective experiences that can only give individuals a faulty security. All tenets of belief must be vigorously investigated so one is fully convinced by overwhelming evidence for those beliefs. Please see the *Appendix* on the biblical doctrines of our triune God along with expositions on the Father, Son, and Holy Spirit. In the next chapter, we will investigate the origins of the teachings that Seventh-day Adventists hold if they are a member of that church.

2

ANALYSIS OF THE ARIAN AND SEMI-ARIAN HERESIES

Where did the various altered views of Jesus Christ originate that we commonly see amongst Seventh-day Adventists, Jehovah's Witnesses, Christadelpians and others like them? Arianism is a fourth century heresy which denied the divinity of Jesus Christ. It defined God as being not only uncreated but also unbegotten, hence only the Father is truly God, because the Scriptures say Jesus is begotten of the Father. The Son is considered divine only by grace or adoption, but is really only a human being, though admittedly the most perfect human being. He had a beginning; its founder, Arius, was fond of saying, "There was a time when he was not."

ARIANISM

The doctrine of the Arians, or Eusebians, Aëtians, Eunomians, as they were called after their later leaders, or

Exukontians, Heteroousiasts, and Anomoeans, as they were named from their characteristic terms, is in substance as follows:

The Father alone is God; therefore He alone is unbegotten, eternal, wise, good, and unchangeable, and is separated by an infinite chasm from the world. He cannot create the world directly, but only through an agent, the Logos. The Son of God is pre-existent, [1] before all creatures, and above all creatures, a middle being between God and the world, the creator of the world, the perfect image of the Father, and the executor of His thoughts, and thus capable of being called in a metaphorical sense God, and Logos, and Wisdom. [2] But on the other hand, He Himself is a creature, that is to say, the first creation of God, through whom the Father called other creatures into existence; he was created out of nothing [3] (not out of the essence of God) by the will of the Father before all conceivable time; He is therefore not eternal, but had a beginning, and there was a time when He was not. [4]

Arianism rises far above Ebionism, Socinianism, deism, and rationalism, in maintaining the personal pre-existence of the Son before all worlds, which were His creation; but it agrees with those systems in lowering the Son to the sphere of the created, which of course includes the idea of temporalness and finiteness. It at first ascribed to Him the predicate of unchangeableness also, [5] but afterwards subjected Him to the vicissitudes of a created being. [6] This contradiction, however, is solved, if need be, by the distinction between moral and physical unchangeableness; the Son is in His nature (φυϖσει) changeable, but remains good (καλοϖϖ) by a free act of His will. Arius, after having once robbed the Son of divine essence, [7] could not consistently allow Him any divine attribute in the strict sense of the word; he limited His duration, His power, and His knowledge, and expressly asserted that the Son does not perfectly know the Father, and therefore cannot perfectly reveal Him. The Son is essentially distinct from the Father, [8] and—as Aëtius and Eunomius afterward more strongly expressed it—unlike the Father; [9] and this dissimilarity was by some extended to all moral and metaphysical attributes and conditions. [10] The dogma of the essential deity of Christ seemed to Arius to lead of necessity to Sabellianism or to the Gnostic dreams of emanation. As to the humanity of Christ, Arius ascribed to Him only a human body, but not a rational soul, and on this point Apollinarius came to the same conclusion, though from orthodox premises, and with the intention of saving the unity of the divine personality of Christ.

The later development of Arianism brought out nothing really new, but rather revealed many inconsistencies and contradictions. Thus, for example, Eunomius, to whom clearness was the measure of truth, maintained that revelation has made everything clear, and man can perfectly know God; while Arius denied even to the Son the perfect knowledge of God or of Himself. The negative and rationalistic element came forth in ever greater prominence, and the controversy became a metaphysical war, destitute of all deep religious spirit.

The eighteen formulas of faith which Arianism and semi-Arianism produced between the councils of Nicea and Constantinople are leaves without blossoms; branches without fruit. The natural course of the Arian heresy is downward, through the stage of Socinianism, into the rationalism which sees in Christ a mere man, the chief of His kind.

Arguments used for and against this error

a. The Arians drew their exegetical proofs from the passages of Scripture which seem to place Christ in any way in the category of that which is created, [11] or ascribe to the incarnate (not the pre-temporal, divine) Logos growth, lack of knowledge, weariness, sorrow, and other changing human affections and states of mind, [12] or teach a subordination of the Son to the Father. [13] Athanasius disposes of these arguments somewhat too easily, by referring the passages exclusively to the human side of the person of Jesus. When, for example, the Lord says He knows not the day nor hour of the judgment, this is due only to His human nature. For how should the Lord of heaven and earth, who made days and hours, not know them! He accuses the Arians of the Jewish conceit, that divine and human are incompatible. The Jews say how could Christ, if He were God, become man and die on the cross? The Arians say how can Christ, who was man, be at the same time God? We, says Athanasius, are Christians; we do not stone Christ when He asserts His eternal Godhead, nor are we offended in Him when He speaks to us in the language of human poverty. But it is the peculiar doctrine of Holy Scripture to declare everywhere a double thing of Christ: that He, as Logos and image of the Father, was ever truly divine, and that He afterwards became man for our salvation. When Athanasius cannot refer such terms as *made*, *created*, or *became* to the human nature, he takes them figuratively for *testified*, *constituted*, or *demonstrated*. [14]

As positive exegetical proofs against Arianism, Athanasius cites almost all the familiar proof-texts which ascribe to Christ divine names, divine attributes, divine works, and divine dignity, and which it is unnecessary here to mention in detail.

Of course his exegesis, as well as that of the fathers in general, when viewed from the level of the modern grammatical, historical, and critical method, contains a great deal of allegorizing caprice and fancy and sophistical subtlety. But it is in general far more profound and true than the heretical.

b. The theological arguments for Arianism were predominantly negative and rationalizing. The amount of them is that the opposite view is unreasonable, is irreconcilable with strict monotheism and the dignity of God, and leads to Sabellian or Gnostic errors. It is true, Marcellus of Ancyra, one of the most zealous advocates of the Nicene homoousianism, fell into the Sabellian denial of the tri-personality, [15] but most of the Nicene fathers steered with unerring tact between the Scylla of Sabellianism, and the Charybdis of Tritheism.

Athanasius met the theological objections of the Arians with overwhelming dialectical skill, and exposed the internal contradictions and philosophical absurdities of their positions. *Arianism teaches two gods, an uncreated and a created, a supreme and a secondary god,* and thus far relapses into *heathen polytheism. It holds Christ to be a mere creature,* and yet the creator of the world; as if a creature could be the source of life, the origin and the end of all creatures! It ascribes to Christ a pre-mundane existence, but denies Him eternity, while yet time belongs to the idea of the world, and is created only therewith, [16] so that before the world there was nothing but eternity. It supposes a time before the creation of the pre-existent Christ; thus involving God Himself in the notion of time; which contradicts the absolute being of God. It asserts the unchangeableness of God, but denies, with the eternal generation of the Son, also the eternal Fatherhood; thus assuming after all a very essential change in God. [17] Athanasius charges the Arians with dualism and heathenism, and accuses them of destroying the whole doctrine of salvation. For if the Son is a creature, man remains still separated, as before, from God; no creature can redeem other creatures, and unite them with God. If Christ is not divine, much less can we be partakers of the divine nature and children of God. [18]

SEMI-ARIANISM

The *semi-Arians*, [19] or, as they are called, the Homoiousiasts, [20] wavered in theory and conduct between the Nicene orthodoxy and the Arian heresy. Their doctrine makes the impression, not of an internal reconciliation of opposites which in fact were irreconcilable, but of diplomatic evasion, temporizing compromise, flat, half and half *juste milieu*. They had a strong footing in the subordination of most of the ante-Nicene fathers; but now the time for clear and definite decision had come.

Their doctrine is contained in the confession which was proposed to the council of Nicaea by Eusebius of Caesarea, but rejected, and in the symbols of the councils of Antioch and Sirmium from 340 to 360. Theologically, they were best represented first by Eusebius of Caesarea, who adhered more closely to his admired Origen, and later by Cyril of Jerusalem, who approached nearer the orthodoxy of the Nicene party.

The signal term of semi-Arianism is homoi-ousion, in distinction from homo-ousion and hetero-ousion. The system teaches that Christ is not a creature, but co-eternal with the Father, though *not of the same, but only of like essence*, and subordinate to him. It agrees with the Nicene Creed in asserting the eternal generation of the Son, and in denying that He was a created being; while, with Arianism, it denies the identity of essence. Hence, it satisfied neither of the opposite parties, and was charged by both with logical incoherence. Athanasius and his friends held, against the semi-Arians that like attributes and relations might be spoken of but not like essences or substances; these are either identical or different. It may be said of one man that he is like another, not in respect of substance, but in respect of his exterior and form. If the Son, as the semi-Arians admit, is of the essence of the Father, He must be also of the same essence. The Arians argued: There is no middle being between created and uncreated being; if God the Father alone is uncreated, everything out of Him, including the Son, is created, and consequently of different essence, and unlike Him.

But Arianism survived for a long time, no small thanks to having a strong foothold within the new kingdoms of the Germanic tribes. It made a resurgence through the Seventh-day Adventists, Jehovah's Witnesses, Christadelpians and the Worldwide Church of God (Armstrongism) which still remains today with the exception of the repentance of the Worldwide Church of God who accepted the historical view of Jesus Christ's deity. With this as our heretical backdrop, let us proceed and evaluate our modern-day heretical religious movements for what they really are.

3

THE NATURE OF THE SEVENTH-DAY ADVENTIST'S CHRIST IN QUESTION

THE NATURE OF CHRIST

Why it is important to examine it and how do we explain it to others?

We have learned that the human nature of Christ is an important truth. We will conclude with a brief overview of the history of the doctrinal change. It was only a few decades ago that the Seventh-day Adventist Church was teaching an error on this point; but now, for the most part, the truth is being taught about Christ's sinless nature.

From its earliest days, the Seventh-day Adventist Church has taught that when God partook of humanity, He took, not the perfect, sinless nature of man before the fall, but the fallen, sinful, offending, weakened, and degenerated nature of man after the fall of Adam. The inclinations and tendencies to sin that are in fallen man's flesh were in His flesh; but that, by complete dependence upon His Father, His mind held its integrity and never, not even by a shadow of a thought, responded to the weakness or sinful cravings of the flesh.

While it was considered that this view of Christ's human nature in no way denied or contradicted the SDA stand on the complete deity and absolute sinlessness of Jesus Christ, the very opposite was true. Can we have a sinful and a fallen God? How could He atone for our sins when He had the same sinful nature as us? As late as 1949, this was accepted SDA teaching as presented in denominationally published lesson quarterlies, books, and periodicals. But, during the fifteen-year period between 1940 and 1955, the words *sinful* and *fallen*, with reference to Christ's human nature, were largely eliminated from denominationally published materials. Since 1952, phrases such as *sinless human nature*, *nature of Adam before the fall* and *human nature defiled* have taken the place of the former terminology. These phrases are interpreted to mean that the human nature of Christ was *sinful*, *fallen*, or *degenerated*, only in the sense of weakness and frailty of the physical organism. It is said that these weaknesses and frailties of the physical organism were not innately and intrinsically a part of Christ's human body but were borne vicariously.

Let us now consider, in more detail, the history of the changeover in the doctrine of the human nature of Christ from being a fallen, sinful being to a righteous, unfallen being in the Seventh-day Adventist Church. This is a critical transformation.

IN THE NINETEENTH CENTURY

This great heresy about the human nature of Christ was shared by the pioneer writers in the Advent movement. Here are a few examples, penned by some of the leading men in the Seventh-day Adventist Church:

[Jesus] was made in all things like unto those whom He came to save. In all points He was made like His brethren. And what the Law could not do, Christ came in the likeness of sinful flesh to do. By His life He has shown that sin in the flesh is condemned, and He has destroyed it, for in Him the body of sin is destroyed. He has taken away this sinful nature—taken it upon Himself that we might be delivered from it.[1]

The garment was woven in Jesus, in the same flesh that you and I have, for He took part of the same flesh and blood that we have. In my flesh; it was my flesh that He had; it was your flesh that He had. The Lord Jesus Christ, who came and stood where I stand, in the flesh in which I live,[2] Christ came the first time, clothed with humanity, taking not upon Himself the nature of angels, but the seed of Abraham, that He might be made like ourselves, subject to temptation, pain, and death, that by His connection with humanity He might sympathize with His fallen creatures.[3]

Very few of us realize how nearly the Divine nature approached the human in the person of Jesus of Nazareth. More properly speaking it is impossible for us even to conceive of the infinite condescension that was necessary in order that the Son of God, the associate of the Father, should appear in mortal flesh and participate in human experiences, with all their trials and weaknesses. But "He was tempted in all points like as we are": consequently He must have partaken of our nature. Should any think that this expression is too strong, let them read verse 16 of Hebrews 2: "For verily He took not on Him the nature of angels; but He took on Him the seed of Abraham." His faultless life under those circumstances becomes a constant reprover of our sins as well as an encouragement to our weakness.[4]

By partaking of our nature, His human arm encircles the fallen race.[5]

He took upon Him sinful flesh to suffer and die for guilty man.[6]

But if He [Christ] comes no nearer to us than in sinless nature, that is a long way off. It is true He is holy; He is altogether holy. But His holiness is not that kind that makes Him afraid to be in company with people who are not holy, for fear He will get His holiness spoiled.[7]

The second Adam came not at the point where the first Adam stood when he failed but at the point at which mankind stood at the end of four thousand years of degeneracy.[8]

So you see that what the Scripture states very plainly is that Jesus Christ had exactly the same flesh that we bear flesh of sin, flesh in which we sin; flesh, however, in which He did not sin. But He bore our sins in that flesh of sin. And what flesh could He take but the flesh of the time? Not only that but it was the very flesh He designed to take; because you see, the problem was to help man out of the difficulty into which he had fallen, and man is a free moral agent. He must be helped as a free moral agent. Christ's work must be, not to destroy him, not to create a new race, but ... to recreate man, to restore him in the image of God.[9]

In the section, just below, we will quote more extensively from that sermon by W. W. Prescott, a prominent historical Adventist.

> He did not come to this world and take upon Himself Adam's condition, but He stepped down lower, to meet man as he is, weakened by sin, polluted in his own iniquity.[10]

> Infinitely superior in every respect to Boaz, yet He stooped to marry the lost race.[11]

> [Waggoner:] We begin with the ninth verse: "We see Jesus." Where are we looking?
> [Voice:] To man in his fallen state.
> [Waggoner:] Yes, our gaze is directed to man's first dominion; as we look, we see him fail, and still looking, we see Jesus taking man's fallen condition.[12]

> He brought divinity from the courts of glory into fallen humanity.[13]

> And that this is likeness to man as He is in His flesh, sinful nature, and not as He was in His original [heavenly] sinless nature, is made certain by the Word: "We see Jesus who was made a little lower than the angels, for the suffering of death." Therefore, as man is since he became subject to death; this is what we see Jesus to be, in His place, as man.[14]

> Moreover, the fact that Christ took upon Himself the flesh, *not of a sinless being,* but of sinful man; that is, the flesh which He assumed and all the weaknesses and sinful tendencies to which fallen nature

is subject, is shown by the statement that He "was made of the seed of David according to the flesh."[15]

Many, many more examples could be cited!

PRESCOTT'S SERMON

On Sunday evening, October 31, 1895, W. W. Prescott preached a powerful sermon on the nature of Christ at the Armadale camp meeting, in Victoria, Australia. It contained twenty-five statements, that Christ took our nature in His birth and life on this planet. Twice in that sermon, Prescott stated that Christ did not take the unfallen nature of Adam.

Ellen White was present and heard that sermon; and, in eight manuscripts and letters, soon after expressed grateful appreciation for that lecture (manuscripts 19, 23, 47 and 52, 1895; and letter 25, 32, 83, and 84, 1895). It was only a couple months later that she wrote that letter to W. L. H. Baker, which we will discuss shortly, reproving him for teaching that Christ had sinned.

Prescott's sermon was printed in the January 6 and 13, 1896, issues of the Bible Echo (SDA's Australian journal). Here are portions of that History of the Change Over sermon. You will see why she valued it so highly:

> The theme of redemption will be the science and the song of the eternal ages, and well may it occupy our minds during our short stay here. There is no portion of this great theme that makes such a demand on our minds in order to appreciate it in any degree as the subject we shall study tonight. The Word became flesh and dwelt among us. Through Him all things became; now He Himself became. He, who had all glory with the Father, now lays aside His glory and becomes flesh. He *lays aside His divine mode of*

existence, and takes the human mode of existence, and God becomes manifest in the flesh. This truth is the very foundation of all truth. Let us consider, first, what kind of flesh, for this is the very foundation of this question as it relates to us personally (Hebrews 2:14-18, quoted).

Ellen G. White states that Jesus Christ laid aside His divine mode of existence and took on the human mode of existence. This suggestion of switching modes is an error. Jesus Christ never ceased being God when He took on human nature at the incarnation. To remove the deity of Jesus implies that He is not eternal and thus not God to begin with. This points to another jesus mentioned in 2 Corinthians 11:4, who is a false Christ.

By suggesting that Jesus had a sinful and fallen nature nullifies the purpose and significance of His virgin birth. The virgin birth made a provision for Jesus to be humanly born without the Adamic nature of sin.

> He came and took the flesh of sin that this family had brought upon itself by sin, and wrought out salvation for them, condemning sin in the flesh. To redeem man from the place into which he had fallen, Jesus Christ comes, and takes the very flesh now borne by humanity; He comes in sinful flesh, and takes the case where Adam tried it and failed.

> Christ came and after a forty days fast the devil tempted Him to use His divine power to feed Himself. And notice, it was in sinful flesh that He was tempted, not the flesh in which Adam fell. This is wondrous truth, but I am wondrously glad that it is so. It follows at once that by birth by being born into the same family, Jesus Christ is my brother in

the flesh "for which cause He is not ashamed to call them brethren" (Hebrews 2:11). He has come into the family, identified Himself with the family, is both father of the family and brother of the family. As father of the family, He stands for the family. He came to redeem the family, condemning sin in the flesh, uniting divinity with flesh of sin. "For there is one God, and one mediator between God and men, the man Christ Jesus" (1 Timothy 2:5). There is a man in heaven now, the man Christ Jesus, bearing our human nature; but it is no longer a flesh of sin; it is glorified. Having come here and lived in a flesh of sin, He died; and in that He died, He died unto sin; and in that He lives, He lives unto God. When He died, He freed Himself from the flesh of sin, and He was raised glorified. Jesus Christ, our own brother, the man Christ Jesus, is in heaven, living to make intercession for us. This union of the divine and the human has brought Jesus Christ very near to us. There is not one too low down for Christ to be there with him. He identified Himself completely with this human family. One version reads, "Inasmuch as ye have done it unto one of the least of these My little brothers, ye have done it unto Me." Christ looks upon every one of the human family as His. When humanity suffers, He suffers. He is humanity; He has joined Himself to this family.

Jesus Christ thus united Himself with the human family that He might be with us by being in us, just as God was with Him by being in Him. The very purpose of His work was that He might be in us, and that, as He represented the Father, so the children, the Father, and the Elder Brother might be united in Him. "Lo, I am with you always, even unto the end of the world" (Matthews 28:20). By being in us, He is with us always and that this might be possible, that He might be in us, He came and took our flesh. This also is the way in which the holiness of Jesus works. He had a holiness that enabled Him to come and dwell in sinful flesh, and help sinful flesh by His presence in it; and that is what He did, so that when He was raised from the dead, He was glorified. His purpose was that having purified sinful flesh by His indwelling presence, He might now come and purify sinful flesh in us, and glorify us. He "shall change our vile body, that it may be fashioned like unto His glorious body according to the working whereby He is able even to subdue all things unto Himself" (Philippians 3:21).

Let us enter into the experience that God has given Jesus Christ to us to dwell in our sinful flesh, to work out in our sinful flesh what He worked out when He was here. He came and lived here that we might through Him reflect the image of God. This is the very heart of Christianity.

By following where He leads, we shall know what Christian experience is, and what it is to dwell in the light of His presence. I tell you, this is a wondrous truth. Human language cannot put more into human thought or language than is said in these words: "The Word became flesh, and dwelt among us." This is our salvation. Nothing short of it will meet what we have to meet the world, the flesh and the devil. But He that is for us is mightier than he that is against us. Let us have in our daily lives Jesus Christ, "the Word" that "became flesh." [16]

Therefore, just as certainly as we see Jesus lower than the angels, unto the suffering of death, so certainly it is by this demonstration that, as man, Jesus took the nature of man as he is since death entered: and not the nature of man as he was before He became subject to death.[17]

E. J. Waggoner wrote,

> Here is the same mystery as that the Son of God should die. The spotless Lamb of God, who knew no sin, was made to be sin. Sinless, yet not only counted as a sinner, but actually taking upon Himself sinful nature.[18]

> When sin entered, death came; so when man sinned, death came upon him. God stayed with him; therefore, in that He stayed with man. although man had sinned, God took upon Himself sinful flesh. And so He took upon Himself death, for death had passed upon all the world (General Conference Bulletin; *Studies in the Book of Hebrews*).[19]

> Christ taking fallen sinful humanity upon Him is Christ crucified...[20]

> The fact that He came in fallen humanity is an evidence of God's presence and His presence to give life.[21]

FIRST HALF OF THE TWENTIETH CENTURY

Throughout the first half of the twentieth century, SDA speakers and writers continued to teach the falsehood about the human nature of Christ.

Over a period of years this view of Christ's human nature continued to reach the majority of church members through the medium of the Sabbath School Lesson Quarterlies. Sample quotations are given below.

> Many hold that from the nature of Christ it was impossible for Satan's temptations to weaken or overthrow Him. Then Christ could not have been placed in Adam's position, to go over the ground where Adam stumbled and fell; He could not have gained the victory that Adam failed to gain. If man has in any sense a more trying conflict to endure than had Christ, then Christ is not able to succor him when tempted. Christ took humanity with all its liabilities. He took the nature of man, capable of yielding to temptation; and with the same aid that man may obtain, He withstood the temptations of Satan and conquered the same as we may conquer. He assumed human nature, being the infirmities and degeneracy of the race. It is not true that humanity has trials to bear which the Son of God has not experienced."[22]

> Jesus was *God acting in sinful flesh* on behalf of the sinner. He made Himself one with humanity.[23]

> By assuming sinful flesh, and voluntarily making Himself dependent upon His Father to keep Him from sin while He was in the world, Jesus not only set the example for all Christians, but also made it possible for Him to minister for sinful flesh the gift of His own Spirit and the power for obedience to the will of God.[24]

> That Son took the flesh of sinful man, and overcame where man failed, overthrew sin in the flesh.²⁵
>
> Christ assumed not the original unfallen, but our fallen humanity. In this second experiment, He stood not precisely where Adam before Him had, but as has already been said, with intense odds against Him.²⁶
>
> As the Son of man, He accepted the limitations and conditions of our common humanity.²⁷
>
> Christ took upon Himself the infirmities and sins of the flesh but to every sin He died, every lust He crucified, every selfish desire He denied Himself and all for our sakes.²⁸

In 1924, Southern Publishing Assocation published a book by the SDA evangelist Carlyle B. Haynes, in which (pages 80, 83) he unequivocally states that as a people, Adventists believe and teach that *Christ took sinful fallen flesh.* He points out that there really was *no need for Christ to come at all unless He was to take such flesh.*

Through the efforts of colporteur evangelists, this Seventh-day Adventist teaching regarding Christ's human nature entered thousands of non-Adventist homes tucked between the covers of Bible readings for the Home Circle. This 1942 book, under the heading, *A Sinless Life*, contained the following note: "In His humanity Christ partook of our sinful, fallen nature. If not then He was not 'made like unto His brethren' was not 'in all points tempted like as we are' did not overcome as we have to overcome, *and is not, therefore, the complete and perfect Savior man needs and must have to be saved.* On His human side from His very conception

He was begotten and born of the Spirit" (p.174, emphasis added).

How can we ever get to the point to suggest that our Savior wasn't the complete and perfect Savior for our salvation? Who then can save us?

It was apparently with a similar view of Christ's sinful flesh but sinless life that L. A. Wilcox wrote in the *Signs of the Times* in 1927:

> He came where I was, He stood in my place. In His veins was the incubus of a tainted heredity like a caged lion ever seeking to break forth and destroy. For four thousand years the race had been deteriorating in physical strength, in mental power, and in moral worth: and Christ took upon Him the infirmities of humanity at its worst.[29]

> In every temptation that assails, it is strength to know that just such a temptation in all its overwhelming force attacked Him in unexpected times and ways; and that, with equal tendencies toward evil, in spite of bad blood and inherited meanness, by the same power to which I have access, He conquered.[30]

Seventh-day Adventists teach that, like all mankind, Christ was born with a sinful nature.

> This plainly indicates *"that His heart, too, was 'deceitful above all things and desperately wicked.'"* In harmony with this, they also teach "that *Christ might have failed while on His mission to earth as man's Savior* that He came

> into the world *at the risk of failure and eternal loss*," But the Bible repeatedly states that Christ was holy, that "He knew no sin," and that He would "not fail nor be discouraged..."[31]

> In part the author replied that the "distinguishing mark of fallen mankind (that is, a deceitful heart or mind) is not necessarily involved in the possession of a human nature that is capable of sin"[32]

He cites as an example, Adam, who as a human being was capable of sin but who did not sin until he exercised his will in the wrong direction:

> In other words, Adventists believe that Christ, the "last Adam," possessed on His human side, a nature like that of the "first man Adam," a nature free from every defiling taint of sin, but capable of responding to sin, and that nature was handicapped by the debilitating effects of four thousand years of sin's in-roads on man's body and nervous system and environment...[33]

In 1950, Southern Publishing Association printed the book, *Drama of the Ages*. Authored by the General Conference President William Branson, this book was distributed and sold all over the English-speaking world. On page 70 of this missionary book, Branson wrote that Christ "had taken upon Himself the nature of fallen man."

THE CHANGE IN BIBLE READINGS

On the next two pages of *Drama of the Ages*, (pages 68-69; in printed book only), documentary reprints of four pages from Bible readings for the Home Circle will be found. A brief overview of the printing history of that book: in 1888 the first edition of *Bible Readings* came off the Review presses. Those who have read John Martin's book, *Editions of Great Controversy*, will know that the Review managers pushed that book ahead of the 1888 edition of *Great Controversy* because the several authors of *Bible Readings* relinquished royalty payments, whereas Ellen White refused to do so. She had been instructed that she should receive that money so it could be used to help Adventist work in various areas where needed. For this reason, the 1888 edition of *Great Controversy* did not come off the presses at the Review until 1889 and at Pacific Press until 1890. (See John Martin's book, *Editions of Great Controversy* for the full story of the history of that most important book in all its editions.)

On page 174 of the 1915 edition of *Bible Readings*, a note was added to the chapter "A Sinless Life" which clearly stated that Christ took our nature. But in the late 1940s, the decision was made to revise *Bible Readings*. On pages 143-144 of the 1949 edition, that note was changed to downplay the idea that Christ took our nature. It questioned "how far that 'likeness' [to sinful flesh] goes."

In this new edition, the statement which had circulated with the book for thirty years was omitted because "it was recognized as being out of harmony with our true position" (Roy A. Anderson, "Human—Not Carnal"; *The Ministry*, September 14, 1956). It was replaced by the following statement: "Jesus Christ is both Son of God and Son of man. As a member of the human family "it behoved Him to be made like unto His brethren' in the likeness of sinful flesh." Just how far that 'likeness' goes is a mystery of the incarnation which men have never been able to solve.[34]

In that same September 1956, *Ministry* magazine article, Anderson discussed the revision in *Bible Readings*, and gave the reason why the change had been made because non-Adventists did not like it! "In fact, this particular point in Adventist theology had drawn severe censure from many outstanding Biblical scholars both inside and outside our ranks."[35]

R. A. Anderson went on to state that the idea that on His human side Christ partook of man's sinful, fallen nature was eliminated because it did not represent our "true position."[36]

Although that statement had first appeared in *Bible Readings* in 1915, we have observed that it correctly represented the SDA's "true position" held down through the years from the time of its earliest pioneers. In addition, the terms "sinful nature" and "fallen nature" were repeatedly in the writings of Ellen G. White.

THE EVANGELICAL CONFERENCES

John Martin's review of the Evangelical Conferences and their aftermath (The Beginning of the End—Part 1–18 [*Doctrinal History* 101-118]) is the most extensive analysis of the subject available anywhere. (At the present time, it is included as Section 2 in the Adventist Doctrinal History Tract Book.)

As Walter Martin and Donald Barnhouse later wrote in evangelical magazines, the conferences (many of which were held at the Seventh-day Adventist's General Conference building in Washington, D.C.) began when Dr. Walter Martin, a Baptist writer, approached SDA leaders and told them he was going to write an in-depth book exposing the doctrinal errors of the SDA denomination.

As he later wrote, they entered into a series of discussions with him that lasted two years, during which they vigorously denied that the Adventist denomination still held to earlier doctrines which the evangelicals did not like. It was obvious that the men on the other side of the table were determined to gain acceptance by Protestants!

There were eighteen conferences, lasting one to three days and usually with three sessions a day. These were held periodically in Washington, D.C., Reading, Philadelphia and New York City over a period of eighteen months.[37]

The two men in charge of what became a doctrinal sell-out were Leroy Edwin Froom and Roy Allen Anderson. Walter Martin would come to the meetings with questions to be answered; and in collaboration with Anderson, Froom would write those answers. Anderson's key work was keeping Reuben Figuhr, the general conference president, contented with the progress of the conferences.

Froom later described the first conference:

> The first conference with Walter Martin and Cannon [Dr. George Cannon. Greek professor at a college in the Hudson Valley of New York], followed by others, took place in an available office at the SDA General Conference headquarters in Takoma Park, Washington D.C. Martin came armed with a formidable list of definitely hostile and slanted questions, most of them drawn from well-known critics of Seventh-day Adventists among them the inevitable Canright, on down to the late defector...[38]

The outcome of the evangelical conferences and the book which, in agreement with Walter Martin, the *Review* published, radically altered church doctrine for all time. That book, *Seventh-day Adventists Answer Questions on Doctrine* (commonly referred to as *Questions on Doctrine*), undermined the Adventist historic teaching on the atonement, the nature of Christ, and several other points. (For an in-depth analysis of these matters, we refer you to two books, Doctrine Tract book and Doctrinal History Tract book, which contain all the relevant material.)

On a second visit [to the General Conference], he [Walter Martin] was presented with scores of pages of detailed theological answers to his questions. Immediately it was perceived that the Adventists were strenuously denying certain doctrinal positions which had been previously attributed to them. "He pointed out to them that in their bookstore adjoining the building [The ABC on Carroll Avenue] in which these meetings were taking place, a certain volume published by them and written by one of their ministers categorically stated the contrary to what they were now asserting. The leaders sent for the book, discovered that Mr. Walter Martin was correct, and immediately brought this fact to the attention of the general officers, that this situation might be remedied and such publications be corrected.

This same procedure was repeated regarding the nature of Christ while in the flesh which the majority of the denomination has always held to be sinless, holy and perfect despite the fact that certain of their writers have occasionally gotten into print with contrary views completely repugnant to the church at large. They further explained to Mr. Walter Martin that they had among their number certain members of their 'lunatic fringe' even as there are similar wild-eyed irresponsibles in every field of fundamental Christianity. This action of the Seventh-day

Adventists was indicative of similar steps that were taken subsequently."[39]

Dr. Donald Barnhouse had founded *Eternity* magazine, which had proven to be a very successful inter-denominational publishing venture. His organization had sponsored Walter Martin's talks with the Adventists. In September 1956, this (in their own words) "bombshell article" came off the presses. Unfortunately, only a few of the Adventist people ever heard about it. Both Barnhouse and Martin wrote articles in it, exposing the Adventist doctrinal sell-out, and promising that the Adventists planned to publish a book which would discuss their new doctrinal positions.

In the above-quoted statement, you will note that the SDA leaders used a confusion of terms to get their point across. They told Walter Martin that the Adventist people always believed Christ was sinless. But they said it in such a way that Walter Martin believed they said that Christ had a sinless nature. Evangelicals Martin, Barnhouse, and Cannon thought they were receiving "clear statements," but they were actually reading words designed to camouflage traditional Adventist doctrines. Walter Martin had a powerful mind, was a fast reader, had something of a photographic memory, and had scanned through many of the Seventh-day Adventists books, including those by Ellen White, but it wasn't enough to prevent the deception that Seventh-day Adventism exercised on him.

The Adventist men assured him that statements about a "sinful nature" or "fallen nature" would henceforth not be found in their new publications and this was done. In the years since the mid-1950s, "sinful nature" has seldom if ever appeared in Adventist journals and new books. At the same time, terms such as "Adam's nature" and "sinless nature" have appeared more frequently.

THE *MINISTRY* MAGAZINE ARTICLES

As head of the Ministerial Association, R. A. Anderson was editor-in-chief of *Ministry* magazine, which is published worldwide for Adventist ministers and workers. In 1956 and 1957, a series of articles, intended to soften the blow for the changeover, were released. Here are some examples:

> Christ did indeed partake of our nature, our human nature with all its physical limitations, but not of our carnal nature with all its lustful corruptions. His was not a corrupt, carnal nature. When He took upon Him sinless human nature, He did not cease to be God, for He was God manifest in the flesh![40]

> He was indeed a man, but withal He was God manifested in the flesh. True, He took our human nature, that is, our physical form, but He did not possess our sinful propensities.[41]

> When God became man He partook of the same moral nature that Adam possessed before the fall. Adam was created holy, and so was Christ, for He became the second Adam.[42]

> When the incarnate God broke into human history and became one with the race. It is our understanding that He possessed the sinlessness of the nature with which Adam was created in Eden.[43]

These quotations, illustrating a comparatively recent emphasis upon the perfection and "sinlessness" of Christ's human nature, present a striking contrast to earlier statements on this subject. For example, the Sabbath School lesson for May 17, 1913, entitled, "God Manifest in the Flesh," quoted a Roman Catholic statement; and then stated unequivocally that it was erroneous: "God the Son. By assuming this perfect human nature, which He took from the blessed virgin, was born in the flesh."[44]

> Thus by shutting Christ away from the same flesh and blood which we have (compare Hebrews 2:14), modern Babylon really denies the vital truth of Christianity, although pretending to teach it. Such is the mystery of iniquity...[45]

> By its dogma concerning the immaculate conception of the virgin Mary, the Roman Catholic Church gives to the Son of God in the incarnation a perfect human nature: and thereby separates Him from those He came to save. "This denial of the perfect union of Christ with sinful flesh opens the way for a series of subsidiary mediators whose duty it is to bring the sinner into saving touch with Christ."[46]

The belief that Christ had the "sinless" human nature of Adam before the fall rather than the "sinful" nature of fallen man is clearly expressed in an article in a *Ministry* magazine article, entitled, "The Immaculate Christ."

> Before Adam fell, he was pure and clean, without taint of sin. He possessed human nature, undefiled, as God created it. When Jesus, 'the second man: 'the last Adam' (1 Corinthians 15:45–47) came, in addition to His divine nature, He also possessed human nature, undefiled, as God originally created it.[47]

From 1955 to 1958, John Martin attended the Adventist seminary which at that time was next door to the General Conference building, where many of the evangelical conferences were held. He was beginning to hear hints of the doctrinal change over in the classes; and, outside of class, students were quietly discussing the matter. When the bombshell *Eternity* article came out, as well as the 1956 and 1957 *Ministry* magazine articles, everyone, students, and faculty were quietly sending for copies. John Martin argued many times with Edward Heppenstall in various classes over some of these changes, but to no avail.

QUESTIONS ON DOCTRINE

Leroy Edwin Froom (1890–1974) was held in the highest respect at the General Conference. As their in-house theologian and church historian, he had produced the four-volume *Faith of Our Fathers* and the two-volume *Conditionalist Faith of Our Fathers*. During and following the evangelical conferences which on the Adventist side Froom led out in, Walter Martin also viewed him with the highest respect, especially since it was obvious that Froom, the pivotal Adventist leader in the talks, went out of his way to doctor SDA teachings so they would be received by the evangelicals.

As part of the agreement, Dr. Walter Martin's forthcoming book, *The Truth about Seventh-day Adventism*, exonerating Adventists as "Christians" was to be released at the same time as a book published by the *Review*, titled *Seventh-day Adventists Answer Questions on Doctrine*. When *Questions on Doctrine* was released in 1957, Roy Anderson, who was extremely influential, arranged for thousands of free copies to be mailed to every Christian college and seminary in the world. Multiplied thousands of free copies were also mailed to various denominational headquarters, leaders, and pastors. The cost of this (*Questions on Doctrine* was a full-size, cloth-bound book) was immense. For many more details, see John Martin's documentary on the evangelical conferences, *The*

Beginning of the End, now in the SDA Doctrinal History Tract book.

> Many thousands of copies have been placed with clergymen and theology teachers not of our faith in a few instances thousands in a single conference. And they have had their wholesome effect. Its total circulation by 1970 had exceeded 138,000.[48]

In *Questions on Doctrine*, Froom (the author) very skillfully explained away the fact that Ellen White used the words "sinful," "fallen," and "deteriorated human nature" in referring to Christ: "It could hardly be construed, however, from the record of either Isaiah or Matthew, that Jesus was diseased or that He experienced frailties to which our fallen human nature is heir. But He did bear all this? Could it not be that He bore this vicariously also, just as He bore the sins of the whole world?

> These weaknesses, frailties, infirmities. Failings are things which we, with our sinful, fallen natures, have to bear. To us they are natural, inherent; but when He bore them, He took them not as something innately His but He bore them as our substitute. He bore them in His perfect, sinless nature. Again we remark, Christ bore all this vicariously, just as vicariously He bore the iniquities of us all. "It is in this sense that all should understand the writings of Ellen G. White when she refers occasionally to sinful, fallen, and deteriorated human nature.[49]

Froom puts words in the mouth of Ellen White, trying to make her say that Christ did not take our nature, but that He only took it "vicariously" as our "substitute." The dictionary defines vicarious as "experienced or enjoyed by imaginary sharing in the experience of another."

> Anyone acquainted with L. E. Froom's writings knew he was a master of vocabulary. Here is a companion statement in that book: All that Jesus took, all that He bore, whether the burden and penalty of our iniquities, or the diseases and frailties of our human nature—all was taken and borne vicariously. Just as bearing vicariously the sins of the whole world did not taint His perfect, sinless soul neither did bearing the diseases and frailties of our fallen nature taint Him in the slightest degree with the corrupting influences of sin.[50]

The following passage from the book clearly teaches the error that Christ took an immaculate nature rather than the nature you and I inherit:

> Although born in the flesh. He was nevertheless God, and was exempt from the inherited passions and pollutions that corrupt the natural descendants of Adam. He was 'without sin,' not only in His outward conduct, but in His very nature. [He was] sinless in His life and in His nature...[51]

Of course, we all believe that Christ never sinned. But, in the above passage, Froom says that Christ inherited none of the negative factors which we inherit.

From the beginning, the two books (Walter Martin's and the SDA's) were to be released simultaneously and to be sold in each other's bookstores. This did not happen. After *Questions On Doctrine* was released, extensive revisions were done on Martin's book; it was not published until three years later (1960). Because it contained so many perceived attacks on Adventists, the SDA Adventist Book Centers refused to carry it

FROOM'S MOVEMENT OF DESTINY

As Leroy Edwin Froom neared the end of his life, he wrote a book reviewing doctrinal changes in the SDA denomination. In view of the very serious changes which have occurred, the book, *Movement of Destiny*, could well have been called "Destiny of a Movement." Published in 1971 (Froom died in 1974, at 84), the book uses the same wordy style found in *Questions on Doctrine* and his *Faith of Our Fathers* books.

The first chapter of *Movement of Destiny* is remarkable in the way it hints at so much. Froom was obviously quite pleased with his central role, and wanted the reader to recognize the pivotal nature of his activities. He said he could not write the book until enough people had died off. The book culminated in a defense of the evangelical conferences, the "grand results" they produced. Froom said he was thankful that all his research *resulted in opportunities to lecture before various Protestant* and Catholic groups; so they could recognize that *Adventists were, indeed, Christians*, sharing similar beliefs.

> The church groups included Episcopalian, Presbyterian, Methodist, Baptist, Reformed, Congregationist, United Brethren, and even Pentecostal and Unitarian faiths as well as an organization of converted Roman Catholic priests.
>
> Universities such as Marburg (Germany), Rutgers (NJ) and Pittsburg (PA) extended unusual invitations, with gratifying results from the presentation opportunities, with question periods. And following

these came various dialogues with Roman Catholic student priests but groups and individual which were highly fruitful and refreshingly frank. In one instance the contact was with thirty-eight student priests in-training for the Catholic University of America, in Washington, D.C. an hour for presentation, and an hour for questions. Out of this, smaller follow-up groups of five to eight. Later, I was privileged to address a class of graduate students at the same 'Catholic' on the same theme.[52]

Elsewhere in the book, Froom says that Walter Martin initially complained about four heretical notions; and Froom set to work to clarify these:

According to Walter Martin, the four leading charges commonly brought against Adventism, dealt with in his article [in a Protestant journal], were:

(1) that the atonement of Christ was not completed upon the cross;
(2) that salvation is the result of grace plus the works of the law;
(3) that the Lord Jesus Christ was not a created being, not from all eternity;
(4) and that He partook of man's sinful fallen nature at the incarnation.[53]

It is true that most of the SDA's nineteenth century writers advocated Arianism. Yet Froom set to work to change the SDA historic beliefs on each and every one of them. He succeeded so well, that Walter Martin later wrote, in an evangelical journal, as quoted below by Froom in his book:

Since there is no conceivable doctrinal ground, in the light of verifiable evidence where the fundamental tenets of the historic Gospel are concerned for refusing that outstretched hand. I for one encourage the extension of our hand which will usher in a new era of understanding and spiritual growth among the Church which is Christ's body.[54]

Froom's book, *Movement of Destiny*, gave added respectability to the doctrinal changes in the eyes of many of the SDA's church leaders and pastors. Yet he chopped up and twisted *Spirit of Prophecy* (Ellen G. White) quotations, to support his contention that Ellen White agreed with his version of the human nature of Christ. See *Doctrinal Fraud* (FF-26 now in the SDA's Doctrinal History Tract book) for more on this. Here is a sample:

The reader has now observed that the paragraph [in *Movement of Destiny*] opens with a title line: "Took Sinless Nature of Adam before Fall." This heading is followed by nineteen statements purporting to support its conclusion. Within each statement is a tiny quotation fragment from Ellen White. But as Ellen White wrote these quotations, not a single one of them says that Christ took the nature of Adam before the fall, and some of them say exactly the opposite! Three fragments are all taken from the same paragraph in Ellen White's writings, [which] opens with the unequivocal statement that Christ took the fallen nature of man![55]

So much for the scholarship of Dr. Froom, but he was successful in deceiving Dr. Walter Martin, giving the green light to welcome Adventism into mainstream Christianity.

JOHNSSON AND THE *REVIEW*

When, in the early 1980s, William Johnsson began as editor-in-chief of the *Adventist Review*, major changeovers began to occur in the Adventist denominational paper. Among other changes, articles began appearing which recommended what would have been considered as erroneous doctrines and lowered standards by most Adventists. Photographs and drawings were printed which would never have been seen in the *Review* in earlier decades.

Among the changes which occurred were articles advocating the pre-fall nature of Christ. One example of this was an article in the June 30, 1983 issue, authored by Norman Gulley. Gulley stated that "the church has never taken a stand for or against one or the other" of the two positions on the human nature of Christ. You will recall, earlier in this present book, we quoted Morris Venden's statement in *Insight* that the fallen nature of Christ concept dovetailed with that of the idea that sin was a transgression of the law, and that we can overcome sin in our lives now. Venden said he believed sin is only a broken relationship with God. In his *Review* article, Gulley took this position, saying that the definition of sin "is not so much a breaking of the law as it is a broken relationship that leads to lawbreaking."

Thus both men switched cause and effect. The Bible says that sin is the transgression of the law (1 John 3:4). That is the cause. The Bible also says that the effect of sin is the broken relationship. "But your iniquities have separated between you and your God, and your sins have hid His face from you that He will not hear" (Isaiah 59:2).

THE 1983 GULLEY QUARTERLY AND BOOK

The *Senior Sabbath School Quarterly* for the first quarter of 1983 was entitled "Christ's All-atoning Sacrifice." The lesson help book which accompanied it bore the name, *Christ Our Substitute*. Both were written by Norman R. Gulley, a religion teacher at Southern College (now Southern University), in Collegedale, Tennessee. In an attempt to placate both sides, Gulley taught that Christ had Adam's pre-fall nature, combined with our post-fall physical infirmities.

> Christ took the spiritual nature of man before the fall, and the physical nature of man after the fall.[56]

If that is true, then He did not really take on a fallen nature. Repeatedly, the *Spirit of Prophecy* (Ellen G. White) said Christ took our nature, and that it was a fallen nature; yet, in that nature, He resisted temptation and sin. Then Gulley uses another new theology argument: If Christ had really taken our nature; He would have fallen into sin, since it is impossible for mankind to stop sinning even with God's help!

> He [Christ] had to identify Himself with us as far as His saving mission made it necessary. But He could not go beyond the requirements of His mission or He would have needed a Savior Himself, and therefore His mission would have been a failure.[57]

In support of his position, Gulley quotes a long (long!) list of pagans (Ovid, Euripides, Senaeca, Epictetus, etc.), Catholics (Augustine, Methodius, etc.), and Protestants (Hort, Moule, Barth, Barclay, Schweitzer, etc.

Then Gulley uses still another proof, that Christ could only save us by not taking our nature; he says that *Christ lived 2,000 years before our time, and human nature then would not have been adequate to save us today!* "If Jesus lived four thousand years after Adam we live two thousand years farther down the line. *Surely we have a much harder time than Jesus.*"[58]

Can you imagine such trite being printed on the presses of the *Review* and *Herald* and sold through Adventist bookstores as truth? Gulley caps his arguments by declaring that we have original sin and Christ did not! "In fact, we do not have to do anything wrong to become sinners. We are born that way. But Jesus was born sinless."[59]

THE BOOK WHICH SEVENTH-DAY ADVENTISTS BELIEVE

The book, *Questions on Doctrine* went out of print in 1980. In March 1983, Walter Martin gave a lecture at Napa, California, in which he announced that he had written letters to the Adventist leaders in Takoma Park, threatening to negatively revise his book, *The Truth about Seventh-day Adventists* if they did not reprint *Questions on Doctrine* or issue a new book to take its place, which also had the same doctrinal changes. Dr. Walter Martin was very blunt and forceful about this. John Martin reprinted sizeable portions of that lecture, and also noted:

> He [Walter Martin] said that if Seventh-day Adventists continued to believe they are the remnant church, that Christ did not have a sinless nature, and that the atonement was not finished at the cross, they will be classed with the cults. [He said] that Reuben Figuhr and the Holy Spirit had transformed the church. They will have so much to lose if they do not take the correct position, as stated in *Questions on Doctrine*.

> [He said] We must fight for our Seventh-day Adventist brethren, that the church will take the right position. *Questions on Doctrine* has been suppressed, and now voices are *teaching heresy which the church originally*

repudiated. This must be remedied. Adventism is answerable to the authority of the Word of God, not to those who would perpetuate heresy. He stated that he had submitted a list of questions to the General Conference, to be answered by the hierarchy, and not the lunatic fringe, so that he will know what information to put in his forthcoming book and tapes...[60]

THE CRITICAL QUESTION

Dr. Walter Martin asked the following critical question in the 1983 General Conference, but it was never answered:

Do you regard the interpretation of the Bible by Ellen G.White to be infallible, that is, to be the infallible rule of interpreting Scripture? For instance, if an issue comes up where you are debating something and Mrs. White speaks on it, is that the infallible voice?

This question may never be answered with a firm yes or no. To answer yes would deny the repeated statements that the Bible alone is used to derive Adventist doctrine. a no would, for many in the church, deny the special gift of prophecy that was given to God's last-day messenger, Ellen G. White, for the purpose of leading this denomination further into the light of the "present truths" revealed through her. The new annotated *Questions on Doctrine,* however, affirms that Adventism has never modified its doctrines. Indirectly, this new volume affirms Adventists' dependence upon Ellen G.White by supporting all of the church doctrines and traditional interpretations.

According to *Adventist Currents,* October 1985 in "The Travail of William Johnsson", Dr. Walter Martin strongly stated that the label "cult" may again be applied to the Seventh-day Adventist Church or perhaps the *label never should have been removed as it was becoming apparent that he may have been deceived* by a well-meaning minority of men in leadership in the 1950's. I don't quite understand how Dr. Walter Martin could have considered the concept of a well-meaning deception.

The SDA brethren at world headquarters set to work to please Martin; and, in 1988, a new Adventist doctrinal book entitled *Seventh-day Adventists Believe*, rolled off the presses. It is highly unfortunate that Adventists have had only two official doctrinal books in their history and both were written to please Walter Martin and the evangelicals! Here we see the motive of the Seventh-day Adventist leaders to pacify and become more acceptable with the evangelicals, even though their historical doctrines, including the role of Ellen G. White's continuing authoritative writings, were not compatible with historical Christianity.

Chapter 4 of *Seventh-day Adventists Believe* dealt with the human nature of Christ. A strong attempt was made to please all sides. This is understandable, since its primary author was Norman Gulley, who wrote the infamous 1983 Gulley Quarterly and in his accompanying book, *Christ Our Substitute*, he believes in a pre-fall nature of Christ:

> Jesus Christ took upon Himself our nature with all its liabilities, but He was free from hereditary corruption.[61]

> He possessed the essential characteristics of human nature...[62]

> Christ's humanity was not Adamic humanity, that is, the humanity of Adam before the fall, nor fallen humanity; that is in every respect the humanity of Adam after the fall. It was not the Adamic because it had the innocent infirmities of the fallen; it was

not the fallen, because it had never descended into moral impurity. It was, therefore, most literally our humanity, but without sin...[63]

The above statement cleverly sidesteps the key issue in the nature of Christ controversy. It does this by equating fallen nature with actual sinning. Two pages later, another clever statement is made, which says that Christ took our fallen nature, but then denies that He did:

The Bible portrays Jesus' humanity as sinless. His birth was supernatural—He was conceived by the Holy Spirit. As a newborn baby He was described as "that Holy One." He took the nature of man in its fallen state [that is, He took our fallen nature], bearing the consequences of sin, not its sinfulness [that is, He did not take our fallen nature]. He was one with the human race, except in sin.[64]

How can two diametrical opposed positions be presented within a quote and be accepted as truth? The new theology can be subtle in the extreme. They will not come out and say the truth about the human nature of Christ, but they fear to pronounce the error. They talk about the actions of Jesus as though they were the nature of Jesus. Classic cult double-talk!

In the midst of conflict of the history of Adventism, George R. Knight, an accomplished professor of history at Andrews University, the Adventist theological seminary in the United States, made several revealing statements. In his book, *Questions on Doctrine* (Adventist Classic Library, Historical and Theological Introduction to the Annotated Edition), Andrews University Press, 2003, he makes the following admissions:

Questions on Doctrine easily qualifies as the most divisive book in Seventh-day Adventist history. A book published to help bring peace between Adventism and conservative Protestantism, its release brought prolonged alienation and separation to the Adventist factions that grew around it. ... *Questions on Doctrine* has been vilified by many Adventists and has probably done more to cause theological division in the Adventist Church than any other in its more than 150-year history.[65]

Concerning Jesus' deity, the church had revised and published *22 Fundamental Beliefs of Seventh-day Adventists* in 1931, *Fundamentals* two and *Fundamentals* three included statements on the Trinity and the full deity of Christ, yet it was well into the 1940's that debates continued within the church on the deity of Christ. It wasn't until 1985 that the wording of "Holy, Holy, Holy" in the church hymnal was re-worded to include the traditional trinitarian phrase, "God in three persons, blessed Trinity," replacing the Adventist emendation "God over all Who rules eternally." In the 1941 edition of the Seventh-day Adventist Hymnal, there is only one hymn out of 703 hymns, that made reference to the Triune God. This isolated reference is found in the fifth stanza of #680 Ancient of Days. On the subject of the Seventh-day Adventist Hymnal, the 1941 edition eliminated the second stanza about "the Incarnate Word." and replaced the beginning of the fourth stanza with "Thou are the Mighty One." These are the following changes made to standardize the SDA Hymn Book, 1985 edition.

Come, Thou Almighty King

Come, Thou Almighty King
help us Thy name to sing, help us to praise!
Father all glorious, over all victorious,
come and reign over us, Ancient of Days

Come, Thou incarnate Word
gird on Thy mighty sword, our prayer attend!
Come, and Thy people bless, and give Thy Word
    success,
Spirit of holiness, on us descend!

Come, holy Comforter,
Thy sacred witness bear in this glad hour.
Thou Who almighty art, now rule in every heart,
and ne'er from us depart, Spirit of power!

To Thee, great One in Three,
eternal praises be, hence, evermore.
Thy sovereign majesty may we in glory see,
and to eternity love and adore!

In "When We Survey The Wondrous Cross", the following changes had been corrected in the SDA Hymn Book, 1985 edition from the 1941 edition.

Forbid it Lord, that I should boast
save in the death of *Christ, my God*
All the vain things that charm me most
I sacrifice them to His blood.

While the above verse was instated in the 1985 edition, the hymn know to the Adventists as "Praise Ye The Father" is the original song called "Praise Ye The Triune God" In both the 1941 and 1985 editions of the SDA Hymnal, the song, "Now The Day Is Over" has several stanzas missing including the sixth which reads as follows,

> "Glory to the Father,
> Glory to the Son,
> And to you, blest Spirit
> While the ages run."

Why would this Trinitarian stanza be missing on both editions unless it doesn't reflect the Seventh-day Adventist's view of God? Another hymn that has an unusual modification is, "On Jordon's Stormy Banks I Stand", in the original, there are seven stanzas. In the Adventist edition, several stanzas have omitted. In stanza two, (Adventist edition) the term, "God the Son" has been changed to "Christ the Sun". To the unsuspecting listener, this discrepancy would go undetected.

Are these just random oversights and modified without any change of doctrinal intent or is it possible that these changes were made by design to really reflect a pattern of what the Adventist body as a whole was to adhere to right into the twenty first century?

By the 1950's, the church stated that it was to be recognized as a truly trinitarian denomination. The way this doctrine was stated in the 1957 *Questions on Doctrine* was deceptive and false.

> Our people have always believed in the deity and the pre-existence of Christ, most of them quite likely unaware of any dispute as to the exact relationships of the Godhead. ... we have statements from Ellen G. White, at least from the 1870's and the 1880's, on the deity of Christ and on His oneness and equality with

God; and from about 1890 on she expressed herself with increasing frequency...[66]

THE BOOK, ISSUES

The November 5, 1992 issue of *Adventist Review* contained a sixteen-page booklet, entitled *Issues: The Seventh-day Adventist Church and Certain Private Ministries*. Within a few months, a full-sized purple cover book, with the same title, was printed and widely sold. (We will here refer to it simply as *Issues*.)

Having changed the SDA's doctrinal beliefs nearly thirty years before, during the evangelical conferences, leadership now asked that those pleading for a return to historic beliefs should be tolerant. The reason given: the *denomination has never decided what it believes on those points!*

In other words, be tolerant on those points that the church has left open.[67]

Neither has the church ever "formally" adopted a position on perfection and the precise nature of human obedience.[68]

One side stresses Jesus' role as our sinless substitute, arguing that His nature was like Adam's before the fall. The other stresses Jesus' role as our example, *arguing that He came in the "likeness of sinful flesh" with a nature like Adam's after the fall.* But the significant point for the discussion here is *Adventists have never formally adopted a position on the question of just how Jesus' nature compared with Adam's and with ours.* Neither has the church ever "formally" adopted a position on perfection and the precise nature of human obedience...[69]

Thus far we have seen that His unique sinless human nature made it possible for Him to be our substitute. We shall see that the same unique nature qualified Him to be our example.[70]

In this article, Gulley attempts to show that Christ could still be our example, even though He was not like us; that is, did not take our nature. One cannot but wonder how Gulley intends to do that. Here is the faulty logic he uses:

> Clearly Jesus did not have a sinful nature; He had no sinful passions or any taint of sin. By contrast, all the rest of us are born into the world with these liabilities. On the surface, at least, *this looks like a huge advantage for Christ, and calls into question His ability* to be our example.[71]

First, Gulley explains *that Christ did not come into this world to overcome in our place,* but in unfallen Adam's place! Yet the very opposite is true, Christ came into this world to overcome on our behalf.

> Satan had charged God with Adam's sin. *The Creator became a created being.* Jesus came as the second Adam sinless, to show that Satan's charge was false. Adam need not have sinned. Like Adam, He had nothing sinful within to respond to Satan's temptations but He could be tempted from an appeal to use His sinless passions and drives in an unlawful way. He withstood the tempter.[72]

In other words, Christ did not come to be our substitute, but unfallen Adam's substitute! Such flawed logic is all the more remarkable, in view of the fact that Gulley's key phrase, which in 1983 he used as the title of his book is *Christ our*

Substitute. But, following Gulley's logic, Christ is not our substitute. Christ is only unfallen Adam's substitute.

Following this, Gulley declares that the immaculately born Christ, with His pre-fall nature is our example, because He kept the law. Obviously, his statement is pointless. How would Christ's sinless obedience, wrought out in a nature which supposedly cannot sin, be an example to us in natures which can? And this Gulley admits:

> Because His humanity was sinless, Jesus could not experience the inner sinful urgings of sinful humans. But it was necessary that He, as our example, experience an equivalency in intensity while remaining a sinless human.[73]

Gulley then claims that Christ reached "the lowest depths" and suffered as we *do at one time in His life*: during the last part of the forty-day fast in the wilderness! According to Gulley, at that one time and no other, Christ suffered as we do. In these words Gulley describes the one time Christ suffered "equivalent" to us:

> To be hungry was not a sin; it was a proper desire. But through 40-day intensification, His *gnawing hunger became equivalent to the worst sinful drives ever experienced by humans.*[74]

> The human became so emaciated and stressed out, through a nearly six-week fast, that His consuming passion to eat became equivalent to sinful passions of men.[75]

Second, Gulley uses the rehashed argument in History of the Change Over that, throughout Jesus' earthly life, the only real temptation He faced was to use His divine power to help Himself! What kind of useful example is that to us? None at all.

> He had received honor in the heavenly courts, and was familiar with absolute power. *It was as difficult for Him to keep the level of humanity as it is for men to rise above the low level of their depraved natures,* and be partakers of the divine nature.[76]

> Can we understand His supreme struggle? Never! But we must try to grasp its depths. He had exercised absolute power from eternity! This power He had by nature; it was inherent. If we grumble about our inheritance by nature, think of His. If we say we have habits that bind us, think of His, a habit with eternal use back of it! Can you get any greater urge than that? Our habits, measured by His, are but drops of water compared to a shoreless sea. He knows the human struggle in temptations because His were infinitely greater and precisely because of His unique divine nature rather than from an identical human nature.[77]

Gulley summarizes the terrible "weight" that was on Christ:

> What an inexplicable intensification this staggering load brought to the agonizing struggle of the emaciated One! In view of this unparalleled experience, can anyone question the genuineness of His example? No! His temptations were infinitely harder than man's![78]

Is the burden that Christ bore identified as the restraint of not exercising His deity? Here we see the misplaced role that Jesus Christ exercised according to the Seventh-day Adventist beliefs. The burden that Jesus Christ bore was the sins of mankind throughout history—past, present and future—at Calvary's cross, while He remained sinless.

Under threats and strong duress from Walter Martin, from 1954 to 1957, the SDA leaders agreed to make definite changes. These changes were printed in the first official doctrinal book in SDA's history.

The 1960s and 1970s constituted a time of adaptation to the changes. The work of retraining Adventist pastors in retreats went on quietly. Their future leaders were, with much struggle, being initiated into new teachings in the colleges.

During the 1980s as these new teachings were integrated, strong pleas for patience and toleration for other views were frequently heard.

During the 1990s those advocating and pleading for a return to historic beliefs are still very strong within Adventism. One only needs to look to the work of the Clear Word Bible to see that the SDA historical beliefs are alive and well within the Seventh-day Adventist Church. They are still preaching the identifying error of Revelation 14:6-12 (the third angel's message) everywhere and requiring obedience by faith in the *Spirit of Prophecy* (Ellen G. White).

> ... the denomination in the closing years of the twentieth century and the opening years of the twenty-first has witnessed a resurgence of anti-Trinitarianism and semi-Arianism on the basis that the earliest founders held those views.[79]

Note that this resurgence is not on the basis of Scripture, but on what the early SDA founders believed.

a) SDA'S JESUS' "FALLEN, SINFUL HUMAN NATURE"

With the above statements in mind, we can better evaluate Dr. Martin's comments regarding the SDA's teaching of Jesus' fallen, sinful human nature in his *Kingdom of the Cults*, where he stresses that Christians erroneously charge SDA with a non-Christian view of Christ. Here Martin again refers to *Questions on Doctrine*, which most SDA's repudiate today, but where they supposedly deny the above teaching. The problem is affirmed to have begun with an article in their *Signs of the Times*, March 1927, in which F. M. Wilcox stated Jesus had a sinful human nature, and in December 1928 saying, "Jesus took humanity with all its liabilities, with all its dreadful risks of yielding to temptation."

Later, in April 1956, Wilcox explained that he was young when writing that, and only later realized his error. So it appears the denomination is being faulted for Wilcox's mistake. Dr. Martin says, *"Nearly every critic of Seventh-day Adventism also uses a statement quote from* Bible Readings for the Home *1944 edition, page 174 even though in 1945 the statement was expunged by the Adventists because it was not in line with official Adventist Theology."*

Yet Wilcox's statement virtually echoes Ellen G. White in *Desire of Ages*: "Our Saviour took humanity with all its liabilities, He took the nature of man with the possibility of yielding to temptation" (p. 49). Surely Wilcox should not be spanked for his words, while Ellen White wasn't! If and since sinfulness is one of the liabilities of man's nature, then Ellen had said the same thing as Wilcox later recited. But it wasn't just Wilcox's writing that showed this to be their official position, for this was published in *Bible Readings* for over thirty years as SDA's explicit doctrinal catechism from 1915 until 1949! It wasn't a mere slip of the pen of some young minister, for most SDA theologians agreed with this continued printing for all these years, and none ever complained about Ellen's words in *Desire of Ages*, for they'd lose their positions if they did! Also, *Bible Readings* adds that if He did not have a sinful human nature "then He was not made like unto His brethren, and was not tempted in all points as we are," and "did not overcome as we have to overcome, and therefore is not the complete and perfect Saviour man needs and must have in order to be saved." *Thus in essence, without Jesus having a fallen and sinful human nature, you have NO Saviour!*

In Bible Readings for the Home Circles, chap.39, 1914 edition, it states, "The idea that Christ was born of an immaculate or sinless mother, inherited no tendencies to sin, and for this reason did not sin, removes him from the realm of a fallen world and from the very place of help where needed. On His human side, Christ inherited what every child of Adam inherits—a sinful nature. On the divine side, from His very conception, He was begotten and born of the Spirit. And all this was done to place mankind on a vantage ground, and to demonstrate that in the same way everyone who is born of the Spirit may gain like victories over sin in his own sinful flesh. Thus each is to overcome as Christ overcame (Revelation 3:21)."

The purpose of this teaching is seen in view of the law as the pivotal point of Adventist doctrine. It's to show we can keep the law, once we are born again, just as Christ did when He was born of the Spirit. Because He proved it can be done with a sinful nature then we have no excuse to sin after our new birth. (We note that teaching He was *born of the Spirit* says He was in fact regenerated from His fallen nature, but it begs the question: *At what age, or when was He born again?*, and implies He was indeed a sinner, before being *born of the Spirit.*)

An evangelical publication, *The Indian Christian*, January 1927, spoke against this heresy, to which Wilcox was responding (above), and in this, the SDA's *Oriental Watchman*, affirmed their teaching was *orthodox to the very core* and that *"If Jesus did not take our fallen nature in His own person by His incarnation, fallen humanity is left without a Saviour..."*

In SDA's *Light Bearers to the Remnant* (page 542–3), we are told this teaching was in Bible Readings and widely circulated until 1949, when they also removed some Arian concepts from Uriah Smith's *Daniel and Revelation* which had been published for sixty years! They tell of Dr. English who troubled the church because of this teaching, but to little avail! But the problem of Jesus' sinful human nature comes from their earlier Arian theology, that He was less than God—i.e. Michael the Archangel. It's from this frame of reference that Ellen White made her statements, not having yet accepted the full deity of Christ first shown by W. W. Prescott in 1896, before *Desire of Ages* was published. Of course she had previously identified Jesus as Michael the Archangel, so this was neither removed from the manuscripts of *Desire of Ages*.

Can *Questions on Doctrine* be held more authoritative for SDA's than Ellen White's very own words, when no minister or theologian dares question *The Spirit of Prophecy* (Ellen G. White), when many loudly dissented *Questions on Doctrine*? Wasn't *Questions on Doctrines* supposed denial of Christ's sinful human nature a new view, attacking one of the pillars of our faith that was received by revelation and God-sustained these fifty years? Evidently so, for though this teaching was initiated by Ellen in the *Review* (Feb. 10, 1885; Dec. 15, 1896) it returned in the *Adventist Review*, March 1977. The conservative SDA's will let her gift stand in the face of *Questions on Doctrine*, which was born only to relieve pressure created by evangelicals like Dr. Barnhouse of *Eternity* magazine and Dr. Walter Martin.

But these *Review* articles were merely the tip of the iceberg, as in Wilcox's case, for while *Questions on Doctrine* supposedly recanted this, it was denominationally upheld by *Answers to Objections* by F. D. Nichol who Dr. Walter Martin interviewed, with continuous printings from 1932 into the 1950s, and greatly expanded in the 1960s. In this official doctrinal defensive publication, nine pages are devoted in apologia for this Adventist teaching! He supplies two additional statements from Ellen White supporting this, which he categorizes as "considered truly authoritative" of their position (from *Desire*; pages 24–49). He declares, "This is Adventist Belief, and we hold this Belief, because we feel it agrees with revelation and reason." By *revelation* he means Ellen White's so-called canonically inspired statements.

George Knight, an Adventist historian states that Jesus took our fallen nature literally which he derived almost verbatim from Ellen G. White's teachings:

> That position of Christ's vicariously bearing fallen human is certainly not set forth in the New Testament. Nor was it the one held by Ellen White ... Thus according to Ellen White, at the incarnation Christ actually, rather than vicariously, took upon Himself ... "fallen, suffering human nature, degraded and defiled by sin."[1]

Note the wording used here, "Thus according to Ellen White..." This again indicates that *she is the final authoritative voice* on doctrinal matters. One will not find a statement such as hers in all of the New Testament.

Also, the SDA *Bible Commentary* in 1958 upholds this view, as did *Bible Readings* in affirming that other churches are modern Babylon, because *"Modern Babylon teaches that God, in the person of His Son, did not take the same flesh with us that is sinful flesh"* (p. 236; 1915 ed.). Quotes from their commentary show they kept this view, which Dr. Martin supposed they had denied in *Questions on Doctrine*, for these were published simultaneously. Here we read:

> "The Son of God came to earth with His divinity veiled in humanity ... our weakened sinful state" (VI, p. 561; Romans 8:3). "For the very first time human nature was led to victory over its natural tendency to sin" (VII, p. 426, Hebrews 4:15). "In fact, one purpose of the incarnation was that Deity might come so close to humanity as to experience the very same problems and infirmities that are our common lot" (ibid). "Our Lord experienced the full weight of every conceivable temptation..." (ibid, 407). "It can never be said that He is a stranger to any temptation ... that men pass through" (ibid). "The Human Nature of Christ felt the full force of temptation" (ibid). "It was also Christ's purpose in assuming our humanity to demonstrate to men ... that sin and Satan may be successfully resisted and that obedience to the will of God may be rendered by human beings in this life" (VI, p. 561, Romans 8:3).

These comments from the SDA *Commentary*, as authoritative SDA doctrine, lead us to wonder, "Did *Questions on Doctrine* really deny this teaching? Or, did they just pad it with redefinitions and double-talk, as in *Answers to Objections*? The answer is revealed in some quotes from *Questions on Doctrine*:

> ...not in possessing like passions. As the sinless One His nature recoiled from evil ... not possessing the passions of our fallen natures ... The Perfect Sinlessness of the Human Nature of Christ (*Questions on Doctrine*, p. 59, SDA *Commentary* V, 1131).

But on page 60:

> He took the nature of man ... He took our sinful nature ... He took our fallen nature ... He took man's nature in its fallen condition ... He took man's nature in its fallen condition.

On pages 654-656 of *Questions on Doctrine*, its authors quote Ellen White:

> Christ took upon His sinless nature our sinful nature. Christ took our nature and its deteriorating condition.

All Ellen's quotes are still upheld by *Questions on Doctrine*, but with redefinitions on page 59! So Jesus' fallen sinful human nature is perfect sinlessness! This double-talk began with Ellen: "He took upon His sinless nature, our sinful nature..." (*Medical Ministry*, p. 181), making Jesus schizophrenic! But they need this to uphold other anti-Christian statements of their false prophet Ellen White! Also, these last four quotes from her *Desire of Ages, Medical Ministry, Special Instructions and Signs...* prove there were more than just one from Ellen, as F. D. Nichol says in *Answers*! But most importantly, *we see* Questions on Doctrine *didn't deny that Jesus had a fallen sinful human nature, as Dr. Martin said.*

Far rather they upheld it—though making it appear as a denial by saying He didn't have like passions as we do. But it's impossible to have a fallen sinful human nature and being man's nature in its fallen condition and yet not have the very same passions which we do! Thus, the *Seventh-day Adventists really deceived Dr. Martin* as to their real position in this area, so they could appear evangelical to his eyes, but strictly from the limited view of *Questions on Doctrine* (page 59; while page 60 and all their other publications show their true colors!).

Lest there are any lingering doubts as to their authoritative position, in 1988 the Ministerial Association published their official doctrines in *SDA Believe* giving exposition on their twenty-seven fundamental doctrines. Over 200 SDA's were involved in developing this book, which was later accepted at their Quadrennial General Conference session. In the chapter "God the Son" we read, "His human nature possessed the same mental and physical susceptibilities as the rest of fallen humanity ... to what extent did He identify with or become identical to fallen humanity ... He was made "in the likeness of sinful flesh" or "sinful human nature" or "fallen human nature"... Adam had the advantage over Christ ... Christ took human nature with all its liabilities, including the possibility of yielding to temptation" (p. 46–47).

This continuous official publication of this view leaves no doubt what their real position is. They uphold Ellen White's view, and will do so, never stating in any article "*We deny or repudiate* that Christ had a fallen sinful human nature." These words are simply nowhere to be found. Nor did the deletion of the words *fallen nature* or *sinful nature* from the 1949 *Bible Readings* constitute denial, but merely temporarily hid that stance! Thus here too, by selectively citing their references and minimizing the materials Dr. Martin researched, the SDA leaders kept him from seeing their real position, so he would give them a favourable review in his book *The Truth about Seventh-day Adventism* and later, *Kingdom of the Cults.*

4

EARLY ADVENTISTS AS ARIANS

a) CONCERNING.THE TRINITY

William Miller is seen as the original founder of the Seventh-day Adventist and interestingly enough he was a trinitarian. It is unfortunate that the other founding members didn't hold to William Miller's view of the godhead. In spite of the strength of the unitarian and Socinian movements in America in the first half of the nineteenth century, Miller, who was regarded as distinctly unorthodox in other respects, abided by the orthodox trinitarian position. Some years after the infant Seventh-day Adventist movement had gained a firm hold on life, James White produced a work entitled Sketches of The Christian Life and Public Labours of William Miller. [1]

James White quotes Miller's statement of faith written at Low Hampton, September 5, 1822:

WILLIAM MILLER

> I hereby acknowledge that I have long believed it my duty ... to leave, for the inspection of my brethren, friends and children, a brief statement of my faith (and which ought to be my practice); and I pray God to forgive me where I go astray. I made it a subject of prayer and meditation, and therefore, leave the following as my faith—reserving the privilege of correction.
> (Signed) William Miller

> I believe in one living and true God, and that there are *three persons in the Godhead*—as there is in man, the body, soul, and spirit. And if any one will tell me how these exist, I will tell him how the *three persons of the Triune God* are connected.[2]

JOSEPH BATES

Joseph Bates' objection to the doctrine of the Trinity evidenced an attitude which was to be reiterated forcefully by later militant Seventh-day Adventist anti-trinitarians. Bates rejected trinitarianism because it involves the complete identification of Father and Son. Of course, trinitarianism does no such thing. William Miller asserted his belief in "one living and true God" composed of "three persons." He understood the "Triune God" to contain "three persons."[3]

This is the true trinitarian understanding of the doctrine, and since Miller wrote in 1822, and Bates objected to trinitarianism on the grounds presented in 1827, it is a justifiable assumption that the concept which trinitarians have today of the relations between members of the deity, was the concept current when Bates wrote. Undoubtedly, there were in vogue in the nineteenth century, as there are today, extreme forms of trinitarianism, against which the early Adventists seriously reacted.

Evidence for this will be presented as we proceed. But this is not an adequate explanation of the extreme anti-trinitarianism of the early Adventists. Bates assumes that, pushed to its logical conclusion, trinitarianism becomes monarchianism, one which the Father is the Son and vice versa. Then he objects to this on the ground that one person cannot possible be another. But he is not objecting to trinitarianism, as he imagined. He is objecting to his interpretation of what trinitarians teach. He is objecting to monarchianism.

Bates wrote his autobiography in 1868. There is no indication in his narration of the events of his past life that his view had changed in the interval since 1827. It is, therefore, reasonable to conclude that, after becoming a Seventh-day Adventist, Bates retained his anti-trinitarian belief.

His father tried unsuccessfully to convince Joseph Bates that in these matters of doctrine the Congregational Church was correct. In regard to the subject of the Trinity, Bates wrote in 1868:

> Respecting the trinity, I concluded that it was impossible for me to believe that the Lord Jesus Christ, the Son of the Father, was also the Almighty God, the Father, one and the same being. I said to my father, "If you can convince me that we are one in this sense, that you are my father, and I your son, and also that I am my father, and you my son, then I can believe in the trinity." ... In a few days I was immersed and joined the Christian Church.[4]

JAMES WHITE

Prior to becoming an Adventist, James White was an ordained minister of the Christian Connection.[5] He wrote his *Life Incidents* in 1868 for the *Review* and *Herald*.[6] He says, "At the age of fifteen I was baptized and united with the Christian Church."[7] Later, he was ordained and carried on revival work for this organization. In 1842 he heard William Miller preach and became an enthusiastic adherent of the Second Advent faith.[8]

Since White came out of the Christian Connection, one would expect to discover that he was, at least early in his career, opposed to trinitarianism. But the evidence is not readily forthcoming, and what is available is inconclusive. It is true that James White was editor of the *Signs of the Times* in 1879. On May 22 of that year there appeared an article strongly opposing trinitarianism written by A. J. Dennis.[9]

It would be easy to conclude that White concurred with the position taken in the article, since he was editor and there is no indication that he, as editor, might have held another view. But James White was a Christian gentleman, and possibly he published a view with which he could not agree simply as a gesture of Christian courtesy. He did not agree with certain workers on some other issues, but remained silent, even when their views were published, simply for the sake of avoiding a serious doctrinal cleavage.

On the other hand, there are certain indications which point in the direction of the view that James White was not a trinitarian. In 1877 he wrote a tract entitled *Christ in the Old Testament* in which the following statement appears:

> The work of emancipating, instructing and leading the Hebrews was given to the One who is called an angel. Exodus 13:21; 14:19, 24; 23:20-23; 32:34; Numbers 20:16; Isaiah 63:9. And this angel Paul

calls "that spiritual Rock that followed them," and he affirms, "That Rock was Christ" (1 Corinthians 10:4). The eternal Father is never called an angel in the Scriptures, while what angels have done is frequently ascribed to the Lord, as they are his messengers and agents to accomplish his work.[10]

We have here a suggested distinction between the eternal Father and Christ. Christ is called an angel in Scripture, the Father is not. Christ is referred to as "the Lord" to distinguish Him from the eternal Father. It would be possible to read between the lines and assume that James White did not regard Christ, the Lord, as eternal in the same sense as the Father; that, in fact, Christ was to some extent inferior in rank to the Father, because he is called an angel and the Father is not. But, in the absence of corroborating evidence, this would not be a fair conclusion.

There is in the James White Memorial Library at Andrew University a thesis which stated that A. T. Robinson declared in an interview that James White was not a trinitarian.[11] Robinson had been acquainted with the Whites. This type of evidence based on the testimony of an old man is hardly to be regarded as entirely satisfactory. But it is nevertheless an additional finger pointing to the same direction as other fragmentary pieces of evidence. At all events, White did not allow his view, whatever it was, to come to the fore, at a time when a major trinitarian controversy might have split the infant Adventist Church.

> The way spiritualizers this way have disposed of or denied the only Lord God and our Lord Jesus Christ is first using the *old unscriptural trinitarian creed,* viz, that Jesus Christ is the eternal God, though they have not one passage to support it, while we have

plain scripture testimony in abundance that He is the Son of the eternal God.[12]

We are told by those who teach the abolition of the Father's law, that the commandments of God mentioned in the New Testament, are not the ten, but the requirements of the gospel, such as repentance, faith, baptism, and the Lord's Supper. But as these, and every other requirement peculiar to the gospel, are all embraced in the faith of Jesus, it is evident that the commandments of God are not the sayings of Christ and his apostles. To assert that the sayings of the Son and His apostles are the commandments of the Father is as wide *from the truth as the old trinitarian absurdity that Jesus Christ is the very and eternal God.* And as the faith of Jesus embraces every requirement peculiar to the gospel, it necessarily follows that the commandments of God, mentioned by the third angel, embrace only the ten precepts of the Father's immutable law which are not peculiar to any one dispensation, but common to all.[13]

Here we might mention the Trinity, which does away the personality of God, and of his Son Jesus Christ, and of sprinkling or pouring instead of being "buried with Christ in baptism," "planted in the likeness of his death:" but we pass from these fables to notice one that is held sacred by nearly all professed Christians, both Catholic and Protestant. It is the change of the Sabbath of the fourth commandment from the seventh to the first day of the week.[14]

The "mystery of iniquity" began to work in the church in Paul's day. It finally crowded out the simplicity of the gospel, and corrupted the doctrine of Christ, and the church went into the wilderness. Martin Luther, and other reformers, arose in the strength of God, and with the Word and Spirit, made mighty strides in the Reformation. The greatest fault we can find in the Reformation is, the Reformers stopped reforming. Had they gone on, and onward, till they had left the last vestige of Papacy behind, such as natural immortality, sprinkling, *the trinity*, and Sundaykeeping, the church would now be free from her unscriptural errors.[15]

J. M. STEPHENSON

Writing in the *Review* and *Herald* in 1854, J. M. Stephenson exposed himself as a militant Arian. In an article entitled *The Atonement*, Stephenson forcefully presented his anti-trinitarian arguments:

The idea of the Father and Son supposes priority of the existence of the one, and the subsequent existence of the other. To say that the Son is as old as the Father, is a palpable *contradiction of term*. It is a natural impossibility for the Father to be as young as the Son, or the Son to be as old as the Father.[16]

He proceeded to point out that the terms Father and Son would not have been used by the Bible writers if they had wished "to convey the idea of the coetaneous existence, and eternity of the Father and Son...."[17]

Stephenson quoted a trinitarian named Fuller who agreed that the Father must have existed prior to the Son. The Son is the first born, said Stephenson, in the sense that He had an origin at a point prior to all other forms of life. Christ was begotten. Therefore, "he must have had a beginning." "God," he wrote, "is the "only supreme ruler." It would be impossible to have two supreme rulers at the same time. Only the Father is "supremely, or absolutely, good."[18]

> Only the Father is, in the absolute sense, immortal. Only the Father is self-existent. The Son is therefore dependent on the Father, for the Father gave "the Son to have life in himself."[19]

Stephenson went so far as to declare that Christ was a created being: Colossians 1:15—"the first born of every creature." Creature signifies creation; hence to be the first born of every creature (creation), he must be a created being, and as such, his life and immortality must depend upon the Father's will just as much as angels, or redeemed men ...[20]

D. W. HULL

Writing in 1859, D. W. Hull presented in the *Review and Herald* a series of two articles discussing the "bible doctrine of divinity." He sees the trinitarian position as subversive of the doctrine of the atonement.[21]

It is clear that he is, to some extent, reacting to certain extreme trinitarian positions, but in the process he attempts to shatter the whole structure of that doctrine. Hull writes:

> The doctrine which we propose to examine, was established by the Council of Nicea [sic], A.D. 325, and ever since that period, persons not believing this particular tenet, have been denounced by popes and priests, as dangerous heretics. It was for disbelief in this doctrine, that the Arians were anathematized in A.D. 513.

As we can trace this doctrine not farther back than the origin of the "man of sin" and as we find this dogma at that time established rather by force, than otherwise, we claim the right to investigate the matter, and ascertain the bearing of Scripture on this subject.[22]

Hull is at pains to point out that "we" believe in the divinity of Christ but adds that "we don't believe, as the m. e. church discipline teaches, that Christ is the very and eternal God; at the same time, very man; that the human part was the Son, and the divine part was the Father."[23]

He then proceeds to repudiate what he calls, "The orthodox view of God" that he is "without body, parts, passions, centre, circumference, or locality." It is not difficult to understand his opposition to this extreme view. He adds, "It certainly appears that such a God as this, must be entirely devoid of an existence."[24]

Hull then begins to investigate all the important passages claimed by trinitarians in support of their view. In answer to the trinitarians' use of Isaiah 9:6, he declares that Christ is here called mighty, but not almighty. The word he believes is used "in a limited sense." Christ is the everlasting Father only in the sense that He is to live everlastingly, certainly not in the trinitarian sense. Hull emphasizes the argument which Joseph Bates used in 1827. If the divine part of Jesus was the Father, if it was the Father who was manifested in the flesh, then God and Christ are one person. Consistently throughout the article, Hull confuses the correct trinitarian position with monarchianism. He argues that trinitarians say there is one God and that Christ is God in the same sense as the Father. Therefore, Christ is the Father. They are one and the same person. But he sees this to be logically impossible and scripturally unsound. Father and Son are one just as are a man and his wife. They are united in interest and purpose. Christ, he says, is not the only and eternal God. He is not as great as the Father, nor did He pretend to be so. His power was delegated. The objection is illustrated as follows:

> What would the reader think of a man who moved from the State of Ohio to Iowa with his family and after enjoying their company for a season talk of going back to Ohio where he could see his family? If you cannot allow inconsistencies in men, how can you accuse the Saviour of leaving the world to go to the Father, and at the same time assert that the Saviour was Jehovah himself? [25]

Hull gives further reasons for rejecting what he calls the trinitarian position. If Father and Son are one person, then the world was three days without a God, for the Bible says that He was "put to death in the flesh." Christ cried, "My God, my God, why hast thou forsaken me?" Trinitarians say that the Godhead had left him. Then Christ must have been alive after the Godhead had departed from Him, and the sacrifice was only a human sacrifice.[26]

But how could a human sacrifice atone for our sins? Thus he objects to the view that Christ's soul did not die. It was necessary for every part of Christ to die that human sin might be adequately atoned for. He quotes 2 Peter 3:18 and adds, "There is no chance of escape here. Christ's soul and every part that dwelt in his flesh was put to death and buried in sheol, or hades."[27]

The trinitarian teaching that Christ's body descended to the grave but his soul or divinity, or whatever it might be termed, ascended to paradise, is rejected as unscriptural and destructive of the possibility of the atonement by Seventh-day Adventists.

The three salient reasons which Hull gives for rejecting trinitarianism are that the doctrine teaches that God lacks bodily parts and emotions, that it identifies Father and Son as one and the same person, and that, because it teaches that the divine in Christ did not die, it renders the sacrifice a human sacrifice, and therefore, an inadequate atonement for the sins of man. It is quite evident that to some extent Hull was opposing an extreme form of trinitarianism, but this is not a sufficient explanation of his anti-trinitarianism. He relegates the decisions of Nicea to the category of false doctrine, but misinterprets the position of the Nicene fathers. They were at pains to avoid the accusation of monarchianism. Hull accuses them of teaching this. Like Joseph Bates, on this particular point, he is opposing not the trinitarian view itself, but his own misconception of what the view is.

> The inconsistent positions held by many in regard to the Trinity, as it is termed, has, no doubt, been the prime cause of many other errors. Erroneous views of the divinity of Christ are apt to lead us into error in regard to the nature of the atonement ... The doctrine which we propose to examine, was established by the council of Nice, A.D. 325, and ever since that period, persons not believing this peculiar tenet, have been denounced by popes and priests, as dangerous heretics. It was for a disbelief in this doctrine. that the Arians were anathematized in A.D. 513 ... As we can trace this doctrine no further back than the origin of the "Man of Sin," and as we find this dogma at that time established rather by force than otherwise, we claim the right to investigate the matter, and ascertain the bearing of Scripture on this subject.[28]

URIAH SMITH

As early as 1859, Uriah Smith stressed the importance of the manifestation of the Holy Spirit in the Church:

> This Spirit is the life-principle of the church of God; and the degree in which that Spirit is possessed by the church marks the exact ratio of her acceptance with him, and the strength of that life which he lives "by faith of the Son of God."[29]

Smith recognizes the Spirit as the source of spiritual power and the surety of the presence of God in the church, and he recoils in horror from the suggestion that there is no Holy Spirit:

> Reader, can you conceive of a more dark and chilly theory, and one better calculated to lie like an iceberg on the heart of the church than the view which some hold, that there is no Holy Spirit? Be it our lot ever to be free from this unhallowed sentiment, and those who hold it.[30]

In the light of these statements it is well to be guarded in our interpretation of Smith's later denials of the personality of the Holy Spirit. He in no way detracts from the importance of the Spirit of God as the source of light and power. He would join trinitarians in praying earnestly for this gift and would emphasize the indispensable nature of the Spirit's work in human redemption. But any attempt to invest the Holy Spirit with personality, Smith met with reasoned opposition.

Later in the century there appeared a regular column in the *Review and Herald* headed "in the question chair." Here the questions of correspondents were answered, and here Smith occasionally found a convenient place to express his views. In 1890 in answer to the question "is the Holy Spirit a person?" Smith wrote:

> But respecting this Spirit, the Bible uses expressions which cannot be harmonized with the idea that it is a person like the Father and the Son. Rather it is shown to be a divine influence from them both, the medium which represents their presence and by which they have knowledge and power through all the universe, when not personally present.[31]

Smith recognizes that in chapters 14 to 16 the Spirit is personified as the comforter. He quotes the use in these chapters of the personal and relative pronouns *he, him,* and *whom* in reference to the Holy Spirit. But these instances he would regard simply as figures of speech, for in most cases in Scripture *it* is spoken of in ways which would deny that *it* is a person, like the Father and the Son "for instance," he writes,

> ...it is often said to be poured out and shed abroad, but we never read about God or Christ being poured out or shed abroad.[32]

When the Holy Spirit has appeared, Uriah Smith points out, it has been in varying shapes and forms. Once it appeared as a dove, once in the form of cloven tongues as of fire as in Acts 2:3-4.

Elsewhere we read of "the seven spirits of God sent forth into all the earth" in Revelation 1:4; 3:1; 4:5; 5:6.

These descriptions would not, in his opinion, be used if the Holy Spirit were to be understood as a person. In March of the following year, 1891, Uriah Smith said in a sermon reported in the *General Conference Bulletin*:

The Holy Spirit is the Spirit of God; it is also the Spirit of Christ. It is that divine, mysterious emanation through which they carry forward their great and infinite work.[33]

He acknowledges that it is the "eternal spirit," it is omniscient and omnipresent, it is the Spirit that had a hand in creation, it can be grieved and quenched. But it is not a person, it is an influence. It is a "mysterious emanation."[34]

The reason for the personification of the Holy Spirit in Scripture is given by Smith in an answer to a question in a later issue of *the Review and Herald*:

2 John 16:13 describes the work of the Holy Spirit, and it is so connected with Father and the Son that it is itself personified and spoken of as doing what the Father and the Son do through it.[35]

In reading the *Review and Heralds* of the 1890s, one gains the decided impression that this subject was, to some extent, challenging the minds of the laity. In September 1892 a questioner again raised the issue, and Uriah Smith answered. The question is significant as an illustration of the type of reasoning which evidently was exercising the minds of some Adventists at that time:

If God is a spirit (John 4:24) and at the same time a person (Dan. 7:9), would not the same reasoning prove the Holy Spirit a person, as referred to in John 14:26?

Answer:
No; for God is elsewhere described and represented as a person; but the Holy Spirit is not. The fact that the Holy Spirit is personified in John 14, and thus

spoken of as acting in a personal and individual manner, does not prove it to be a person, any more than the fact that love is spoken of in 1 Corinthians 13 as performing certain acts and exercising certain emotions, proves that charity, or love, is a person.[36]

Again in October 1896, a questioner probed into the mysterious nature of the Spirit of God. The question: "Do the scriptures warrant the praise or worship of the Holy Spirit? If not, does not the last line of the doxology contain an unscriptural sentiment?"[37]

Smith answered the first question in the negative. "Nowhere in Scripture are we commanded to worship the Holy Spirit, as we are commanded to worship Christ." In answer to the second question, he reasoned that if in the baptismal formula the name of the Holy Spirit is to be used along with that of the Father and the Son, Why could it not properly stand as a part of the same trinity in the hymn of praise, "Praise Father, Son, and Holy Ghost"?[38]

Uriah Smith's argument here and his use of the word trinity may suggest to some that perhaps his view of the nature of the Holy Spirit and of the relations between the members of the Godhead having undergone a change in the direction of trinitarianism, since last he expressed himself on the subject. As will be seen, this is not so. Through these years, his work on Daniel and the Revelation, containing his Arian views, was being printed and circulated. In 1898, his book *Looking Unto Jesus* appeared with its strongly Arian description of Christ. The very next year after Smith's use of the word *trinity* in a *Review and Herald* article, he published, in answer to a questioner, his opinion that

> there are various expressions concerning the Holy Spirit which would indicate that it could not be properly considered as a person such as its being

"shed abroad" in the heart, and "poured out upon all flesh."[39]

It is, therefore, reasonable to conclude that Uriah Smith consistently held that the Holy Spirit is an influence, not a person, nor a member of the deity in a trinitarian sense. No evidence has been discovered that he held any other belief on the subject, or that he changed his position prior to his death in 1903.

SMITH'S VIEW OF CHRIST

Uriah Smith's stand on the subject of the relation between Christ and the Father has been more widely publicized because of its inclusion in his volumes *Daniel and the Revelation*, and *Looking Unto Jesus*. The first issue of his commentary on Revelation came off the press in 1865 under the title, *Thoughts Critical and Practical on the book of Revelation*. Speaking of Christ in his comment on Revelation 3:14-22, Smith wrote:

> Moreover he is "the beginning of the creation of God." Not the beginner, but the beginning, of the creation, the first created being, dating his existence far back before any other created being or thing, next to the self-existent and eternal God. On this expression Barnes makes the following significant admission: "if it were demonstrated from other sources that Christ was, in fact, a created being, and the first that God had made, it cannot be denied that this language would appropriately express that fact."[40]

In the 1882 edition of *Thoughts on the Book of Daniel and the Revelation*, this statement was modified so as to exclude the suggestion that Christ was created in the ordinary sense of the term.[41]

The 1899 edition of the same work altered the statement again so that it now indicated it to be the opinion of Erwin R. Gane that Christ was not created in the ordinary sense, but that there was a time when He did not exist:

> Others, however, and more properly we think, take the word to mean "agent" or "efficient cause," which is one of the definitions of the word, understanding that Christ is the agent through whom God has created all things, but that he himself came into existence in a different manner, as he is called "the only begotten" of the Father. It would seem utterly inappropriate to apply this expression to any being created in the ordinary sense of the term.[42]

The 1907 edition of the work contained the comment in this identical form. The Southern Publishing Association produced "a new edition, revised and annotated" in 1941. For decades the Seventh-day Adventist Church had been supposed trinitarian in belief as will be seen later in the discussion. As would be expected, this comment on Revelation 3:14-22 was revised so as to relegate to the category of error any idea of Christ having been created. But surprisingly, the statement still reads so as clearly to imply "that the Son came into existence." The passage reads as follows:

> Moreover, he is "the beginning of the creation of God." Some attempt by this language to uphold the error that Christ was a created being, dating his existence anterior to that of any other created being or thing, next to the self-existent and eternal God.... Others, however, and more properly we think, take

the word to mean "agent" or "efficient cause," which is one of the definitions of the word, understanding that Christ is the agent through whom God has created all things, but that the Son came into existence in a different manner, as he is called "the only begotten" of the Father. It would seem utterly inappropriate to apply this expression to any created being in the ordinary sense of the term.[43]

The phrase, "and more properly we think," clearly indicates that in the opinion of the author the view that follows, containing the statement "that the Son came into existence," is the correct one. Why the editors should have strengthened the opposition contained in the statement to the position that Christ was created, and yet have failed to delete the teaching that there was a time when He did not exist, is beyond the knowledge of the present writer. It is certainly difficult to understand in view of the official trinitarian declarations of the Church at the time for years before this.[44]

It was not until the 1944 revision that the Arian view was finally excluded from this work. The statement now reads:

Others, however, and more properly we think, take the word, arche, to mean the "agent" or "efficient cause," which is one of the definitions of the word, understanding that Christ is the agent through whom God has created all things.[45]

Daniel and the Revelation in the older editions contained other utterances which were clearly anti-trinitarian in intent. For instance, the 1882 edition contains a comment on Revelation 1:4 which denies eternity of existence to Christ. The phrase, "from him which is and which was, and which is to come," is said to be an "expression which signifies complete eternity, past and future, and can be applicable to God the Father only."[46]

Smith points out that this language is never applied to Christ. On the use of the term "alpha and omega" in Revelation 1:11 he excludes any application of the phrase to Christ by quoting textual evidence for the omission of the words.[47]

Of course, Revelation 22:13 provides an undeniable application of this phrase to Christ, because of verse 16, but Smith explained the usage as follows:

> Christ here applies to himself the appellation of Alpha and Omega. As applied to him, the expression must be taken in a more limited sense than when applied to the Father as in chap. 1:8. Christ is the Alpha and Omega, the beginning and the end, of the great plan of salvation.[48]

In 1898, the same year that Ellen G. White's book *The Desire of Ages* was published, the Review and Herald Publishing Company produced Uriah Smith's work, *Looking Unto Jesus*. It is significant that the leading denominational publishing house should produce in the same year two works, one so markedly anti-Arian and the other so distinctly Arian. Smith renewed and further explained his Arian teaching in this new work. He wrote:

> God alone is without beginning. At the earliest epoch when a beginning could be—a period so remote that to finite minds it is essentially eternity—appeared the Word ... This uncreated Word was the Being, who, in

the fullness of time was made flesh, and dwelt among us. His beginning was not like that of any other being in the universe ...Thus it appears that by some divine impulse or process, not creation, known only to Omniscience, and possibly only to Omnipotence, the Son of God appeared.[49]

Obviously, Smith's 1865 teaching that Christ was a created being was a passing phase. Here again we see that although he recognizes a remote time at which Christ came into being, yet the process by which this took place is regarded as distinct from creation. After having been brought into existence, the Son was given equality with the Father. So Uriah Smith understands Paul's utterance as recorded in Philippians 2:6. He regards deity as having in some mysterious way evolved. "With the Son," he writes, "the evolution of deity, as deity, ceased."[50]

Uriah Smith in his book *Looking Unto Jesus* declared himself as adhering to the position that every part of Christ died on Calvary. In this he was in complete agreement with D. W. Hull. He believed that when Christ left heaven He left His immortality behind also. When He died it was "as a whole, as a divine being, as the Son of God." If this had not been so then the Saviour would have been merely a human one, and the sacrifice merely a human sacrifice, "but the prophet says that "his soul" was made "an offering for sin" (Isaiah 53:10).[51]

Uriah Smith's position on the nature of God is, therefore, clearly Arian. The Holy Spirit is a mere influence. The Son was brought into existence by the Father, and although elevated to a position of equality with the Father, His authority is, at best, a delegated authority. The suggestion that the divine part of Christ did not die on Calvary he rejected as destructive of the possibility of the atonement.

J. N. LOUGHBOROUGH

James White was editor of the *Review and Herald* in 1861. In November of that year, he published J. N. Loughborough's answer to the question, "What serious objection is there to the doctrine of the trinity?" Loughborough replied:

> There are many objections which we might urge, but on account of our limited space we shall reduce them to the following: 1. It is contrary to common sense. 2. It is contrary to Scripture. 3. Its origin is pagan and fabulous.[52]

In enlarging on the first point, Loughborough objected to the idea that three are one, and one, three. He opposes the use of the terms "the Triune God," and "the three-in-one God."[53]

"If Father, Son, and Holy Ghost are each God, it would be three Gods." Under the second point he urges that in Scripture, Father and Son are spoken of as two distinct persons. As indicated by John chapter 17, the oneness between them is the same as that between Christian believers. To believe the doctrine of the Trinity, to Loughborough, would involve acceptance of the idea that "God sent himself onto the world, died to reconcile the world to himself, raised himself from the dead, ascended to himself in heaven...."[54]

Here again we are confronted with anti-trinitarianism based on opposition to what trinitarians did not teach, that the Father was the Son and vice versa.

That Loughborough was opposing trinitarianism, not merely as it appeared in his day, but in its earliest manifestation in the Christian church, is evidenced by his amplification of his third point. The doctrine of the Trinity came into the church, so he argues, about the same time as image worship and Sunday observance. It is simply a renovation of the pagan Persian religion. It was introduced into the Christian church about AD 325 and was an established doctrine by AD 681. Spain adopted it in 589, Africa in 534, and England in 596.[55]

J. N. Loughborough also declared himself on the subject of the Holy Spirit. Writing in 1898 he described the Spirit of God as "God's representative—the power by which he works, the agency by which all things are upheld."[56]

He says that the Spirit of God is recognized in the Bible as the Lord's presence. The Spirit of God, as spoken of in respect to creation, he describes as, "the creative energy of God." Throughout this 1898 article, Loughborough emphasizes that the Holy Spirit is God's power. He expresses no concept of the Spirit as a personality, and consistently uses the pronoun "it" in reference to the third person of the godhead.

> The word Trinity nowhere occurs in the Scriptures. The principal text supposed to teach it is 1 John 5:7, which is an interpolation. Clarke says, "Out of one hundred and thirteen manuscripts, the text is wanting in one hundred and twelve. It occurs in no MS. before the tenth century. And the first place the text occurs in Greek is in the Greek translation of the acts of the Council of Latern, held A.D. 1215."—Com. on John 1, and remarks at close of chap."[57]

Questions for Bro. Loughborough. Bro. White: The following questions I would like to have you give, or send, to Bro. Loughborough for explanation. W. W. Giles, Toledo, Ohio

Question 1. What serious objections is there to the doctrine of the Trinity?

Answer. There are many objections which we might urge, but on account of our limited space we shall reduce them to the three following: 1. It is contrary to common sense. 2. It is contrary to scripture. 3. Its origin is pagan and fabulous... Instead of pointing us to scripture for proof of the Trinity, we are pointed to the trident of the Persians ... This doctrine of the Trinity was brought into the church about the same time with image worship, and keeping the day of the sun, and is but Persian doctrine remodelled. It occupied about three hundred years from its introduction to bring the doctrine to what it is now. It was commenced about 325 A.D., and was not completed till 681. See Milman's Gibbon's Rome (in the original), vol. iv, p. 422. It was adopted in Spain in 589, in England in 596, in Africa in 534.[58]

> The Athanasian creed ... was formulated and the faith defined by Athanasius. Previous to that time there was no settled method of expression, if, indeed, there was anywhere any uniformity of belief. Most of the early writers had been pagan philosophers, who to reach the minds of that class, often made strong efforts to prove that there was a blending of the two systems, Christianity and philosophy. There is abundance of material in their writings to sustain this view. Bingham speaks of the vague views held by some in the following significant terms: "There were some very early that *turned the doctrine of the Trinity into Tritheism,* and, instead of three divine persons under the economy of

Father, Son, and Holy Spirit, *brought in three collateral, coordinate, and self- originated beings,* making them three absolute and independent principles, without any relation of Father or Son, which is the *most proper notion of three gods.* And having made this change in the doctrine of the Trinity, they made another change answerable to it in the form of baptism."[59]

Who can distinguish between this form of expression and that put forth by the council of Constantinople in A.D. 381, wherein the true faith is declared to be that of "an uncreated and consubstantial and co-eternal Trinity?" The truth is that we find the same idea which is here described by Bingham running through much of the orthodox literature of the second and third centuries. There is no proper "relation of Father and Son" to be found in the words of the council, above quoted ... Bingham says this error in regard to a Trinity of *three coordinate and self-originated and independent beings* arose in the church very early; and so we find it in the earliest authors after the days of the apostles.[60]

Surely, we say right, that the doctrine of a *trinity degrades the atonement*, by bringing this sacrifice, the blood of our purchase, down to the standard of socinianism.[61]

E. GOODRICH

E. Goodrich, writing for the *Review* in 1862, expressed his horror at the sentiment that there is no Spirit.[62]

He sees not much of worth left in Bible religion when it is divested of the doctrine of the Holy Spirit. He describes the Spirit as "the living and acting agent" by which God's work for man is accomplished.[63]

> There is no indication as to whether Goodrich regarded this agent as a personally and a member of the deity, or simply as an influence. This much is certain: that an anti-trinitarian possessing the convictions of Uriah Smith, could heartily subscribe to what Goodrich wrote, as indicated by Smith's own discussion of the importance of the Holy Spirit in 1859.[64]

S. B. WHITNEY

S. B. Whitney became a Seventh-day Adventist some short time before 1862. His change of faith was seriously regretted by the Congregational Church at Malone, and two representatives of that congregation, A. Parmalee and J. B. Henck wrote to him with the intention of winning him back to his old faith.

The *Review and Herald* published the letter to Whitney and his reply. The relevant sections for the purpose of this discussion are quoted here. Parmalee and Henck wrote:

> A few words now in regard to the doctrine which you have recently embraced as substitutes for those you once adopted, but have now put away. The doctrine of the Trinity you set aside as not a scripture doctrine. Our creed on this subject is, that there are three persons in one God, not three persons in one

person, and that Christians are required to baptize in the name of these three, as constituting the only true God revealed on the scriptures. (in the original) The doctrine of the Trinity is a doctrine of faith, not of comprehension, nor could we solve the mysteries of this infinite, wonderful Being, if he were presented to us as existing in one person only.[65]

The writers proceed to depreciate Whitney's conduct in "launching out" as had the unitarians and Socinians in an effort to gain knowledge beyond what is revealed in Scripture.

In his reply, S. B. Whitney fails to answer the Congregational creed that, "there are three persons in one God."[66]

Evidently Parmalee and Henck quoted this in their letter in answer to a previous accusation that their teaching involved the notion of "three persons in one person."[67]

They are certainly objecting to this latter concept. Whitney ignores the issues involved on this point and proceeds to prove that God has a form:

> In Exodus xxxiii, 21-23, we read that God told Moses that he would cover him with his hand while he passed by, but that he should see his back parts. Will the Dr. charge God with deception or admit that he has a form? Will he receive Christ's testimony when he speaks of his Father's "shape"? Luke v, 37. Will he admit that Christ went to heaven bodily? Acts i, 9.[68]

There can be no doubt that Whitney was opposing the concept that God lacks bodily parts and form. The point is not even referred to in the Congregational letter. The trinitarian position of three persons in one God is in no way answered in Whitney's reply. It appears reasonable to conclude:

a) that new converts to the Adventist Church at this stage were introduced to anti-trinitarianism. At least this was so in Whitney's case. This was certainly the impression received by the Congregationalists of Malone; and no effort was made in Whitney's reply or elsewhere in the *Review and Herald* to correct this impression. On the contrary, the reply contained renewed opposition to the trinitarian position. Of course, it is dangerous to generalize on this point. There may have been many converts who retained their trinitarianism, but the present writer has not been able to discover evidence for this.
b) S. B. Whitney's reply evidences the reaction to certain extreme statements in the trinitarian creed, which we have noticed in other early Seventh-day Adventist writers, but,
c) There can be no doubt that the trinitarians at this time did not teach, as certain Seventh-day Adventist writers interpreted them as teaching, that Christ and God are one person. The Congregational creed, as referred to by Parmalee and Henck, clearly stated that "there are three persons in one God, not three persons in one person.[69]

D. M. CANRIGHT

Writing for the *Review and Herald* in the period from 1867 to 1878, D. M. Canright confined himself, for the most part, to a very verbal and somewhat polemic reiteration of what his Seventh-day Adventist predecessors had written.

CANRIGHT'S 1867 ARTICLE

In 1867 he produced an article entitled, "Jesus Christ the Son of God." He wrote:

Christ came into existence first of all things ... My grounds for this proposition are John 1:1, 2; Colossians 1:17; Proverbs 8:22, 30. "In the beginning was the Word, and the Word was with God, and the Word was God. The same was in the beginning with God." Here, the existence of the Word, or Christ, is placed as far back as language can place it, even in the beginning with the great God.[70]

Canright understood that Christ was begotten, not created in the same sense as angels and men. We are commanded to worship the Son, and no created being is ever worthy of worship. The Son is not to be regarded as great as the Father for first all things are subdued under the Son and then the Son becomes subject to the Father. Here Canright quotes John 14:28 and 1 Corinthians 15:28. Therefore, he concludes, "The Son is subordinate to the Father."[71]

As did his predecessors, Canright assumes that trinitarians teach that the Father and the Son are one person, and then proceeds to demonstrate the incorrectness of this position. When Christ died, every part of Him died, otherwise the sacrifice was only a human one.

CANRIGHT'S 1878 ARTICLES

In 1878, Canright produced a series of four articles titled "the personality of God," greatly amplifying his views and providing strong opposition to the trinitarian position. He wrote, "Jesus says that his father is the only true God, but trinitarians contradict this by saying that the Son and the Holy Ghost are just as much the true God as the Father is."[72]

Canright opposed the creedal concept of God as "without body, part, or passion."

> I do not believe that any person, whatever his creed may be, ever prays to God without conceiving of him as having a body, form, and shape, and being located upon a throne in heaven.[73]

He provides considerable scriptural quotation as evidence for his belief. He denies the usual distinction between matter and spirit, and regards God as possessing form and parts, even though He is a Spirit.[74]

"It is our opinion," he writes, "founded both in revelation and science, that celestial beings are as material as men, only that they are more highly organized, more refined—matter on a higher plane."[75]

In the same year, 1878, *The Signs of the Times* published an article by Canright entitled "The Holy Spirit not a person, but an influence proceeding from God." He begins:

> All trinitarian creeds make the Holy Ghost a person, equal in substance, power, eternity, and glory with the Father and Son. Thus they claim three persons in the trinity, each one equal with both others. If this is so, then the Holy Spirit is just as truly an individual intelligent person as is the Father or the Son. But this we cannot believe. The Holy Spirit is not a person. In all our prayers we naturally conceive of God as a person, and of the Son as a person, but whoever conceived of the Holy Ghost as being a person, standing there beside the Father and equal with Him?[76]

On the contrary, Canright takes the decided stand that the Holy Spirit is "a divine influence proceeding from the Father and also from the Son, as their power, energy, etc."[77]

The Spirit is personified in the Bible only because it is the Spirit of a person. In a similar way is man's spirit personified.[78]

A. J. DENNIS

It was during James White's term as editor of *The Signs of the Times* that A. J. Dennis in 1879 published his article entitled "One God." He wrote:

What a contradiction of terms is found in the language of a trinitarian creed: "In unity of this Godhead are three persons, of one substance, power, and eternity, the Father, the Son, and the Holy Ghost." There are many things that are mysterious written in the word of God, but we may safely presume the Lord never calls upon us to believe impossibilities. But creeds often do.[79]

A. J. Dennis regarded belief in *two self-existent beings each equal in power, as postulating the existence of two Gods*. But, he says, the Bible teaches the existence of only one. He saw no difficulty in ascribing eternity to both Father and Son if eternity refers to duration without end. In this sense Enoch and Elijah and all the redeemed saints have eternity of existence.[80]

J. M. HOPKINS

J. M. Hopkins, writing for the *Review and Herald* in 1883, attached great importance to the work of the Holy Spirit, but proceeded to define His existence in the following term, "It is that almighty, holy influence operating in the universe of god, by means of which worlds have been formed, physical laws established and maintained..."[81]

God, he believed, has communicated to his people by means of the Spirit, the saints are to be raised by the same power, and the living changed into an incorruptible form ready for translation, by the same Spirit. But the Spirit remains an influence as different from a person, an equal member in the Godhead.[82]

J. E. SWIFT

> Two men wrote for the *Review and Herald* in 1883, leaving the question as to the nature of the Holy Spirit an open one. Neither was prepared to dogmatize and both placed emphasis on the importance of the work of the Holy Spirit. Swift wrote, "Just what the spirit is, is a mooted question among theologians, and we may not hope to give it a positive answer, but we may learn something of its nature, and the part it acts in human salvation."[83]

He proceeded to speak of the work of the Spirit and consistently used the personal pronoun "he" in reference to the Spirit. There is no real indication in the article as to whether Swift believed the Holy Spirit an influence or a person, but the tenor of the article is certainly in the direction of the latter concept.

G. C. TENNEY

G. C. Tenney in his article entitled "The Comforter," asserts that whatever the existence of the Holy Spirit is material or immaterial, whether it is "a personal being, or a representative influence, it exists, clothed with an all-seeing and omnipresent nature, and claims our most sacred respect."[84]

Here again Tenney leaves the question open as to the personality of the Holy Spirit. Later in the century, in 1896, Tenney wrote an answer to a question sent by a correspondent. The question was as follows:

> Please explain 1 John 5:8.
> a) Is the word "spirit" synonymous with the Holy Ghost of verse 7?
> b) What is the Holy Ghost? How do we receive it, through God, or through angels?
> c) Is the Comforter of John 16:7, 8 the Holy Ghost? If so, how can it be alluded to as "him" and "he"?[85]

Tenney disposed of the first question by saying that the last part of verse 7 and the first part of verse 8 is an interpolation which ought not to be in the Scriptures. He added:

> It is not in the Revised Version, and it is well understood by Biblical scholars that these words were inserted by some one who desired to render more prominent an erroneous idea of the dogma of the Trinity.[86]

Of course modern scholarship would not disagree with Tenney's rejection of the 1 John 5:7 and 8 interpolations. But it is clear from his statement that he is not trinitarian. The idea, which the passage would prove, were it genuine, is that the Father, Son, and Holy Spirit are one. This idea Tenney regards as "erroneous."

In spite of this, Tenney does not rule out the possibility that the Holy Spirit is a person. In answer to the second question he wrote, "We cannot tell. We cannot describe the Holy Spirit." He regards the scriptural evidence of such a nature that he is "led to believe he is something more than an emanation from the mind of God." Tenney continues:

> He is included in the apostolic benedictions, and is spoken of by our Lord as acting in an independent and personal capacity as teacher, guide, and comforter. He is an object of veneration, and is a heavenly intelligence, everywhere present, and always present. But as limited beings, we cannot understand the problems which the contemplation of the Deity presents to our minds.[87]

Here we are confronted with a writer who obviously has not accepted the doctrine of the Trinity, but whose doubts in regard to the personality and deity of the Holy Spirit seem to be gradually resolving in the direction of the trinitarian belief. He is not yet thoroughly sure, but is at least prepared to concede that "He," the Spirit of God, "is something more than an emanation from the mind of God."

J. H. WAGGONER

The Pacific Press published J. H. Waggoner's book, *The Atonement*, in 1884. As has been shown Waggoner was by no means the first Seventh-day Adventist writer who regarded the trinitarian view of Christ as subversive of the atonement, but his work underlined and for a time perpetuated this position. He wrote, "...surely, we say right, that the doctrine of a trinity degrades the atonement, by bringing this sacrifice, the blood of our purchase, down to the standard of socinianism."[88]

The point which Waggoner emphasized so often is that in Christ there were not two distinct natures during the incarnation; one, the human, which died, and the other, the divine which, when the human died, ascended again to the Father. This view would render the sacrifice a human one, and therefore an inadequate one for human redemption.

Waggoner regards it as impossible for the self-existent God to die. He says, "...here is a plain declaration that 'the ever-living, self-existent god' died for sinners, which we cannot believe...."[89]

The Father was the self-existent God, Christ was not. Therefore, Christ could die for sinners. Both His human and divine attributes died on the cross. This position led Waggoner to conclude that Christ was subordinate, possessing a derived existence. Christ was pre-existent but not self-existent and therefore God in a subordinate sense. Waggoner wrote:

> The first of the above quotations say the Word was God, and also the Word was with God. Now it needs no proof—indeed it is self-evident that the Word as God, was not the God whom he was with. And as there is but "one God," the term must be used in reference to the Word in a subordinate sense, which is explained by Paul's calling the same pre-existent person the Son of God.[90]

It was this pre-existent, subordinate Son of God who died on Calvary and provided the possibility of atonement. It is clear, therefore, that Waggoner's repudiation of trinitarianism was in view of its apparent contradiction of his understanding of the atonement.

Many theologians really think that the atonement, in respect to its dignity and efficacy, rests upon the doctrine of a trinity. But we fail to see any connection between the two. To the contrary, the advocates of that doctrine really fall into the difficulty which they seem anxious to avoid. Their difficulty consists in this: They take the denial of a trinity to be equivalent to a denial of the divinity of Christ. Were that the case, we should cling to the doctrine of a trinity as tenaciously as any can; but it is not the case. They who have read our remarks on the death of the Son of God know that we firmly believe in the divinity of Christ; but we cannot accept the idea of a trinity, as it is held by trinitarians, without giving up our claim on the dignity of the sacrifice made for our redemption.

> As before remarked, the great mistake of Trinitarians, in arguing this subject, is this: they make no distinction between a denial of a trinity and a denial of the divinity of Christ. They see only the two extremes, between which the truth lies; and take every expression referring to the pre-existence of Christ as evidence of a trinity. The Scriptures abundantly teach the pre-existence of Christ and his divinity; but they are entirely silent in regard to a trinity. The declaration, that the divine Son of God could not die, is as far from the teachings of the Bible as darkness is from light. And we would ask the Trinitarian, to which of the two natures are we indebted for redemption? The answer must, of course, be, to that one which died or shed his blood for us; for "we have redemption through his blood." Then it is evident that if only the human nature died, our Redeemer is only human, and that the divine Son of God took no part in the work of redemption, for he could neither suffer nor die. Surely, we say right, that the doctrine of a trinity degrades the Atonement, by bringing the sacrifice, the blood of our purchase, down to the standard of Socinianism.[21]

Much stress is laid on Isaiah 9:6, as proving a trinity, which we have before quoted, as referring to our

High Priest who shed his blood for us. The advocates of that theory will say that it refers to a trinity because Christ is called the everlasting Father. But for this reason, with others, we affirm that it can have no reference to a trinity. Is Christ the Father in the trinity? If so, how is he the Son? Or if he is both Father and Son, how can there be a trinity? For a trinity is three persons. To recognize a trinity, the distinction between the Father and Son must be preserved. Christ is called "the second person in the trinity;" but if this text proves a trinity, or refers to it at all, it proves that he is not the second, but the first. And if he is the first, who is the second? It is very plain that this text has no reference to such a doctrine.[92]

G. W. MORSE

"The Commentary" section of the *Review and Herald* consisted in 1886 of a column of questions and answers. G. W. Morse, in answering the question as to whether the Father's throne will be in heaven and Christ's on earth, stated that the new earth will be Christ's kingdom. But God the Father will always be the supreme ruler of the universe, governing from His throne in heaven, and reigning "jointly with the Son in the New Earth."[93]

His point seems to be that the Son is a dependent ruler of just a small segment of God's dominions, this earth, while the Father is the supreme ruler of the entire universe. In a previous article of the same year Morse distinguished between Christ, and the "great God" of Titus 2:13. He wrote:

A literal translation of the words italicized reads thus: *"And the appearing of the Lord of the glory of the great God,"* etc. Thus it is seen that it is the glory of the great God as manifested in the appearing of his Son, that we are to look for, and not the great God himself. [24]

Thus he does not regard Christ as the great God, but a a dependent being.

C. P. BOLLMAN

Writing for the *Signs of the Times* in November 1889. C. P. Bollman declared that the Spirit of God "is essentially divine."[25]

But he does not go so far as to portray the Holy Spirit as a distinct personality and member of the deity. This Spirit is the power of God by which the Son created all things. The Spirit is "an essential part of God, and therefore, necessarily divine," but "it" remains to Bollman an impersonal power.[26]

THE 1889 YEARBOOK

The 1889 Yearbook was the first to include a definition of the beliefs of Seventh-day Adventists. The statement of their understanding of God is interesting in that it is such that both trinitarians and anti-trinitarians could subscribe to it without violating their respective convictions. The declaration reads:

a) That there is one God, a personal, spiritual being, the Creator of all things, omnipotent, omniscient, and eternal; infinite in wisdom, holiness, justice, goodness, truth, and mercy; unchangeable, and everywhere present by his representative, the Holy Spirit. Psalm 139:7.

> b) That there is one Lord Jesus Christ, the Son of the Eternal Father, the one by whom he created all things, and by whom they do consist...[97]

The identical statement appeared in the yearbook of 1905. The trinitarian of course could agree with the entire passage. He would interpret it his way, including Christ and the Holy Spirit in the term "one God" in item a). But so could the anti-trinitarian agree with it. He would interpret the passage to mean that only the Father is eternal. He would be, to the Arian, the "one God" referred to in item a). There is no indication in this declaration that the Arian views of the "Smiths, Canrights and Waggoners" in the Adventist Church had been suspended by trinitarianism.

E. J. WAGGONER

Back in 1890, before he left the Adventist Church, E. J. Waggoner expressed himself on the subject of the pre-existence of Christ in a manner consistent with what we have discovered to be the traditional explanation given by Seventh-day Adventist writers up to this time. In his work *Christ and His Righteousness* he wrote, "We know that Christ 'proceeded forth and came from God' (John 8:42), but it was so far back in the ages of eternity as to be far beyond the grasp of the mind of man."[98]

> To E. J. Waggoner, at least at this stage of his career, Christ had a beginning. There was a time when He had not existed. His life was derived from that of the Father. This view was in no way regarded by Waggoner as a contradiction of his remark a little farther on in the same work to the effect that Christ is God by inheritance, possessing the attributes of deity.[99]

Nor would it necessarily be ruled out by what Waggoner wrote in 1900 that, "Jesus Christ and God the Father, who raised him from the dead," are associated on equal terms. "I and my Father are one" John 10:30. They both sit upon one throne. Hebrews 1:3; 8:1; Revelation 3:21."[100]

Even Uriah Smith, for all his Arian pronouncements, conceived of Christ as "the Associate Majesty of Heaven equal with the Father, and sharing equally in the glory..."[101]

This equality was conferred upon Him; hence He is not God in the same sense as the Father. Waggoner's remark in 1900 that both Father and Son "sit upon one throne" is, however, a departure from the position of G. W. Morse that the Father, as Supreme Ruler, has His throne in heaven while the Son has His on this earth.

After leaving the Seventh-day Adventist Church, and shortly before his death, E. J. Waggoner wrote his *Confession of Faith*. In it we read this declaration:

From the simple truth that Christ is "the image of the invisible God"—the shining forth of His glory, the manifestation of His unchangeable character— Himself the same yesterday, and all the yesterdays, and today, and forever, we must believe and know that from the days of eternity of old until now, Christ has exercised the three-fold office of Prophet, Priest, and king.[102]

Had Waggoner altered his former stand so that now he conceived of Christ as a being without beginning? Had he now accepted the trinitarian doctrine of the eternal preexistence of Christ? Taking the statement in isolation from his former utterances, one would probably conclude that. The phrase, "from the days of eternity of old until now," strongly suggests this. But Waggoner had written in 1850 that Christ came into existence "so far back in the ages of eternity..."[103]

The "days of eternity" of the 1916 declaration might well have reference to the infinite period which, in Waggoner's earlier work, time was said to have elasped since Christ "came from God."

D. T. BORDEAU

There can be no doubt but that in 1890 there was no unity of understanding in regard to the nature of God in Adventist circles. D. T. Bordeau wrote in November of that year:

> Although we claim to be believers in, and worshippers of, only one God, I have thought that there are as many gods among us as there are conceptions of the Deity. And how many there are of these, and how limited are most of them! Rather, how limited are all of them! We do not half study the character of God the Father and of God the Son, and the result is that we make Christ such beings as ourselves.[104]

T. R. WILLIAMSON

Almost a year after Bordeau's remark, T. R. Williamson wrote for the *Review and Herald* reiterating the old argument that the Holy Spirit was not a person, but an influence. He could not see that the Bible references to the Holy Spirit intend for us "to conclude that a person is meant, or that any other idea is intended by these terms, than that of an influence."[105]

No one, said Williamson, is ever baptized with or filled with a person. But they are baptized with and filled with the Spirit. He considered the personification of the Holy Spirit in Scripture to be simply a figure of speech.

Williamson repudiated the trinitarian belief that the Holy Spirit is God. He wrote:

> It was said by the Lord Jesus, "I and my Father are one." If there are three persons in the Godhead, why did he not include all three in one? Why did he only say, "I and my Father are one," if the Holy Spirit is a member of the Godhead, one with the Father and Son? Why this ignoring of the third person of the Trinity?[106]

He concludes by repeating that the Holy Spirit "is simply an influence from God."

> It is a manifestation of the power of God which pervades the universe as air pervades the earth.[107]

SAMUEL T. SPEARS

The publication in 1892, by the Pacific Press, of a trinitarian article, written by a non-Adventist writer, would seem to indicate a growing acceptance of this doctrine in the Adventist Church. The article entitled, "The Bible Doctrine of the Trinity," was written by Samuel T. Spear and published in 1889 in the *New York Independent*.[108]

The Pacific Press reprinted it in 1892 as No. 90 at the Bible Student's Library. The Spear article clearly defines the trinitarian position as teaching the unity of the Godhead consisting of three persons:

This doctrine, as held and stated by those who adopt it, is not a system of tri-theism, or the doctrine of three Gods, but it is the doctrine of one God subsisting and acting in three persons, with the qualification that the term "person," though perhaps the best that can be used, is not, when used in this relation, to be understood in any sense that would make it inconsistent with the unity of the Godhead, and hence not to be understood in the ordinary sense when applied to man.[109]

The article thus effectively answered those Seventh-day Adventists who had confused trinitarianism with monarchianism, and those who had confused it with tri-theism. But there is much in the article that would be quite unobjectionable to Adventist anti-trinitarians. The Son is spoken of as "in some respect distinct from and subordinate to God the Father."[110]

This subordination is not said to be simply in regard to his human nature. Spear wrote, "the subordination extends to his divine as well as his human nature."[111]

God acted through Christ in the work of creation. Christ was the subordinate agent. Christ was "sent" into the world and delivered "up for us all." Therefore the Father possessed "some kind of primacy."[112]

Spear quotes 1 Corinthians 15:28 as proving that after Christ's reinstatement in heaven He is subordinate to the Father, and that not in His human nature merely, but in His higher divine nature.[113]

This was certainly a palatable form of trinitarianism for Adventists who had in the past, and who during and after this time, opposed the doctrine. Spear does not go so far as to say that the subordination of the Son to the Father involved the propagation of the Son by the Father back in the eternal ages. There is no suggestion that there was a time when the Son did not exist. In reference to this theory he writes:

> The theory of the eternal generation of the Son by the Father, with the cognate theory of the eternal generation of the Holy Ghost from the Father, or from the Father and the Son, while difficult even to apprehend, and while at best but a mystical speculation, is an effort to be wise, not only above what is written, but also beyond the possibilities of human knowledge.[114]

It is difficult to resolve the contradiction in Spear's judgment that the Son "is truly divine and truly God in the most absolute sense," with his opinion that in His divine nature Christ is subordinate to the Father. He regards the Arian, who views Christ as more than human but less than divine as in error, because of his failure to recognize the absolute divinity of Christ. But Spear himself recognizes, as he asserts, the absolute divinity of Christ, yet proceeds to fall into the Arian dilemma of regarding His divinity as subordinate to that of the Father. Here we have absolute divinity inferior to absolute divinity, which, in the final analysis, is perilously close to the Arian concept of the anti-trinitarian writers of the Adventist Church.

A. T. JONES

A. T. Jones recognized the Holy Spirit as the presence of Christ. His sermon "The Third Angel's Message" was published in the *General Conference Bulletin* in 1895. Jones spoke of the Holy Ghost as "the real presence of christ" to the believer.[115]

He adds, "...can he bring christ to us without bringing the mind of christ to us?—assuredly not."[116]

The remark is not conclusive evidence that Jones accepted the doctrine of the personality of the Holy Spirit, but it seems to indicate that possibly this was so.

A series if editorial articles appeared in the *Review and Herald* in 1900 under the title, "The Faith of Jesus." Uriah Smith and A. T. Jones were co-editors at this time. The serial article is not signed, but the language and style of writing appear to be that of A. T. Jones. The writer sets forth Christ's likeness to God as taught in the first chapter of Hebrews and His likeness to man as indicated by the second chapter. Just as Christ is like the Father "in very nature," of the same substance and form of the Father, so, said Jones, He bears in His human nature a complete likeness to fallen humanity.[117]

> Of course this question of the human nature of Christ was of special concern to Jones as revealed by his emphasis on the subject in his book, *The Consecrated Way to Christian Perfection*.[118]

This serial *Review and Herald* article contains the identical emphasis, and thus provides us with an additional clue to its authorship.

> The important relevant point in this series is that "Jesus and God are—of one flesh, of one nature, of one substance ..."[119]

This was a major departure from the militant opposition to such views by earlier writers.

M. C. WILCOX

M. C. Wilcox explained the scriptural passages that refer to the Holy Spirit as a person, in the light that "It" is the personal representative of both the Father and the Son.[120]

Writing for the *Signs of the Times* in 1898, he failed to credit personality and deity to the Spirit in the trinitarian sense. The Holy Spirit "comes to the believer as a person, the person of Christ Jesus...."[121]

Wilcox wrote an article in 1898 entitled "The Divine Unity." The unity is not presented as the unity of three divine persons, but that of "one God, the Father."[122]

> Christ is depicted as "under God, our Creator and Redeemer."[123]

Once again the reader of the denominational literature is confused by the subordination of the Son to the Father.

A. T. ROBINSON

A. T. Robinson, writing for the *Review and Herald* in 1929, leaves a doubt in the reader's mind as to his true position. He states, "there is 'one God' to whom the sinner must be reconciled, or else go down to eternal death. there is 'one mediator,' through whom alone such reconciliation can be effected."[124]

His article is headed "One God and One Mediator," and, whether intentionally or not, he gives the impression that the one God is the Father only. He is to become the supreme ruler of the universe. "When the Plan of Salvation is completed, there will be a reunion of the 'whole family in Heaven and earth,' over whom one Supreme Father will precide."[125]

As proof he quotes 1 Corinthians 15:28. The reader cannot do otherwise than receive the impression that in the mind of the writer there lingers the doctrine of the subordination of the Son to the Father.

J. S. WASHBURN

On October 14, 1939, W. W. Prescott preached a sermon in the Takoma Park Church on the subject, "The Coming One." He took the position that Jehovah of the Old Testament is Jesus of the New Testament. He urged that the three persons of the Godhead cannot be regarded as separate personalities in the same sense as human beings, because there is a mysterious union between them which is dissoluble.[126]

OPPOSES PRESCOTT'S SERMON

J. S. Washburn took exception to the Prescott sermon, and produced twenty typed pages in answer to the trinitarian position. The first section consists of a polemical attempt to refute trinitarianism, particularly as represented by Prescott's sermon, and the second section comprises a personal attack on Prescott. Washburn exposes himself throughout as a testy supporter of a dying cause. He describes the doctrine of the Trinity as "a cruel heathen monstrosity removing Jesus from the true position of Divine Saviour and Mediator."[127]

> Trinitarianism is of pagan origin and it is characteristic of Roman theology. In fact it is "Satan's 'crowning masterpiece' of apostate counterfeit Christianity."[128]

HIS VIEW OF CHRIST

Washburn's depiction of Christ was identical to that of the older Adventist writers. Christ was brought into being, begotten of the Father. The Father is Jehovah and the Son Adoni.[129]

He accuses Prescott of teaching that the Father and the Son are one person. His illustrations of the absurdity of that view are practically identical to those used by early Adventist writers. Washburn saw the unity between the Father and Christ as entirely analogous to that between Christ and His disciples. If Prescott is correct, says Washburn, the Father was born of the Virgin, and He hung on the cross and died. Obviously the basis of his anxiety is the old problem of J. H. Waggoner and others that the divine in Christ died, but he says, trinitarian teaching renders this impossible and the sacrifice was not an adequate atonement.[130]

HE CONTRADICTS HIMSELF

> Washburn attempts to explain the Ellen G. White statement, "Deity did not sink and die, that would have been impossible."[131]

He quotes Job 34:12, 14-15 and Psalm 36:9 as evidence that when a man dies, God simply takes back the life He has previously given. Just so:

> When Christ was begotten of the Father, He received the life of God, His Father. When Jesus died on the cross, He said, "Father into thy hands I commend my spirit," (or life), and the life of God was given back to the Father, and for a time, three days and nights, that life was with the Father from whence it had come. In the resurrection that life of God is restored to the one who died. Psalm 104:30. But between his death on Friday afternoon, till Sunday morning, *the Son of God was dead.*[132]

Thus Washburn reduces the life of Christ, the pre-existent, divine Christ, to the level of human existence, derived from the Father in the same sense, re-called at death, and re-bestowed in the resurrection, in the same sense. Then Washburn proceeds to quote a *Spirit of Prophecy* statement which contradicts the argument he has just presented. The statement he quotes is as follows:

> When he closed his eyes in death upon the cross, the soul of Jesus did not go at once to Heaven.... All that comprised the life and intelligence of Jesus remained with his body in the sepulchre. And when he came forth it was as a whole being. He did not have to summon his spirit from heaven.[133]

Washburn confidently affirmed, "This squarely contradicts the teaching of Elder Prescott."[134]

But what he had overlooked was that it squarely contradicted J. S. Washburn. He had just announced that "the life of God was given back to the Father..." But the Ellen G. White statement, which he quoted as supporting evidence, has the life of Jesus remaining in the sepulchre. The remainder of Washburn's attack on trinitarianism in general, and Prescott's sermon in particular, consists of a piling up of reasons as to why the Godhead could not be one person. As were the early Adventist Arians, Washburn is opposing monarchianism. Thus he exposes his misunderstanding of what trinitarians teach. He concludes, "The whole Trinity doctrine is utterly foreign to all the Bible and the teachings of the Spirit of Prophecy. Revelation gives not the slightest hint of it."[135]

R. F. COTTRELL

"My reasons for not adopting and defending it are:

1. Its name is unscriptural the Trinity, or the triune, is unknown to the Bible; and I have entertained the idea that doctrines which require words coined in the human mind to express them, are coined doctrines.
2. I have never felt called upon to adopt and explain that which is contrary to all the sense and reason that God has given me. All my attempts at an explanation of such a subject would make it no clearer to my friends..." [136]

He proceeded to affirm that "man is a triune being," consisting of body, soul, and spirit.

> I never heard a Disciple confess faith in the doctrine of the trinity; but why not, if man consists of three persons in one person? Especially, since man was made in the image of God? But the image he said was a moral likeness. So man may be a triune being without proving that God is. But does he mean that one man is three men? I might say that a tree consists of body, bark and leaves, and no one perhaps would dispute it. But if I should affirm that each tree consists of three trees, the assertion would possibly be doubted by some. But if all admitted that one tree is three trees, I might then affirm that there were ninety trees in my orchard, when no one could count but thirty. I might then proceed and say, I have ninety trees in my orchard, and as each tree consists of three trees, I have two hundred and seventy. So if one man is three men, you may multiply him by three as often as you please. But if it takes body, soul and spirit to make one perfect, living man; then separate these, and the man is unmade. [137]

That one person is three persons, and that three persons are only one person, is the doctrine which we claim is contrary to reason and common sense. The being and attributes of God are above, beyond, out of reach of my sense and reason, yet I believe them: But the doctrine I object to is contrary, yes, that is the word, to the very sense and reason that God has himself implanted in us. Such a doctrine he does not ask us to believe. A miracle is beyond our comprehension, but we all believe in miracles who believe our own senses. What we see and hear convinces us that there is a power that affected the most wonderful miracle of creation. But our Creator has made it an absurdity to us that one person should be three persons, and three persons but one person; and in his revealed word he has never asked us to believe it. This our friend thinks objectionable...

But to hold the doctrine of the Trinity is not so much an evidence of evil intention as of intoxication from that wine of which all the nations have drunk. The fact that this was one of the leading doctrines, if not the very chief, upon which the bishop of Rome was exalted to the popedom, does not say much in its favour. This should cause men to investigate it for themselves; as when the spirits of devils working miracles undertake the advocacy of the immortality of the soul. Had I never doubted it before, I would now probe it to the bottom, by that word which modern Spiritualism sets at nought ... Revelation goes beyond us; but in no instance does it go contrary to right reason and common sense. God has not claimed, as the popes have, that he could "make justice of injustice," nor has he, after teaching us to count, told us that there is no difference between the singular and plural numbers. Let us believe all he has revealed, and add nothing to it. [138]

J. B. FRISBIE

We will make a few extracts that the reader may see the broad contrast between the God of the Bible brought to light through Sabbath-keeping, and the god in the dark through Sunday-keeping. *Catholic Catechism Abridged* by the Rt. Rev. John Dubois, Bishop of New York. Page 5. 'Q. Where is God? Ans. God is everywhere. Q. Does God see and know all things? A. Yes, he does know and see all things... Q. Are there more Gods than one? A. No; there is but one God. Q. Are there more persons than one in God? A Yes; in God there are three persons. Q. Which are they? A. God the Father, God the Son and God the Holy Ghost. Q. Are there not three Gods? A. No; the Father, the Son and the Holy Ghost, are all but one and the same God'...These ideas well accord with those heathen philosophers ... We should rather mistrust that the Sunday God [the Trinity] came from the same source that Sunday-keeping did." [139]

A QUESTIONABLE CONCLUSION

Some short time ago, certain updated, unsigned, mimeographed documents were circulated by the Seventh-day Adventist leadership in answer to some of the positions taken by M. L. Andreasen Document 1 entitled, "Uriah Smith's Restricted View of the Atonement," states, "both Smith and Waggoner were in the minority group of Arians, or anti-Trinitarians, as regards the Godhead, following the crisis of 1844." [140]

Document II, entitled, "J. H. Waggoner's Position on the Atonement" states:

> However, it is essential to note, first, that our founding fathers came out of diversified denominational backgrounds. Many were Trinitarians, while a few came from the "Christian Connection," which was militantly Arian, or anti-Trinitarian. But some of these few rose to positions of prominence among us. Smith and Waggoner both held Arian views. Both were writers and editors, and interwove Arian views into their writings. [141]

In light of the evidence presented in this paper, it might justifiably be asked, where is the proof that in the early history of the Seventh-day Adventists "many were trinitarians," or that the anti-trinitarians were a minority? Almost every utterance on the subject published in Adventist literature prior to 1898 was Arian or anti-trinitarian. The Spear article was a notable exception, but it was a reprint of an article written by a non-Adventist writer, and it contained the doctrine of the subordination of the Son to the Father, which was quite acceptable to the Adventist anti-trinitarian, but quite unacceptable to the later believer who concurred with the 1931 statement of belief.

As has been shown, there was prior to 1898 considerable diversity of belief on the subject of the nature of God. Bordeau in 1890 regretted this. But Erwin R. Gane has been unable to discover any evidence that "many were Trinitarians" before 1898, nor has there been found any trinitarian declaration written, prior to that date, by any Adventist writer.

The statement quoted from the document, "J. H. Waggoner's position on the atonement," strongly suggests that it was the few who came from the "Christian Connection," and who rose to "prominence among us," who are regarded as responsible for the dissemination of Arian, or anti-trinitarian views among Adventists. [142]

> Smith and Waggoner are then cited as holding Arian views. But no evidence is given that these men came from the "Christian Connection," as the statement would suggest. As has been shown, James White and Joseph Bates came from this organization, but it is not known who else. And is it to be believed that all the Adventist writers examined in this thesis, who presented Arian opinions, came from the Christian Connection? Of course that was not so. The truth is as stated by the document quoted above, that "our founding fathers came out of diversified denominational backgrounds."[143]

This fact, and the fact that so many were Arians, is sufficient to prove that the origin of a few from the "Christian Connection" is not adequate explanation of the anti-trinitarianism consistently appearing in Adventist literature.

Of course the writers and editors of any church organization will be a minority group. So they were in the Seventh-day Adventist Church. But this minority group happened to present, almost without exception, anti-trinitarian statements in articles and books. This certainly does not look like evidence that "many were trinitarians." If trinitarians were so numerous it is strange indeed that some of them did not put their views in writing. Some would perhaps blame Uriah Smith for preventing this. Then why did not trinitarian articles appear in the years when James White was editor of the *Review and Herald*? And what evidence is there that Uriah Smith exercised such an overriding influence that for decades he succeeded in excluding from publication, in any form, the trinitarian beliefs of the majority of Adventists?

ELLEN G. WHITE

Ellen G. White explains at least in part what happened to the deity element of Christ's nature when He died on Calvary:

> When He closed His eyes in death upon the Cross, the soul of Christ did not go at once to heaven, as many believe, or how could His words be true—"I am not yet ascended to my Father"? *The Spirit of Jesus slept in the tomb with His body, and did not wing its way to heaven,* there to maintain a separate existence, and to look down upon the mourning disciples embalming the body from which it had taken flight. All that comprised the life and intelligence of Jesus remained with His body in the sepulcher; and when He came forth it was as a whole being; He did not have to summon His spirit from heaven.[144]

As further evidence, the circumstances of the resurrection may be cited. Ellen G. White speaks of Christ as a prisoner in the tomb. Only the Father could release Him:

> He who died for the sins of the world was to remain in the tomb the allotted time. He was in that stony prison house as a prisoner of divine justice. He was responsible to the judge of the universe. He was bearing the sins of the world, and His Father only could release Him.[145]

AUSTIN P. COOKE

It appears that the pioneers, not having a theological background, misunderstood the nature of the Trinity. They also had problems in understanding what constitutes a person... It is asserted by the exponents of the revived error that the Holy Spirit is Jesus Christ Himself because He said, "I will come to you." If so, then Jesus in His heavenly state would need to be omnipresent, i.e. everywhere present. This claim clashes with other scriptures and also with the Spirit of Prophecy. Jesus is the Godman. He will be a member of the human race forever. *He surrendered His omnipresence forever* in becoming man in order to redeem the human race. *This limits the presence of Jesus.*[146]

Understandingly my non-Adventist friends were confused. "How could five people belonging to the same church have such different opinions about God?" they asked. A Jewish friend remarked, "That means every time Adventists pray, some are praying to one God, and some to many Gods." "Your church sounds like a confusion," a Muslin interjected. "I don't think that I would want to go to your church."

This incident troubled me for the entire week. I had always believed in the Trinity as stated in the twenty-seven Fundamental beliefs of Seventh-day Adventists, so it never occurred to me that some Adventists believed otherwise. The following Sabbath I went to church and asked various people about their belief about the Trinity. Amazingly I received radically different opinions. It seems clear that we do not know what we believe. If Adventists cannot agree on what is one of our fundamental beliefs, how can we then go into the entire world, and preach the gospel to every creature? [147]

V. R. CHRISTENSEN

> There is no evidence in scripture that the term "Son of God" is applied to Christ in any literal sense ... In biblical times the term "Son of God" was nothing more than a title, in the same sense the term "prophet" is a title. Because the disciples believed Jesus' relationship to God was special, they heightened the meaning of the existing terminology of sonship, and referred to Christ as God's "only" Son. It was the word only not the term begotten, that gave Jesus His unique place in the disciples' eyes. In the NT perception every Christian is "begotten" by God (1 John 5:18), so the term "begotten" has no special meaning of its own, it was the word "only" which set Christ apart. ... In Old Testament revelation, as Yahweh Christ was the Father. In the New Testament He who was first called "Father" fulfilled another role in which He is called the "Son." In biblical testimony the same Jesus is both Father and Son, but at different times ... The Father and Son do not exist as separate beings, they coexist as one God... [148]

If the quotes up to this point haven't been twisted enough, here's a quote from the *Dialogue* magazine out of Loma Linda, California where their managing editor, Gina Foster states:

> God no longer plays parent to our childish irresponsibility. Instead, God treats us as friends, allowing us

to make our own mistakes. *She* suffers with us and celebrates with us. We cry and laugh together. [149]

Later in the Letters to the Editor, Jerry A Garner writes:

Dear Sister Foster,
I am seldom aroused by the published error of others to take a pen in hand; however, I'm impressed to do so now because of your recent remark upon Deity, Himself. Your use of the pronoun "SHE" in reference to God (*Dialogue*, November, 1991; "Responding to God's Suffering," page 7, paragraph 4) is either presumptuous, or, at best simply confused and mistaken; so I will assume for you the best. Please note, for your edification, that in Galatians 4:6 God is referred to in both the Greek and Hebrew as the Father. This reference is consistent with all of Scripture, as any reputable theologian will attest. While God is, at times, characterized in the Bible to have qualities generally considered feminine, like tenderness and nurture, this does not in any way negate that He is the Father of all. After all, where did women get these qualities in the first place, if not from the infinite Creator?

Here's how Gina Foster responded:

Editor's Note:
The use of the pronoun *"SHE" was neither a typographical error nor due to a lack of theological training.*

SUMMARY

The evidence as presented here indicates that prior to 1898 the prevailing opinion in the Seventh-day Adventist Church on the nature of God was anti-trinitarian. It has been shown that a whole series of writers took this position. Those early Adventist writers who expressed themselves on the subject agreed on certain fundamental issues. Christ was consistently regarded as subordinate to the Father and the Holy Spirit as a mere influence. Although all the Adventist Arians aimed at discounting trinitarianism, the arguments they emphasized in opposition to it varied somewhat. Certain writers, such as Bates, Hull, Loughborough, Whitney, and Canright identified trinitarianism with monarchianism. As they saw it, if Christ were absolute deity then He was the Father. Since they repudiated this position, they repudiated trinitarianism. On the other hand some writers saw trinitarianism as postulating the existence of three gods. Loughborough and Dennis so viewed it. Thus the Arians opposed both extremes, monarchianism and tritheism. trinitarianism, they thought, might be identified with one of these extremes, but it certainly is not the truth. To them, Arianism provided a satisfactory mediating position. There is only one supreme God, and that is the Father. There was a time when Christ did not exist, and the Holy Spirit is not a person.

Some writers particularly opposed trinitarianism because it apparently depreciated the efficacy of the atonement. Hull, Smith, Canright, and J. H. Waggoner were in this category. If Christ were absolute God in the same sense as the Father, then His divine nature could not die. Under these circumstances, the sacrifice would have been a human one. Such they regarded as an inadequate atonement for the sins of man.

Some opposed the extreme creedal positions which divested God of bodily parts and form. Hull, Whitney, and Canright were particularly articulate on this point. On the other hand, it is clear that the opposition by early Adventist writers to trinitarianism was not simply a reaction to extreme forms of the doctrine. Both Hull and Loughborough opposed the decisions of Nicea, and Whitney in becoming a Seventh-day Adventist, had evidently repudiated the creedal teaching of the Congregational Church that there are three persons in one God.

Attempts have been made to demonstrate that the Arians among Seventh-day Adventists were a small but influential minority. As indicated, Uriah Smith and J. H. Waggoner are sometimes blamed for the existence of anti-trinitarianism in the Adventist Church. The evidence suggests otherwise. Four Seventh-day Adventist writers declared themselves Arians before publication of Uriah Smith's *Thoughts Critical and Practical on the Book of Revelation* in 1865. Stephenson wrote in 1854, Hull in 1859, Loughborough in 1861, and Whitney in 1862. Although Joseph Bates did not write his autobiography until 1868, in it he clearly demonstrates that he had been an Arian since 1827. The views of such a prominent pioneer were undoubtedly influential. Even Smith's extreme statement in 1865 to the effect that Christ was a created being finds its antecedent in a similar statement by Stephenson in 1854. By the same token, the views expressed by J. H. Waggoner in 1884 were by no means original with him. His anti-trinitarianism and his limited view of the atonement were shared by a considerable stream of writers who preceded him.

The Whitney article proves that in 1862 it was not unusual for a new convert to be inducted into the Arian belief. Evidently by 1890, when Bourdeau deprecated the prevailing diversity of opinion on the subject, the situation had changed in that other views were being seriously considered. The reprinting of the Spear article would indicate that they were. But these other views were not expressed by Adventist writers, with the exception of Ellen G. White, until 1898 and following. Jones' statement on the Holy Spirit back in 1895 was at best only an approximation to the trinitarian view.

Why was Arianism the prevailing doctrine up to 1898? As has been demonstrated, some of the pioneers were influenced by the Christian Connection which was opposed to trinitarianism. To what precise extent the religious background of these few influenced the positions of later writers would be difficult to determine. The Adventists, coming as they did from diversified denominational backgrounds, rejected many of the major beliefs of their former communions. It would appear that trinitarianism became associated in their thinking with other theological views they thought unscriptural and pagan. Sunday observance was introduced by the papacy, but so was trinitarianism. Were not the decisions of Nicea and Chalcedon largely the result of papal influence? And was not papal dogma leavened by pagan error? Then whatever the Bible teaches it could not possibly teach pagan-papal trinitarianism. So reasoned the pioneers of the Adventist Church.

It appears that what the Bible does actually teach on this subject was not seriously considered in the early years of Seventh-day Adventism. Immediately after the disappointment of 1844, the founding fathers of the church were occupied with what was termed *"present truth."* Of course, the primary emphasis was on the second coming of Christ. Since a correct understanding of the cleansing of the sanctuary explained the mistake of 1844, the emphasis on the scriptural teaching of the sanctuary service became a vital issue. The Bible was studied with new zest and as new beliefs developed, Ellen G. White confirmed them. But the subject of the nature of God did not come to the forefront. This fact is underlined by the relatively few articles on the subject in the *Review and Herald* in the second half of the nineteenth century, by comparison with the huge volume of material published on the distinctive Seventh-day Adventist doctrines. Whenever an Adventist writer declared himself on the nature of God the declaration was anti-trinitarian, including Ellen

G. White. This indicates a prevailing concept of Arianism. Seventh-day Adventists have no creed. This is why the prevailing belief on the *doctrine of God could change.*

It would appear that the early Seventh-day Adventist writers were to some extent influenced by the nineteenth-century Arminian, Unitarian and Socinian reaction to the Calvinistic theology of certain leading Protestant denominations. Trinitarianism was a tenet of Calvinism. Had not Calvin burned Servetus for his anti-trinitarian declarations? Therefore the Arminian, Unitarian, and Socinian reaction to predestinarianism, and other aspects of Calvinism, became associated with anti-trinitarianism. It would have been unusual if the early Adventists had not been influenced to some extent by this movement. They rejected predestinarianism and many of them came out of well-established Calvinistic communions.

What changed the prevailing Seventh-day Adventist view from Arianism to trinitarianism? It has been led to believe that the publication of the trinitarian declarations of Ellen G. White in the last decades of the nineteenth century initiated the change. It would appear that she wrote little before the early 1890s which could have led to serious questioning of the prevailing Arian view. Most of her statements which appeared before 1890 could have been interpreted to agree with the Arian doctrine. But from the early 1890s on, Ellen G. White produced increasingly what appeared to be trinitarian statements, but *could also have been interpreted as being tritheistic.* She exalted the eternally pre-existent, *self-existent Son,* who at every stage of His existence was absolutely equal with the Father. The Holy Spirit she depicted as a person, in as real a sense as Christ and the Father are persons. According to Ellen, *Lucifer* was considered to be, *next to Christ, the most honoured of God* and was higher in power and *glory compared with the Holy Spirit.* From this statement, we see that *she didn't understand the nature of* the Triune Godhead. Her statement that *the Son is self-existent, implies that He is a separate God from God the Father resulting in the heresy of either ditheism or tritheism.*

> *Sin originated with him who, next to Christ, had been most honoured of God* and was highest in power and glory among the inhabitants of heaven.[150]

A more recent quote by Austin P. Cooke discloses that Jesus *has lost His omnipresence forever.* With this implication, his Jesus is not God. Not only is He not God now, but He never was due to the fact that the nature of God never changes. V. R. Christensen is espousing *a modalistic form of the Godhead* in that Jesus Christ was the Father in one of His roles and the Son in another. The Oneness Pentecostals espouse a similar *modalistic heresy.* The Seventh-day Adventist's respected Bible scholar Raoul Dederen from Andrews University sums it quite well when he states that the persons mentioned above do not worship the God of the Holy Scriptures. In the Seventh-day Adventist *27 Articles of Faith*, in #17, Ellen G. White as the Lord's Messenger, *her writings are a continuing and authoritative source of truth* which provides for the *church comfort, guidance, instruction and correction.* The Trinity lies at the root of a genuine Christian's theology and affects his whole creed and practice. In other words, the early Adventists and the more recent Adventist people's quotes indicate that they are and were *worshipping a false God.*

Why were Ellen G. White's statements on the subject so relatively late in appearing? It has been considered that had they appeared in the early phase of denominational history they might well have been the subject of considerable division and that the church needed to be firmly established before such difficult and controversial matters could be introduced. If a church misunderstands the foundation of the whole nature of who God is, they have everything else wrong. When Ellen G. White wrote on the nature of God it was her intent not only to answer Arianism, but also to answer the pantheistic concepts which were being propagated by J. H. Kellogg. But this pantheistic threat did not seriously arise until late in the nineteenth century. It was a more serious danger to the stability of the developing movement than Arianism. The Arians were not so militant due to their stranglehold on the SDA church and thus were loyal to the denomination and, as subsequent events proved; many of them were quite open to conviction on the subject. *Essentially, there isn't much difference between Arianism, semi-Arianism and the new proposed doctrine of tritheism or ditheism. They both believe in the two- or three-god theory.*

No doubt the enlarging missions program of the church late in the nineteenth century emphasized the need of careful statement of faith. If an attempt to correct Arianism were unwise in the earliest period, it would have been even more unwise to wait until this doctrine was held by thousands of Seventh-day Adventists the world around.

> God is a spirit; yet He is a personal being, for man was created in His image. As a personal being, God has revealed Himself in His Son.... The express image of His person.[151]

> We have been brought together as a school, and we need to realize that the Holy Spirit, who is as much a person as God is a person, is walking through these grounds...[152]

> John 3:34-36. In this Scripture God and Christ are spoken of as two distinct personalities, each acting in their own individuality.[153]

John 17:20-21. These words present God and Christ as two distinct personalities [154]

If it be said that the Spirit of the Father, and the Son, and the Holy Ghost is one Spirit, with this we'll agree. But if it be said that the *Father, and the Son, and the Holy Ghost are three persons in one person*, making in all one God without body or parts, with an idea so inconsistent we cannot agree. The oneness of Christ with the Father may be plainly seen by any one who will refer to John 17:22. "That they [that believe] may be one, even as we are one." Who could believe that Christ prayed that his disciples should be one disciple? Yet this would be no more inconsistent than the idea of some that Christ and his Father are one person. In accordance with the doctrine that three very and eternal Gods are but one God, how may we reconcile Matthew 3:16, 17? Jesus was baptized, the Spirit of God descended like a dove, and the Father's voice heard from heaven, saying, This is my beloved Son, &c. The Father in heaven, the Son on earth, the Spirit of God descending from one to the other. Who could ever suppose for a moment that *these three were one person without body or parts*, unless it was by early training? See other texts which appear equally absurd, if such doctrine be true. Matthew 28:18; Acts 10:38. "How God anointed Jesus with the Holy Ghost," &c. First person takes the third person and anoints the second person with a person being at the same time one with himself.

> That three are one, and one are three,
> Is an idea that puzzles me;
> By many a learned sage 'tis said
> That three are one in the Godhead.

The Father then may be the Son,
For both together make but one;
The Son may likewise be the Father.

Without the smallest change of either. Yea, and the blessed Spirit be the Father, Son and trinity; This is the creed of Christian folks, who style themselves true orthodox, All which against plain common sense, we must believe or give offence. [155]

When we have accepted Christ, and in the name of the Father, and of the Son, and of the Holy Spirit have pledged ourselves to serve *God, the Father, Christ, and the Holy Spirit—the three dignitaries and powers of heaven*—pledge Themselves that every facility shall be given to us if we carry out our baptismal vows ... When we are true to our vows, He says, "I will receive you."[156]

There are *three living persons of the heavenly trio*; in the name of these three great powers—the Father, the Son, and the Holy Spirit...[157]

You are baptized in the name of the Father, of the Son, and of the Holy Ghost. You are raised up out of the water to live henceforth in newness of life—to live a new life. You are born unto God, and you stand under the sanction and the power of the three holiest beings in heaven, who are able to keep you from falling...[158]

We are to co-operate with the *three highest powers in heaven*—the Father, the Son, and the Holy Ghost—and these powers will work through us, making us workers together with God. [159]

...in the name of these *three great powers*—the Father, the Son, and the Holy Spirit—those who receive Christ by living faith are baptized, and these powers will co-operate with the obedient subjects of heaven in their effort to live the new life in Christ.[160]

Please see also these Bible texts regarding all three: Isaiah 48:16-17; Matthew 28:19; Mark 12:36; Luke 1:35, 3:22; John 14:16, 15:26, 16:15; Acts 2:33; Romans 8:27, 15:16; 2 Corinthians 13:14; Ephesians 2:18; Colossians 2:2-3; Hebrews 9:14; 1 Peter 1:2; Jude 20-21.

When you took these vows, you pledged yourself, in the name of the Father, the Son, and the Holy Spirit, that you would live unto God, and you have no right to break this pledge. The help of the *three great powers* is placed at your disposal.[161]

On that occasion [baptism] we pledge ourselves, in the presence of the *three great heavenly powers,* to come out from the world and be separate.[162]

By our baptismal pledge we avouched and solemnly confessed the Lord Jehovah as our ruler. We virtually took a solemn oath, and in the name of the Father, and of the Son, and of the Holy Ghost, that henceforth our lives would be merged into the life of these *three great agencies*, that the life we should live in the flesh would be lived in faithful obedience to God's sacred law.[163]

The *three powers of the Godhead* have pledged Their might to carry out the purpose that God had in mind when He gave to the world the unspeakable gift of His Son.[164]

Our sanctification is the work of the Father, the Son, and the Holy Spirit ... Have you been born again? Have you become a new being in Christ Jesus? Then cooperate with *the three great powers of heaven* who are working in your behalf.[165]

In the name of the Father, the Son, and the Holy Spirit, man is laid in his watery grave, buried with Christ in baptism, and raised from the water to live the new life of loyalty to God. The *three great powers in heaven* are witnesses; They are invisible but present.[166]

The rite of baptism is administered in the name of the Father, and of the Son, and of the Holy Ghost. These *three great powers* of heaven pledge Themselves to be the efficiency of all who submit to this ordinance, and who faithfully keep the vow they then make.[167]

The *three powers of the Godhead,* the Father, the Son, and Holy Spirit, are pledged to be their strength and their efficiency in their new life in Christ Jesus.[168]

As Christians submit to the solemn rite of baptism, He registers the vow that they make to be true to Him. This vow is their oath of allegiance. They are baptized in the name of the Father and the Son and the Holy Spirit. Thus they are united with the *three great powers of heaven*. They pledge themselves to renounce the world and to observe the laws of the kingdom of God. Henceforth they are to walk in newness of life. No longer are they to follow the traditions of men. No longer are they to follow dishonest methods. They are to obey the statutes of the kingdom of heaven. They are to seek God's honour. If they will be true to their vow, they will be furnished with grace and power that will enable them to fulfill all righteousness. "As many as received Him, to them gave He power to become the sons of God, even to them that believe on His name."[169]

"Let us not forget our baptismal vow. In the presence of the *three highest powers of heaven*—the Father, the Son, and the Holy Spirit—we have pledged ourselves to do the will of Him who, over the rent sepulcher of Joseph, declared, "I am the resurrection and the life."[170]

There is to be the imprint of the sacred name, baptizing the believers in the name of the *threefold powers in the heavenly world*. The human mind is impressed in this ceremony, the beginning of the Christian life. It means very much. The work of salvation is not a small matter, but so vast that the highest authorities are taken hold of by the expressed faith of the human agency.... The three great and glorious heavenly characters are present on the occasion of baptism. All the human capabilities are to be henceforth consecrated powers to do service to God in representing the Father, the Son, and the Holy Ghost upon whom they depend. All heaven is represented by these three in covenant relation with the new life.[171]

We are ordained unto God to bear fruit. Was this not our experience when we were led down into the water and baptized in the name of the Father, and of the Son, and of the Holy Ghost? What did that mean? —it meant that the *three great powers in heaven* were pledged to keep us so long as we remain one with Christ, united to the vine.[172]

In the name of whom were you baptized? You went down into the water in the name of the three great Worthies in heaven—the Father, the Son, and the Holy Ghost.... Those who have been baptized can claim the help of the *three great Worthies of heaven* to keep them from falling, and to reveal through them a character that is after the divine similitude.... When I feel oppressed, and hardly know how to relate myself toward the work that God has given me to do, I just call upon the three great Worthies...[173]

In whose name are we baptized? In the name of the Father, and of the Son, and of the Holy Ghost the *three highest powers* in the heavenly courts.[174]

We are baptized in the name of the Father, Son, and the Holy Ghost, and these *three great, infinite powers* are unitedly pledged to work in our behalf if we cooperate with them.[175]

...at our baptism we pledged ourselves to Him [Jesus], and received the ordinance in the name of the Father, and of the Son, and of the Holy Ghost, *these three great powers* of heaven pledged themselves to work in our behalf, not only to begin, but to finish our faith.[176]

The *three highest powers* in the universe are pledged to labour with those who will seek to save the lost.[177]

The presence of the Father, the Son, and the Holy Spirit, the *three highest powers* in the universe and those in whose name the believer is baptized, is pledged to be with every striving soul. It will impart grace and strength to all who will watch unto prayer, to all who will purify the soul by obedience to the truth. And it will make the believer instrumental in leading other souls to accept Christ by faith.[178]

The Father, the Son, and the Holy Spirit, the *three holy dignitaries of heaven*, have declared that They will strengthen men to overcome the powers of darkness.[179]

Those who submit to the solemn rite of baptism pledge themselves to devote their lives to God's service; and the *three great powers of heaven*, the Father, the Son, and the Holy Spirit, pledge themselves to cooperate with them, to work in and through them. As men and women thus enter into covenant relation with God, they take the name of Christian. Henceforth they are to live the life of Christ. They have been buried with Him, and they are to seek those things which are above, where Christ sitteth on the right hand of God. [180]

...the *three great powers of heaven* pledged Themselves to co-operate with you in your efforts to live the new life in Christ.[181]

As a Christian submits to the solemn rite of baptism, the *three highest powers* in the universe—the Father, the Son, and the Holy Spirit—place Their approval on this act, pledging Themselves to exert Their power in his behalf as he strives to honour God.[182]

The *three great powers* of heaven pledge themselves to furnish to the Christian all the assistance he requires. The Spirit changes the heart of stone to the heart of flesh. And by partaking of the word of God, eating the flesh and drinking the blood of His

Son, Christians obtain an experience that is after the divine similitude. When Christ abides in the heart by faith, the Christian is the temple of God. Christ does not abide in the heart of the sinner, but hearts that are susceptible to the influence of Heaven's instrumentalities, and have been sanctified by obedience to the truth, are representatives of His righteousness.[183]

When you gave yourself to Christ, you made a pledge in the presence of the Father, the Son and the Holy Spirit the *three great personal dignitaries of heaven.*[184]

Those who proclaim the third angel's message must put on the whole armour of God, that they may stand boldly at their post, in the face of detraction and falsehood, fighting the good fight of faith, resisting the enemy with the word, "It is written." Keep yourselves where the *three great powers* of heaven, the Father, the Son, and the Holy Spirit, can be your efficiency. These powers work with the one who gives himself unreservedly to God. The strength of heaven is at the command of God's believing ones. The man who takes God as his trust is barricaded by an impregnable wall.[185]

They pledge themselves to devote their lives to God's service; and the *three great powers* in heaven, the Father, the Son, and the Holy Spirit, pledge Themselves to cooperate with them, to work in and through them.[186]

Those who have been baptized and have taken their stand on the Lord's side, separating from the enemy, have pledged themselves to the service of God. When you went down into the water and were baptized in the name of the Father, the Son, and the Holy Spirit, these *three great powers* of heaven pledged themselves to give you power and grace to resist every temptation to dishonour God. When you rose from the water, you represented the resurrection of Christ.[187]

No requirement is laid upon man that Christ has not obeyed. We can overcome as He overcame, if we will avail ourselves of the help of the *three great powers* of heaven, who are waiting to answer the demand made upon Them by God's people for power to defeat satanic agencies.[188]

This is one of the chief proof texts Adventists use today to prove trinitarianism. However, a study of Ellen White's writings reveals that she did not use the terms "being" and "person" interchangeably as some do today. She stated that Christ was "*the only being* that could enter into all the counsels and purposes of God" (*Patriarchs and Prophets*, p. 34). This denotes only two "beings." *If the Holy Spirit was a "being" in the same sense as Christ, then why was the Holy Spirit not able to enter into all the "counsels and purposes of God"?* Further, there is a distinction that can be made between "person" and "personality" and the manner in which "personality" can be defined. In a letter dated January 24, 1935, Elder H. W. Carr wrote to W. C. White requesting Willie White's understanding of his "mother's position in reference to the personality of the Holy Spirit." Elder White responded in part:

This I cannot do because I never clearly understood her teachings on the matter. There always was in my mind some perplexity regarding the meaning of her utterances which to my superficial manner of thinking seemed to be somewhat confusing. ... My perplexities were lessened a little when I learned from the dictionary that one of the meanings of personality, was characteristics. It is stated in such a way that I concluded that there might be personality without bodily form which is possessed by the Father and the Son.[189]

It is perceived within Adventism that if they support the doctrine of either trinitarianism or tritheism, they would be out of harmony with these texts. They go on to say that one of the most basic truths of the Bible is that *there is one supreme being* and that Jesus taught us to address this being as "Our Father." Because this truth is so basic to the Scriptures and to the plan of salvation (see John 17:3), according to Adventism, they fail to see that the one true God of John 17:3 is the Triune God. Another misconception is that the doctrine of the Trinity teaches that Jesus is not really the Son of God, but rather He is a co-equal with God who plays the role of a son. By this misunderstanding, they see Jesus to be a different God than the Father.

The Athanasian Creed states in part:

1. Whosoever will be saved: before all things it is necessary that he hold the Catholic Faith:
2. Which Faith except every one do keep whole and undefiled: without doubt he shall perish everlastingly.
3. And the Catholic Faith is this: That we worship one God in Trinity, and Trinity in unity;
13. So likewise the Father is Almighty: the Son Almighty: and the Holy Ghost Almighty.
14. And yet they are not three Almighties: but one Almighty.

17. So likewise the Father is Lord: the Son Lord: and the Holy Ghost Lord.
18. And yet not three Lords: but one Lord.
25. And in this Trinity none is afore, or after another: none is greater, or less than another.
26. But the whole three persons are coeternal and coequal.
44. This is the Catholic Faith: which except a man believe faithfully, he can not be saved.[190]

This Catholic doctrine is blasphemy and does not measure up to God's Word. The Scriptures plainly state: "But to us there is but one God, the Father, of whom are all things, and we in him; and one Lord Jesus Christ, by whom are all things, and we by him." (1 Corinthians 8:6) The Bible says nothing about *one in three or three in one*; but rather declares "one God the Father" and "one Lord Jesus Christ" the Son of the "only true God." (see John 17:3) This is not a "Jesus Only" creed nor is it a trinitarian creed. Shall we believe the creeds and councils of devil-inspired men instead of the sacred words of truth inspired by the Holy Spirit? God forbid! The Bible plainly declares that "God, who at sundry times and in divers manners spake in time past unto the fathers by the prophets, Hath in these last days spoken unto us by his Son, whom he hath appointed heir of all things, by whom also he made the worlds." (Hebrews 1:1, 2) The testimony of Jesus agrees: "There is a personal God, the Father; there is a personal Christ, the Son."[191]

Brother E. Everts writes from Round Grove, Whiteside Co., Ill.:

We find some who have ears to hear, some who acknowledge the truth as we present it, and some half dozen have decided to keep all the commandments. We find more who are looking for the coming of the Lord than we expected; and we find some who were keeping the Sabbath, who appear to delight in so-doing; but O how deformed they appear with their errors, of the "Spirit-Land," the conscious, living dead, and a "Triune God." How incomprehensible to attempt to comprehensible to attempt to comprehend living dead men; and, Father and Son, one person![192]

David Clayton, the author of The Divinity of Christ states that others, notably the Seventh-day Adventist Church, have concluded that the word, *"God" is a collective noun, which really refers to three Gods (!)* working together in unity. The SDA church will deny that it teaches or believes in three Gods. However, semantics will not deny the truth. *The SDA belief in three co-equal, co-eternal, co-omnipotent Beings who are not related to each other clearly teaches Tritheism, a doctrine of three Gods*, even though it is claimed that the three are one in the sense that they are united in character, goals and purposes.

The doctrine of the Trinity is a cruel heathen monstrosity, removing Jesus from his true position of Divine Saviour and Mediator. It is true we can not measure or define divinity. It is beyond our finite understanding, yet on this subject of the personality of God the Bible is very simple and plain. The Father, the Ancient of Days, is from eternity. Jesus was begotten of the Father. Jesus speaking through the Psalmist says: "The Lord (Jehovah) has said unto me, Thou art my son, this day have I begotten thee." -

Psalm 2:7. Again in Proverbs (where Jesus is spoken of under the title of wisdom, See 1 Corinthians 1:24), we read: Satan has taken some heathen conception of a *three-headed monstrosity*, and with deliberate intention to cast contempt upon divinity, has woven it into Romanism as our glorious God, an impossible, absurd invention. This monstrous doctrine transplanted from heathenism into the Roman Papal Church is seeking to intrude its evil presence into the teachings of the Third Angel's Message. ... And the fact that Christ is not the mediator in the Roman Church demonstrates that the Trinity destroys the truth that Christ is the one, the only mediator. The so-called Christian Church, the Papacy, that originated the doctrine of the Trinity, does not recognize him as the only mediator but substitutes a multitude of ghosts of dead men and women as mediators. *If you hold the Trinity doctrine, in reality, Christ is no longer your mediator.* ... Seventh-day Adventists claim to take the word of God as supreme authority and to have "come out of Babylon," to have renounced forever the vain traditions of Rome. If we should go back to the immortality of the soul, purgatory, eternal torment and the Sunday Sabbath, would that be anything less than apostasy? If, however, we leap over all these minor, secondary doctrines and accept and teach the very central root, doctrine of Romanism, the Trinity, and teach that the son of God did not die, even though our words seem to be spiritual, is this anything else or anything less than apostasy, and the very Omega of apostasy? ... However kindly or beautiful or apparently profound his sermons or articles may be, when a man has arrived at the place where he teaches the heathen Catholic doctrine of the Trinity, and denies that the Son of God died for us, is he a true Seventh-day Adventist? Is he even a true preacher of the Gospel? And when many regard him as a great teacher and accept his unscriptural theories, absolutely contrary to the Spirit of Prophecy, it is time that the watchmen should sound a note of warning. ...[193]

Adventist beliefs have changed over the years under the impact of "present truth." Most startling is the teaching regarding Jesus Christ, our Saviour and Lord. Many of the pioneers, including James White, J. N. Andrews, Uriah Smith, and J. H. Waggoner, held to *an Arian or semi-Arian view* that is, the Son at some point in time before the Creation of our world was generated by the Father.... Likewise, the Trinitarian understanding of God, now part of our fundamental beliefs, was not generally held by the early Adventists. *Even today a few do not subscribe to it*".[194]

A plan of salvation was encompassed in the covenant made by the Three Persons of the Godhead, who possessed the attributes of Deity equally. In order to eradicate sin and rebellion from the universe and to restore harmony and peace, one of the divine Beings accepted, and entered into the role of the Father, another the role of the Son. The remaining divine Being, the Holy Spirit, was also to participate in effecting the plan of salvation.[195]

Considering that this comment came from a prominent Seventh-day Adventist magazine, we see that there is a vast confusion as to who God is, including God's gender. If they don't know who God is, how can they be trusted on any doctrine—because every doctrine one holds is a derivative from one's view of God.

> If the Trinity is true then those who deny it do not worship the God of the scriptures ... it is not merely speculation, but lies at the root of every man's theology and affects his whole creed and practice.[196]

With the evidence of at least ten different prominent Seventh-day Adventist leaders, we see by looking at their quotes that they were not in agreement with addressing God as the Triune God. All the early Adventists either had an Arian or semi-Arian view of God where Jesus was either created or at the least, didn't have the same nature as God the Father. It is interesting that Ellen G. White referred to the Father, Son, and Holy Spirit as being the three great powers, the heavenly trio. In the worse case, this could be understood a tritheism view of the Godhead, but at best, leaving the interpretation open to all kinds of views of the Godhead with this sloppy language. Unlike the Seventh-day Adventist Church today, she did not believe that persons meant exactly the same as beings. The term being referred exclusively to the Father and the Son who were personal beings. According to the first chapter of "Why Was Sin Permitted?" in *Patriarchs and Prophets*, the *third highest being in heaven* before the entrance of sin, *was Lucifer*.

How can one ever believe Ellen was a trinitarian, when history so clearly declares that her husband and all the pioneers of the SDA Church were semi-Arian? She was married to her husband for thirty-five years and never once did she rebuke him for his belief. Never once did she ever teach against the semi-Arian doctrine. In fact, she never used the term Trinity, and she taught decidedly against it. As a matter of fact, when you look at the language that Ellen G. White and other Adventists used, it would be fairly safe to say that the Adventist movement didn't become trinitarians in 1896, but rather tritheistic in their view of the Godhead. While the modern Seventh-day Adventists claim to hold to a trinitarian view point of the Godhead, they have not resolved the issues of heresy set forth by their predecessors in the Adventist movement of the tritheism heresy.

We know that Ellen White didn't believe in or teach the Trinity because:

a) In 10,000 manuscripts; 100,000 pages; 25 million words about theological issues, she *never once used the word "Trinity"* to describe her view of the Godhead.

b) In her writings, while she copied profusely from hundreds of theological writers, many of whom were trinitarian, in some cases word for word, page for page; yet she never included the word Trinity which those she copied from had occasion for the word.

c) She had scores of Arian references to Jesus as the Son of God before or at original creation, or as lesser deity from the Father.

d) She had hundreds—if not more—references to the Godhead, yet never used the word Trinity to describe the Christian God.

e) There are scores of references to the three persons, or powers, etc. of the Godhead, yet never the word Trinity to describe the three.

f) In her seventy years of prophetic ministry, with scores of SDA leaders who publicly spoke and wrote against the Trinity, whose words she publicly endorsed, she never once corrected their false anti-trinitarian views in favour of the triune God.

g) However, she does have a blatant statement against all other fallen Babylonish Protestant and Catholic churches that "All their prayers and professions are an abomination to God" whereby *she has condemned the profession of the Trinity*, which is one of the primary confessions of the historic Christian Faith.

From the above, no other conclusion can be drawn than this than that *Ellen G. White did not believe in or uphold or teach the full deity of Jesus Christ and the Triune God.*

b) CONCERNING.THE FATHER

JAMES WHITE

To assert that the sayings of the Son and his apostles are the commandments of the Father, is as wide from the truth as the *old Trinitarian absurdity* that Jesus Christ is the very and eternal God.[1]

The Father is the greatest in that he is first. The Son is next in authority because He has been given all things.[2]

J. N. ANDREWS

That God is the fountain and source of immortality is plain from the statement of Paul. He speaks thus of God the Father: "Who only hath immortality, dwelling in the light which no man can approach unto; whom no man hath seen nor can see; to whom be honour and power everlasting; Amen." 1 Timothy 6:16. This text is evidently designed to teach that the self existent God is the only being who, of himself, possesses this wonderful nature. Others may possess it as derived from him, but he alone is the fountain of immortality. Our Lord Jesus Christ is the source of this life to us. "For as the Father hath life in himself, so hath he given to the Son to have life in himself." John 5:26. "As the living Father hath sent me, and I live by the Father; so he that eateth me, even he shall live by me." John 6:57. The Father gives us this life in His Son. "And this is the record, that God hath given to us eternal life and this life is in his Son. He that hath the Son hath life; and he that hath not the Son of God hath not life." 1 John 5:11, 12. These Scriptures do clearly indicate that Christ is the source of endless life, and that those only have this who have Christ.[3]

D. M. CANWRIGHT

Text: "But to us there is but one God, the Father, of whom are all things." 1 Corinthians 8:6 ... At the time when the Bible was written, nearly the whole world had adopted either Polytheism or Pantheism. Polytheism taught that there were many gods ... In opposition to that, Moses and the prophets set forth the grand fact that this doctrine of many gods was a lie, and that there was but one God, Jehovah the living God ... "Hear, O Israel: The Lord our God is one Lord." Deuteronomy 6:4. Here we strike the key-note of the doctrine of the Deity. "The Lord our God is ONE Lord." Not many, not a thousand, not a hundred, not ten, not three, but only ONE—one God... (Exodus 20:3; Deuteronomy 4:35; 2 Samuel 7:22; 2 Kings 19:15; Nehemiah 9:6; Psalm 86:10; Isaiah 43:10; 44:6, 8; 45:5, 22; quoted). No comments of ours can make these declarations plainer. There is just one eternal God and no more, one who is the Author and Father of all things.

Turning to the New Testament, we find the same doctrine taught just as plainly as in the Old. Neither Moses nor the prophets ever set forth the unity of God more strongly than Jesus himself. He taught it and reiterated it many times. Thus he says: "The first of all the commandments is, Hear, O Israel: The lord our God is one Lord; and thou shalt love the Lord thy God with all thy heart, and with all thy soul ... And the scribe said unto him, Well, Master, thou hast said the truth; for there is one God; and there is none other but he." Mark 12:29-32. "The scribe said, 'There is one God, and there is none other but he.' To this declaration Jesus assented. 'And this is life eternal, that they might know thee the only true God, and Jesus Christ, whom thou has sent.'" John 17:3. Jesus says his Father is the only true God. But trinitarians contradict this by saying that the Son and Holy Ghost are just as much the true God as the Father is... (1 Corinthians 8:4-6 quoted). Says the great apostle, "There is none other God but one," and "there is but one God, the Father, of whom are all things." He tells us who this one God is. It is not the Holy Ghost; it is not Jesus Christ, but it is the Father. Galatians 3:20; 1 Timothy 1:17.

There is, then, only one wise God. 1 Timothy 2:5; Deuteronomy 6:4. Those who are familiar with the Bible will see that I have selected only a few of the plainest texts upon this doctrine. How the doctrine of the Trinity, of three Gods, can be reconciled with these positive statements I do not know. It seems to me that nothing can be framed which more clearly denies the doctrine of the Trinity, than do the Scriptures above quoted.

And then the Bible never uses the phrases, 'Trinity,' 'triune God,' 'three in one,' 'the holy three," 'God the Holy Ghost,' etc. but it does emphatically say there is only one God, the Father. And every argument to prove three Gods in one person, God the Father, God the Son, and God the Holy Ghost, all of them of one substance, and every way equal to each other, and all three forming but one, contradicts itself, contradicts reason, and contradicts the Bible ... God is self-existent, and the source and author of all things, of angels, of men, of all the worlds, of everything. Thus Paul says, "For of him and through him and to him, are all things; to whom be glory forever. Amen." Romans 11:36. He is the source of all life and immortality. Thus, speaking of the Father, Paul says, "Who only hath immortality, dwelling in the light which no man can approach unto." 1 Timothy 6:16. Notice that this glorious God is the only one who, in himself, possesses immortality. That is, he is the fountain head, the source of all life and immortality ... "For as the Father hath life in himself; so hath he given to the Son to have life in himself." John 5:26. This statement is unequivocal. The Father has life in himself, and in his great love for his Son he bestows the same gift upon him; but it will be noticed that the Father is the one from whom the gift came ... How carefully Paul distinguishes between the Father and the Son. He says, "The Father, of whom are all things," and "Jesus Christ, by whom are all things." The Father is the source of everything. Jesus is the one through whom all things are done. All the authority, the glory, and the power of Christ he received from his Father...

A belief in this doctrine is very important. Indeed, it cannot be too strongly insisted upon. Jesus even declares that the knowledge of this truth is necessary to eternal life. "And this is life eternal, that they might know thee the only true God, and Jesus Christ, whom thou has sent." John 17:3. We must know the Father as the only true God. Then there is no true God besides the Father. But we must also know his Son Jesus Christ, whom he has sent. How simple and plain is this doctrine, and how abundantly sustained by the Holy Bible.[4]

A. T. JONES

In 1890 Jones wrote:

Again, speaking of the appearing of Jesus Christ, the Word says: "In His times He shall show, who is the blessed and only Potentate, the King of Kings, the Lord of Lords; who only hath immortality, dwelling in the light which no man can approach unto; whom no man hath seen, nor can see." 1 Timothy 6:15-16. Christ has brought this immortality to light ... Now as immortality is to be sought for, and as God is the only one who has it, and as Christ is the only one who has brought it to light, it follows that immortality must be sought of God, through Christ.[5]

E. J. WAGGONER

Christ and His Righteousness.

We are mindful of Paul's words, that "to us there is but one God, the Father, of whom are all things, and we in Him; and one Lord Jesus Christ, by whom are all things and we by Him" (1 Corinthians 8:6); just as we have already quoted, that it was by Him that God made the worlds. All things proceed ultimately from God, the Father; even Christ Himself proceeded and came forth from the Father...[6]

There isn't much question to how the early Adventists were opposed to the trinitarian God. They considered the doctrine of the Trinity to be an absurdity.

c) CONCERNING THE SON

JAMES WHITE

The Father is the greatest in that he is first. The Son is next in authority because He has been given all things.[1]

Paul affirms of the Son of God that he was in the form of God, and that he was equal with God. "Who being in the form of God thought it not robbery to be equal with God." Phil. 2:6. The reason why it is not robbery for the Son to be equal with the Father is the fact that he is equal ... The inexplicable Trinity that makes the godhead three in one and one in three, is bad enough; but that ultra Unitarianism that makes Christ inferior to the Father is worse. Did God say to an inferior, "Let us make man in our image??"[2]

"Beloved, when I gave all diligence to write unto you of the common salvation, it was needful for me to write unto you and exhort you that ye should earnestly contend for the faith which was once delivered unto the saints..." Jude 3-4 ... The exhortation to contend for the faith delivered to the saints, is to us alone. And it is very important for us to know what the apostle meant, that we may know what for and how to contend. In the 4th verse he gives us the reason why we should contend for THE faith, a particular faith; "for there are certain men," or a certain class who deny the only Lord God and our Lord Jesus Christ ... The way spiritualizers this way have disposed of or denied the only Lord God and our Lord Jesus Christ is first using the old unscriptural Trinitarian creed, viz., that Jesus Christ is the eternal God, though they have not one passage to support it, while we have plain scripture testimony in abundance that he is the Son of the eternal God.[3]

Here we might mention the Trinity, which does away with the personality of God, and of His Son Jesus Christ...[4]

J. N. ANDREWS

And as to the Son of God, he would be excluded also, for he had God for his Father, and did, at some point in the eternity of the past, have beginning of days. So that if we use Paul's language in an absolute sense, it would be impossible to find but one being in the universe, and that is God the Father, who is without father, or mother, or descent, or beginning of days, or end of life.[5]

C. W. STONE

> The Word, then, is Christ. This text speaks of his origin. He is the only begotten of the Father. Just how he came into existence, the Bible does not inform us any more definitely; but by this expression and several of a similar kind in the Scriptures, we may believe that Christ came into existence in a manner different from that in which other beings first appeared; that he sprang from the Father's being in a way not necessary for us to understand.[6]

E. J. WAGGONER

> In arguing the perfect equality of the Father and the Son, and the fact that Christ is in very nature God, we do not design to be understood as teaching that the Father was not before the Son. It should not be necessary to guard this point, lest some should think that the Son existed as soon as the Father; yet some go to that extreme, which adds nothing to the dignity of Christ, but rather detracts from the honour due him, since many throw the whole thing away rather than accept a theory so obviously out of harmony with the language of Scripture, that Jesus is the only begotten Son of God. He was begotten, not created. He is of the substance of the Father, so that in his very nature he is God; and since this is so "It pleased the Father that in him should all fullness dwell." Colossians 1:19 ... While both are of the same nature, the Father is first in point of time. He is also greater in that he had no beginning, while Christ's personality had a beginning.[7]

"The Word was in the beginning." The mind of man cannot grasp the ages that are spanned in this phrase. It is not given to men to know when or how the Son was begotten; but we know that He was the Divine Word, not simply before He came to this earth to die, but even before the world was created... [Micah 5:2 quoted]. We know that Christ "proceeded forth and came from God" (John 8:42), but it was so far back in the ages of eternity as to be far beyond the grasp of the mind of man.[8]

As the Son of the self-existent God, he has by nature all the attributes of Deity. It is true that there are many sons of God; but Christ is the "only begotten Son of God," and therefore the Son of God in a sense in which no other being ever was, or ever can be. The angels are sons of God, as was Adam (Job 38:7; Luke 3:38), by creation; Christians are the sons of God by adoption (Romans 8:14, 15); but Christ is the Son of God by birth.[9]

All things proceed ultimately from God, the Father; even Christ Himself proceeded and came forth from the Father...[10]

The Scriptures declare that Christ is "the only begotten Son of God." He is begotten, not created. As to when He was begotten, it is not for us to inquire, nor could our minds grasp it if we were told. The prophet Micah tells us all that we can know about it, in these words: "But thou, Bethlehem Ephratah, though thou be little among the thousands of Judah, yet out of thee shall He come forth unto Me that is to be ruler in Israel; whose goings forth have been from old, from the days of eternity." Micah 5:2, margin.

There was a time when Christ proceeded forth and came from God, from the bosom of the Father (John 1:18; 8:42), but that time was so far back in the days of eternity that to finite comprehension it is practically without beginning.[11]

W. W. PRESCOTT

As Christ was twice born, once in eternity, the only begotten of the Father, and again here in the flesh, thus uniting the divine with the human in that second birth, so we, who have been born once already in the flesh, are to have the second birth, being born again of the Spirit, in order that our experience may be the same, the human and the divine being joined in a life union.[12]

A. T. JONES

He was born of the Holy Ghost. In other words, *Jesus Christ was born again.* He came from heaven, God's first-born, to the earth, and was born again, but all in Christ's work goes by opposites for us: he, the sinless one, was made to be sin, in order that we might be made the righteousness of God in him. He, the living one, the prince and author of life, died that we might live. He whose goings forth have been from the days of eternity, the first-born of God, was born again, in order that we might be born again.

If Jesus Christ had never been born again, could you and I have ever been born again? No. But he was born again, from the world of righteousness into the world of sin; that we might be born again, from the world of sin into the world of righteousness. He was born again, and was made partaker of the human nature, that we might be born again, and so made partakers of the divine nature. He was born again, unto earth, unto sin, and unto man, that we might be born again unto heaven, unto righteousness, and unto God.[13]

He who was born in the form of God took the form of man. "In the flesh he was all the while as God, but he did not appear as God." "He divested himself of the form of God, and in its stead took the form and fashion of man." "The glories of the form of God, He for awhile relinquished." [14]

J. M. STEPHENSON

To be the only begotten Son of God must be understood in a different sense than to be a Son by creation; for in that sense all the creatures he has made are sons. Nor can it refer to his miraculous conception, with the virgin Mary, by the Holy Ghost; because he is represented by this endearing title more than four thousand years before his advent in the village of Bethlehem. Moreover, he is represented as being exalted far above the highest orders of men and angels in his primeval nature. He must therefore be understood as being the Son of God in a much higher sense than any other being. His being the only begotten of the Father supposes that none except him were thus begotten; hence he is, in truth and verity the only begotten Son of God; and as such he must be Divine; that is, be a partaker of the Divine nature.

This term expresses his highest, and most exalted nature... "The idea of Father and Son supposes priority of the existence of the one, and the subsequent existence of the other. To say that the Son is as old as his Father, is a palpable contradiction of terms. It is a natural impossibility for the Father to be as young as the Son, or the Son to be as old as the Father. If it be said that this term is only used in an accommodated sense, it still remains to be accounted for, why the Father should use as the uniform title of the highest, and most endearing relation between himself and our Lord, a term which, in its uniform signification, would contradict the very idea he wished to convey. If the inspired writers had wished to convey the idea of the coetaneous existence, and eternity of the Father and Son, they could not possibly have used more incompatible terms. And of this, Trinitarians, had the honesty to acknowledge, in the conclusion of his work on the Son-ship of Christ, that, "in the order of nature, the Father must have existed before the Son."[15]

The Trinitarian view, I think is equally exceptionable. They claim that the Son of God had three distinct natures at the same time; viz., a human body, a human soul, united with his Divine nature: the body being mortal, the soul immortal, the Divinity co-equal, co-existent, and co-eternal with the everlasting Father. Now, none of the advocates of this theory, claim that either his soul or Divinity died, that the body was the only part of this triple being which actually died "the death of the cross;" hence, according to this view (which makes the death of Christ the grand atoning sacrifice for the sins of the world) we only have the sacrifice of the most inferior part—the human body—of the Son of God. But it is claimed that his soul suffered the greater part of the penalty—yet it did not suffer "the death of the cross:"

it deserted the body in its greatest extremity, and left it to bear alone the death penalty; hence, the death of the cross is still only the death of a human body. But even admitting that in his highest nature as a human being, he suffered, all of which his nature, as such, was susceptible, during his whole life, and then died the ignominious death of the cross—even then, such a sacrifice would come almost infinitely short of the demands of God's just and holy law, which has been violated by all of Adam's race, (infants excepted) and trodden under foot with impunity, for so many thousands of years.

Of this Trinitarians themselves are sensible; hence, they represent his Divinity as the altar upon which his humanity was sacrificed; and then estimate the intrinsic value of the sacrifice by that of the altar upon which it was offered. But if I understand the theory under consideration, the Divine nature of Jesus Christ had no part nor lot in this matter; for this nature suffered no loss, indeed, made no sacrifice whatever. Suppose a king to unite the dignity of his only son with one of his poorest peasants, so far as to call him his son; and then should subject this peasant under the character of his own son, to a life of poverty, privation and suffering, and then crucify him under the character of a malefactor, while his real son enjoyed all the blessings of life, health, ease, honor and glory of his father's court—would any one contend in such case, that because he was called after the name, and clothed with honorary titles of the king's son, and died in this character, that therefore his suffering and death would be entitled to all the dignity and honour of his real son? In this case, all the sacrifice is made by the peasant. The son has no part nor lot in the matter. It is emphatically the offering of a peasant, and worth just as much as he is worth, had just as much dignity, and no more. The same is true in reference to the sacrifice of Christ, according to the above view. His humanity suffered all that was suffered, made all the sacrifice that was made; his privation, suffering and death are, therefore, entitled to all the value, dignity and honour, this nature could confer upon it, and no more. Hence, according to this theory, we have only a human sacrifice; and the question still remains to be answered, how can the life of one human being make an adequate atonement for the lives of thousands of millions of others?

So, after all that has been said and written by these two schools, it appears that there is no real difference in their respective theories, in reference to the atonement; both have, in fact, only a human sacrifice: but with reference to their views of the highest nature of the Son of God, they are as far asunder as finitude, and infinitude, time and eternity. The former makes the "only Begotten of the Father," a mere mortal, finite man; the latter makes him the Infinite, Omnipotent, All-wise, and Eternal God, absolutely equal with the Everlasting Father. Now, I understand the truth to be in the medium between these two extremes. I have proved, as I think conclusively,

1st, that the Son of God in his highest nature existed before the creation of the first world, or the first intelligent being in the vast Universe;

2nd, that he had an origin; that "he was the first born of every creature ... the beginning of the creation of God" [Revelation 3:14]

3rd, that, in his highest nature, all things in heaven and in earth were created, and are upheld, by him;

4th, in his dignity, he was exalted far above all the angels of heaven, and all the kings and potentates of earth;

5th, in his nature he was immortal, (not in an absolute sense) and Divine;

6th, in his titles and privileges, he was "the only begotten of his Father," whose glory he shared "before the world was;" the "image of the invisible God;" "in the form of God;" and "thought it not robbery to be equal with God;" "the likeness of his Father's glory and express image of his person;" "the Word" who "was in the beginning with God" and who "was God."

This was the exalted, and dignified, personage, who was sacrificed for the sins of the world—these are the privileges he voluntarily surrendered; and although "rich, for our sake he became poor:" "he made himself of no reputation," and became man; and "being found in fashion as a man, he humbled himself and became obedient unto death, even the death of the cross," to declare the righteousness of God, "that he might be just and the justifier of him that believeth in Jesus."

Here was real humility; not a mere pretence or show; here, we behold the amazing spectacle of the well-beloved and "only begotten Son of God," "the first born of every creature," voluntarily divesting himself of "the glory he had with the Father before the world," coming down from heaven, his high and holy habitation, and though "rich" becoming so poor that he had "no where to lay his head," the blessed Word who "was in the beginning with God," and who was God, actually becoming flesh, in the ignoble garb of a servant—subjecting himself to all the privations, temptations, sorrows, and afflictions, to which poor fallen humanity is subjected; and then to complete this unprecedented sacrifice, we see this once honoured, but now humbled—this once exalted, but now abased personage, expiring, as a malefactor, upon the accursed cross; and last of all descending into the depths of the dark and silent tomb—a symbol of the lowest degree of humiliation. *This, this, is the sacrifice, the "only begotten of the Father" offered as an atonement* for the sins of the world; this is the being who was actually sacrificed, and this the price the Son of God actually paid for our redemption. Hence, in reference to its dignity, it is the sacrifice of the most exalted and dignified being in the vast empire of God; nay, the sacrifice of the King's only begotten Son. In reference to its intrinsic value, who can estimate the worth of God's darling Son? It is, to say the least of it, an equivalent for the dignity, the lives, and eternal interests of the whole world; nay further, it is equal in value to all the moral interest of the whole intelligent creation, and equal in dignity and honour to the moral government of the Supreme Ruler of the Universe. In reference to its nature, it is Divine; hence we have a Divine sacrifice, in contradistinction to the Trinitarian and Unitarian views, which make it only a human sacrifice. In reference to its fullness, it is infinite, boundless. Yes, thank God, there is enough for each, enough for all, enough for ever more; enough to save an intelligent Universe, were they all sinners; and lastly, in reference to its adaptation to man's conditions and necessities, it is absolutely perfect.[16]

R. F. COTTRELL

Men have gone to opposite extremes in the discussion of the doctrine of the Trinity. Some have made Christ a mere man, commencing his existence at his birth in Bethlehem; others have not been satisfied with holding him to be what the Scriptures so clearly reveal him, the pre-existing Son of God, but have made him the "God and Father" of himself.[17]

JOHN MATTESON

Christ is the only literal son of God. "The only begotten of the Father." John 1:14. He is God because he is the Son of God; not by virtue of His resurrection. If Christ is the only begotten of the Father, then we cannot be begotten of the Father in a literal sense. It can only be in a secondary sense of the word.[18]

URIAH SMITH

The Scriptures nowhere speak of Christ as a created being, but on the contrary plainly state that he was begotten of the Father. (See remarks of Revelation 3:14, where it is shown that Christ is not a created being.) But while as the Son he does not possess a coeternity of past existence with the Father, the beginning of his existence, as the begotten of the Father, antedates the entire work of creation, in relation to which he stands as joint creator with God. John 1:3; Hebrews 1:2.

Could not the Father ordain that to such a being worship should be rendered equally with himself, without its being idolatry on the part of the worshiper? He has raised him to positions which make it proper that he should be worshipped, and has even commanded that worship should be rendered him, which would not have been necessary had he been equal with the Father in eternity of existence.

Christ himself declares that "as the Father hath life in himself, so hath he given to the Son to have life in himself." John 5:26. The Father has "highly exalted him, and given him a name which is above every name." Philippians 2:9. And the Father himself says, "Let all the angels of God worship him." Hebrews 1:6. These testimonies show that Christ is now an object of worship equally with the Father; but they do not prove that with him he holds an eternity of past existence.[19]

God alone is without beginning. At the earliest epoch when a beginning could be—a period so remote that to finite minds it is essentially eternity—appeared the Word. "In the beginning was the Word, and the Word was with God, and the Word was God." John 1:1. This uncreated Word was the Being, who, in the fullness of time, was made flesh, and dwelt among us. His beginning was not like that of any other being in the universe. It is set forth in the mysterious expressions, his [God's] only begotten Son" (John 3:16; 1 John 4:9), "the only begotten of the Father" (John 1:14), and "I proceeded forth and came from God." John 8:42. Thus it appears that by some divine impulse or process, not creation, known only to Omniscience, and possible only to Omnipotence, the Son of God appeared.[20]

When Christ left heaven to die for a lost world, he left behind, for the time being, his immortality also, but how could that be laid aside? That it was laid aside is sure, or he could not have died; but he did die, as a whole, as a divine being, as the Son of God, not in body only, while the spirit, the divinity, lived right on; for then the world would have only a human Saviour, a human sacrifice for its sins; but the prophet says that "his soul" was made "an offering for sin." Isaiah 53:10.[21]

JOSEPH BATES

My parents were members of long standing in the Congregational church, with all of their converted children thus far, and anxiously hoped that we would also unite with them. But they embraced some points of faith which I could not understand. I will name two only: their mode of baptism, and doctrine of the Trinity. My father, who had been a deacon of long standing with them, laboured to convince me that they were right in points of doctrine ... I said to my father, "If you can convince me that we are one in this sense, that you are my father, and I your son; and also that I am your father, and you my son, then I can believe in the Trinity.'... In a few days I was immersed and joined the Christian church.[22]

D. W. HULL

The inconsistent positions held by many in regard to the Trinity, as it is termed, has, no doubt, been the prime cause of many other errors. Erroneous views of the divinity of Christ are apt to lead us into error in regard to the nature of the atonement.[23]

G. W. AMADON

In Revelation 1:8, occurs a passage which has presented some difficulty to those who reject the doctrine of the trinity. The text, with its foregoing connection, reads as follows: "Behold, he cometh with clouds; and every eye shall see him, and they also which pierced him: and all kindreds of the earth shall wail because of him. Even so, Amen. I am Alpha and Omega, the beginning and the ending, saith the Lord, which is, and which was, and which is to come, the Almighty." Verses 7 and 8. The question has often arisen here, In what sense is Jesus Christ "the Almighty?" To us this inquiry is very easily answered. We do not believe that Christ is at all meant by the phrase, the Almighty, and for this belief we will give a few short reasons.

a) We think there are two persons brought to view in these texts—the Saviour, in the seventh verse; and the Father, in the eighth.
b) There is another most august title in verse 8 which never refers to the Son. It is the phrase—"Which is, and which was, and which is to come." This title points out the eternity of the being to whom it refers.

We will notice the use of this title, as the passages in which it occurs very plainly show that it belongs to "the High and lofty One which inhabits eternity." Beginning with verse 4 of this chapter it reads—

"John to the seven churches which are in Asia: Grace be unto you, and peace, from Him which is, and which was, and which is to come; and from the seven spirits which are before his throne; and from Jesus Christ, who is the faithful Witness, and the first-begotten of the dead, and the Prince of the kings of the earth." Here are two personages pointed out—the everlasting God under the fitting title, "Which is, and which was, and which is to come, the Almighty," and Jesus Christ by the no less appropriate titles of "the faithful Witness," "the first-begotten of the dead," and "the Prince of the kings of the earth." We will now present three other texts where this phrase is found, and which all readily admit speak of the immortal Father. Revelation 4:8.

"And the four beasts had each of them six wings about him; and they were full of eyes within: and they rest not day and night, saying, Holy, holy, holy, Lord God Almighty, which was, and is, and is to come." Chapter 11:16, 17. "And the four and twenty elders, which sat before God on their seats, fell upon their faces, and worshipped God, saying, We give thee thanks, O Lord God Almighty, which art, and was, and art to come; because thou hast taken to thee thy great power, and hast reigned." Chapter 16:5, 7. "And I heard the angel of the waters say, Thou art righteous, O Lord, which art, and was, and shalt be; because thou hast judged thus. And I heard another out of the altar say, Even so, Lord, God Almighty, true and righteous are thy judgments." With these passages we dismiss the point, as it can serve no purpose to the trinitarian, and to us seems so plain that the wayfaring man need not err therein.[24]

ELLEN G. WHITE

There is no one who can explain the mystery of the incarnation of Christ. Yet we know that He came to this earth and lived as a man among men. The man *Christ Jesus was not the Lord God Almighty*, yet Christ and the Father are one. The Deity did not sink under the agonizing torture of Calvary, yet it is nonetheless true that "God so loved the world, that he gave his only begotten Son, that whosoever believeth in him should not perish, but have everlasting life."[25]

When Jesus was awakened to meet the storm, He was in perfect peace. There was no trace of fear in word or look, for no fear was in His heart. But *He rested not in the possession of almighty power.* It was not as the "Master of earth and sea and sky" that He reposed in quiet. That power He had laid down, and He says, "I can of Mine own self do nothing." John 5:30. He trusted in the Father's might. It was in faith—faith in God's love and care—that Jesus rested, and the power of that word which stilled the storm was the power of God.[26]

Abraham saw the incarnate Saviour, and rejoiced ... Before Abraham was, I AM." Christ is the pre-existent, *self-existent* Son of God.[27]

He is the eternal, *self-existent* Son.[28]

Still seeking to give a true direction of her faith, Jesus declared, "I am the resurrection, and the life." In Christ is life, *original, unborrowed, underived.*[29]

He clothed His divinity with humanity. He was all the while as God, but He did not appear as God. He veiled the demonstrations of Deity which had commanded the homage, and called forth the admiration, of the universe of God. He was God while upon earth, but He divested Himself of the form of God, and in its stead took the form and fashion of a man ... He was God, but the glories of the form of God He for a while relinquished ... He humbled Himself, and took mortality upon Himself. As a member of the human family He was mortal, but as a God He was the fountain of life to the world. He could, in His divine person, ever have withstood the advances of death, and refused to come under its dominion; but He voluntarily laid down His life, that in so doing He might give life and bring immortality to light. He bore the sins of the world, and endured the penalty which rolled like a mountain upon His divine soul. He yielded up His life a sacrifice, that man should not eternally die.

Wondrous combination of man and God! He might have helped His human nature to withstand the inroads of disease by pouring from His divine nature vitality and undecaying vigour to the human. But He humbled Himself to man's nature ... What humility was this! It amazed angels. The tongue can never describe it; the imagination cannot take it in. The eternal Word consented to be made flesh! God became man![30]

The Word existed as a divine being, even as the eternal Son of God, in union and oneness with His Father. From everlasting He was the Mediator of the covenant ... Before men or angels were created, the

Word was with God, and was God ... Christ was God essentially, and in the highest sense. He was with God from all eternity, God over all, blessed forevermore. The Lord Jesus Christ, the divine Son of God, existed from eternity, a distinct person, yet one with the Father.[31]

It is quite apparent that the early Adventists saw Jesus Christ as someone who had a point-in-time origin after the Father, thus not being eternal and labelled Him as being essentially God. To be "essentially" something means that the object is not quite, but almost something. In other words, Jesus isn't quite God, but He is almost. Translation: Jesus Christ is not God! How could Jesus, being in the form of God, divest Himself of the form of God? The term "God" implies eternality so for Jesus not to be God for a period of time indicates that the Seventh-day Adventist Jesus never was God. Labelling Jesus Christ as someone who was born again sounds a lot like our modern day Word Faith cult. Either they didn't understand what the biblical precedence was for the term born again, in relation to themselves, or they were implying that there was something wrong with Jesus' nature, thus being in need of being born again. Both are serious errors! Jesus Christ is not the Lord God Almighty! How much more blasphemous can one get? Who is the Alpha and the Omega, the Almighty, in Revelation 1:8? This same Alpha and Omega is the First and the Last, the beginning and the end in Revelation 22:13. How many First and Lasts are there? I believe it is safe to conclude that this First and Last is Almighty God in Revelation 1:17-18 who was dead, but is alive forevermore! Jesus Christ is Almighty God!

d) CONCERNING THE HOLY SPIRIT

J. N. LOUGHBOROUGH

The Spirit of God is spoken of in the Scriptures as God's representative, the power by which he works, the agency by which all things are upheld. This is clearly expressed by the Psalmist ... Psalm 139:7-10. We learn from this language that when we speak of the Spirit of God we are really speaking of his presence and power.[1]

M. C. WILCOX

God is the source of all life ... God's life is eternal life, even as He is "the eternal God." ... But God is a person; how can His life be everywhere present? God is everywhere present by His Spirit ... The presence of God is therefore His Holy Spirit; and the Holy Spirit is therefore the life of God. And so we read of the Spirit of life (Romans 8:2), that the Spirit is life because of righteousness (verse 10); that the Spirit giveth life (2 Corinthians 3:6).[2]

The Personality of the Spirit Question: Some say the Holy Spirit is a person; others say He is a personality; and others, a power only. Till how long should this be a matter of discussion? Answer: The personality of the Holy Spirit will probably be a matter of discussion always. Sometimes the Spirit is mentioned as being "poured out," as in Acts 2. All through the Scriptures, the Spirit is represented as being the operating power of God ... The reason why the Scriptures speak of the Holy Spirit as a person, it seems to us, is that it brings to us, and to every soul that believes, the personal presence of our Lord Jesus Christ...

Because of the lack of faith, it was 'expedient,' necessary, that He should go away; for He declared, "If I go not away, the Comforter will not come unto you; but if I go, I will send Him unto you." John 16:7. His disciples could not realize the presence of the Spirit of God as long as Christ was with them personally. In that sense, He could be with those only who were in His immediate presence. But when He went away, and the Spirit came, it could make Christ present with everyone, wherever that one was with Paul in Athens, Peter in Jerusalem, Thomas in India, John in Patmos.

These are simply illustrations. Wherever God's children are, there is the Spirit—not an individual person, as we look upon persons, but having the power to make present the Father and the Son. That Spirit is placed upon God's messengers, the angels; but the angels are not the Spirit. That Spirit is placed upon God's servants, His human messengers; but the human messengers are not the Spirit. They are possessed by the Spirit, and used by the Spirit, and have within them the power of the Spirit; but they are not the Spirit. The Spirit is independent of all these human or material agencies. Why not leave it there? Why not know that the Spirit, the Spirit of God, the Spirit of Christ, the Spirit of Deity, goes out into all the earth, bringing the presence of God to every heart that will receive it?[3]

The Holy Spirit and Ministering Spirits. "What is the difference between the Holy Spirit and the ministering spirits (angels), or are they the same?" Answer. The Holy Spirit is the mighty energy of the Godhead, the life and power of God flowing out from Him to all parts of the universe, and thus making a living connection between His throne and all creation. As is expressed by another: "The Holy Spirit is the breath of spiritual life in the soul. The impartation of the Spirit is the impartation of the life of Christ." It thus makes Christ everywhere present.

To use a crude illustration, just as a telephone carries the voice of a man, and so makes that voice present miles away, so the Holy Spirit carries with it all the potency of Christ in making Him everywhere present with all His power, and revealing Him to those in harmony with His law. Thus the Spirit is personified in Christ and God, but never revealed as a separate person.

Never are we told to pray to the Spirit; but to God for the Spirit. Never do we find in the Scriptures prayers to the Spirit, but for the Spirit.[4]

And yet there is order observed in God's working; there is the regular channel through which His life force flows to the children of men, and by which His blessed Spirit does its work. We read: "The revelation of Jesus Christ, which God gave unto Him, to show unto His servants things which must shortly come to pass; and He sent and signified it by His angel unto His servant John; who bare record of the Word of God, and of the testimony of Jesus Christ." Revelation 1:1, 2. Here we have the order of divine procedure: (1) The Father; (2) Jesus Christ; (3) Christ's angel; (4) John the apostle and prophet; (5)

the church. And as respects the latter, the messages to the church are given through the ministers, or watchmen, of that church. "God in His wisdom can work and does work in other ways, because conditions of men demand it, but this is the regular way." The glory supreme and insupportable of the Godhead is represented in the Father. 1 Timothy 6:16. Jesus Christ has forever blended the divine with the human, and from Him flows out the Spirit of life to all His children. The angels are the mediums, the ganglia, on these great currents of God's life to re-enforce so to speak, these life currents. They can bear without exaltation God's Spirit and its outshining glory, and in themselves bring the presence of God to His children, and drive back the angels of evil which seek to destroy them.[5]

E. J. WAGGONER

Finally, we know the Divine unity of the Father and the Son from the fact that both have the same Spirit. Paul, after saying that they that are in the flesh cannot please God, continues: "But ye are not in the flesh, but in the Spirit, if so be that the Spirit of God dwell in you. Now if any man have not the Spirit of Christ, he is none of His." Rom. 8:9. Here we find that the Holy Spirit is both the Spirit of God and the Spirit of Christ.[6]

A. J. MORTON

The Holy Spirit is divine because it proceeds from divinity. You can no more separate divinity from the Spirit of God and Christ than you can separate divinity from God and Christ. It is, therefore, the presence of the Spirit in the words of God's promises which enable us to receive the divine nature from those promises.[7]

URIAH SMITH

J.W.W. asks: "Are we to understand that the Holy Ghost is a person, the same as the Father and the Son? Some claim that it is, others that it is not." Answer— The terms "Holy Ghost," are a harsh and repulsive translation. It should be "Holy Spirit" (*hagion pneuma*) in every instance. This Spirit is the Spirit of God, and the Spirit of Christ; the Spirit being the same whether it is spoken of as pertaining to God or Christ. But respecting this Spirit, the Bible uses expressions which cannot be harmonized with the idea that it is a person like the Father and the Son. Rather it is shown to be a divine influence from them both, the medium which represents their presence and by which they have knowledge and power through all the universe, when not personally present. Christ is a person, now officiating as priest in the sanctuary in heaven; and yet he says that wherever two or three are gathered in his name, he is there in the midst. Matthew. 18:20. How? Not personally, but by his Spirit.

In one of Christ's discourses (John, chapters 14, 15, and 16) this Spirit is personified as "the Comforter," and as such has the personal and relative pronouns, "he," "him," and "whom," applied to it. But usually it is spoken of in a way to show that it cannot be a person, like the Father and the Son. For instance, it is often said to be "poured out" and "shed abroad." But we never read about God or Christ being poured out or shed abroad.

If it was a person, it would be nothing strange for it to appear in bodily shape; and yet when it has so appeared, that fact has been noted as peculiar. Thus Luke 3:22 says: "And the Holy Ghost descended in a bodily shape like a dove upon him." But the shape is not always the same; for on the day of Pentecost it assumed the form of "cloven tongues like as of fire." Acts 2:3, 4. Again we read of "the seven Spirits of God sent forth into all the earth." Revelation 1:4; 3:1; 4:5; 5:6.

This is unquestionably simply a designation of the Holy Spirit, put in this form to signify its perfection and completeness. But it could hardly be so described if it was a person. We never read of the seven Gods or the seven Christ's.[8]

J. H. WAGGONER

There is one question which has been much controverted in the theological world upon which we have never presumed to enter. It is that of the personality of the Spirit of God. Prevailing ideas of person are very diverse, often crude, and the word is differently understood; so that unity of opinion on this point cannot be expected until all shall be able to define precisely what they mean by the word, or until all shall agree upon one particular sense in which the word shall be used.

But as this agreement does not exist, it seems that a discussion of the subject cannot be profitable, especially as it is not a question of direct revelation. We have a right to be positive in our faith and our statements only when the words of Scripture are so direct as to bring the subject within the range of positive proof. "We are not only willing but anxious to leave it just where the word of God leaves it. From it we learn that the Spirit of God is that awful and mysterious power which proceeds from the throne of the universe, and which is the efficient actor in the work of creation and of redemption."[9]

JAMES WHITE

Only one being in the universe besides the Father bears the name of God, and that is His Son, Jesus Christ.[10]

The Holy Spirit is Christ's representative, but divested of the personality of humanity, and independent thereof. Cumbered with humanity, Christ could not be in every place personally. Therefore it was for their interest that He should go to the Father, and send the Spirit to be His successor on earth. No one could then have any advantage because of his location or his personal contact with Christ. By the Spirit the Saviour would be accessible to all. In this sense He would be nearer to them than if He had not ascended on high.... The disciples still failed to understand Christ's words in their spiritual sense, and again He explained His meaning. By the Spirit, He said, He would manifest Himself to them.[11]

In the plan of restoring in men the divine image, it was provided that the Holy Spirit should move upon human minds, and be as the presence of Christ, a molding agency upon human character.[12]

The work of the Holy Spirit is immeasurably great. It is from this source that power and efficiency come to the worker for God; and the Holy Spirit is the comforter, as the personal presence of Christ to the soul.[13]

But no distance, no circumstances can separate us from the Comforter. Wherever we are, wherever we may go, He is there, always a Presence, a Person connected with heaven, One given us in Christ's place,to act in His stead.[14]

THE HOLY SPIRIT IS THE BREATH OF GOD

There is a great work to do; and the Spirit of the living God must enter into the living messenger, that the truth may go with power. Without the Holy Spirit, without the breath of God, there is torpidity of conscience, loss of spiritual life. Unless there is genuine conversion of the soul to God; unless the vital breath of God quickens the soul to spiritual life; unless the professors of truth are actuated by heaven born principles, they are not born of the incorruptible seed, which liveth and abideth forever. Unless they trust in the righteousness of Christ as their only security; unless they copy his character, labour in his spirit, they are naked; they have not on the robe of righteousness. The dead are often made to pass for the living; for those who are working out what they term salvation after their own ideas, have not God working in them to will and to do of His good pleasure.[15]

THE HOLY SPIRIT IS THE LIFE OF CHRIST

The Indwelling of the Spirit. The influence of the Holy Spirit is the life of Christ in the soul. We do not see Christ and speak to Him, but His Holy Spirit is just as near us in one place as in another. It works in and through everyone who receives Christ. Those who know the indwelling of the Spirit reveal the fruits of the Spirit—love, joy, peace, long-suffering, gentleness, goodness, faith.[16]

Christ declared that, after His ascension, He would send to His church, as His crowning gift, the Comforter, who was to take His place. This Comforter is the Holy Spirit—the soul of His life, the efficacy of His church, the light and life of the world. With His Spirit, Christ sends a reconciling influence and a power to take away sin.[17]

The Holy Spirit is the breath of spiritual life in the soul. The impartation of the Spirit is the impartation of the life of Christ. It imbues the receiver with the attributes of Christ. Only those who are thus taught of God, those who possess the inward working of the Spirit, and in whose life the Christ-life is manifested, are to stand as representative men, to minister in behalf of the church.[18]

The influence of the Holy Spirit is the life of Christ in the soul. We do not see Christ and speak to Him, but His Holy Spirit is just as near us in one place as in another. It works in and through everyone who receives Christ. Those who know the indwelling of the Spirit reveal the fruits of the Spirit—love, joy, peace, long-suffering, gentleness, goodness, faith.[19]

Through the Holy Spirit, that voice which was speaking from the fisherman's boat on the Sea of

Galilee would be heard speaking peace to human hearts to the close of time.[20]

When He (Christ) should come forth from the tomb, their sorrow would be turned to joy. After His ascension He was to be absent in person; but through the Comforter He would still be with them, and they were not to spend their time in mourning ... but by faith they were to look to the sanctuary above, where Jesus was ministering for them; they were to open their hearts to the Holy Spirit, His representative, and to rejoice in the light of His presence ... when Christ was not personally with them (after His ascension), and they failed to discern the Comforter, then it would be more fitting for them to fast.[21]

Keep cheerful. Do not forget that you have a Comforter, the Holy Spirit, which Christ has appointed. You are never alone. If you will listen to the voice that now speaks to you, if you will respond without delay to the knocking at the door of your heart, "Come in, Lord Jesus, that I may sup with Thee, and Thee with me," the heavenly Guest will enter. When this element, which is all divine, abides with you, there is peace and rest ... Remember the words of Christ, remember that He is an unseen presence in the person of the Holy Spirit.[22]

The Holy Spirit is a free, working, independent agency. The God of heaven uses His Spirit as it pleases Him; and human judgment, and human methods can no more set boundaries to its working, or prescribe the channel through which it shall operate.[23]

The Holy Spirit of the early Adventists was nothing more than the omnipresence of God the Father and Jesus Christ. The Jehovah's Witnesses, who are a daughter church to the Seventh-day Adventists, identify the Holy Spirit as God's active force. We can see where they got that idea. By impersonalizing the Holy Spirit as the breath or life of God or the life of Christ, this nullifies the belief in the Trinity, thereby creating a false view of the Godhead. We see the impersonal and independent relationship between the Holy Spirit and God as God uses the Holy Spirit as it pleases God. According to Ellen G. White, even *Lucifer ranks higher in power than the Holy Spirit.*

e) ELLEN WHITE'S ARIAN VIEWS

Ellen G. White often called Jesus as "The Son of God" at original creation. We read these statements not seeing them as the Arian views they are, for they evoke the question *How was He* "the Son of God"? John 1:1-3 and Hebrews 1:10 show He was *Yhwh*, the Word at creation, but *became Son of God* and Son of Man *at His incarnation* (Hebrews 1:5-6) when the Father said "I will *become* to Him a father, and He will *become* to me a Son" (cf Luke 1:35). Arians teach he was the 'Son of God' by *being created* or *begotten* by the Father, then God created other things *through* him. So He was only *a lesser deity*, whose pre-eminence over the angels was *conferred* to Him, by the Father. Ellen G. White also held this Christ-debasing view:

> ...yet, Jesus, *God's dear Son*, had the pre-eminence over all the angelic host. He was one with the Father before the angels were created. Satan was envious of Christ and gradually assumed command which devolved on Christ alone. "The great Creator assembled the heavenly host, that *he might in the presence*

> *of all the angels confer special honour upon his Son ...The Father then make known that it was ordained by himself that Christ, his Son, should be equal with himself."*[1]

The article "Trinity?" acknowledges this implies that "he was not equal to the Father before that time," for Jesus' command was only devolved or was handed down from the Father, and His equality was conferred or positional equality—rather than being equal by nature, as necessary for true deity (Galatians 4:8).

f) MOVING TO THE DEITY OF CHRIST AND THE SUPPOSED TRINITY

Dr. Walter Rea says that in 1896 W. W. Prescott identified Jesus as the "I AM" of John 8:58 and Exodus 3:14, beginning the move toward Christ's true deity and the Trinity (SDA Forum, Feb. 14, 1982).

> "Trinity?" says "The breakthrough came with the publication of Ellen White's article "Christ the Lifegiver" in *Signs of the Times* in 1897, and the book *The Desire of Ages* in 1898 ... she says, "In Him was life original, unborrowed, underived." In *Desire of Ages* ... she quotes Jesus' answer to the Jews in John 8:58: "Most assuredly, I say to you, before Abraham was I AM" ... "He was equal with God, infinite and omnipotent ... He is the eternal self-existing Son."[1]

"Trinity?" dubs these changing views "she received more light" and "increasing light leading to a clearer understanding" (p. 3). On page seven they say "Ellen White in 1905 ... *unambiguously* endorsed the Trinity doctrine" citing *Evangelism* (p. 614-615) where she calls the Father, the Son and the Holy Spirit "the fullness of the God-head" individually, saying, "There are three living persons of the heavenly trio..." Yet by 1919 SDA leaders had not united on Christ's full deity or the Trinity (1919 Bible Conference, p. 57). Their 1915 *Bible Readings for the Home* only held Jesus' "essential deity," limiting His equality with God to "proprietorship" of the angels, saints, etc. (p. 68); but failed to give any teaching of the Trinity at all! These had to be because Ellen's 1897, 1898, and 1905 words were ambiguously modified by other statements!

The belief that the plan of salvation was not completed with the atonement on the cross, coupled with the understanding of the humanity of Jesus, separated Seventh-day Adventists from most evangelical bodies until the mid 1950's. Prior to the mid 1950's, most evangelicals considered Seventh-day Adventists to be a cult. It was the work of Donald Barnhouse and Walter Martin that opened the way for the church to have the stigma of culthood removed. With the blessing of the then General Conference President R. R. Figuhr, Martin, Barnhouse, and George Cannon met with T. E. Unruh, Roy A. Anderson, LeRoy Froom, and W. E. Read to try to resolve supposed misunderstandings between Adventists and evangelicals. Unruh, writing in *The Adventist Heritage,* stated:

> A series of conferences between Seventh-day Adventist and Evangelical leaders, begun in the spring in 1955 and running into the summer of 1956, led to the publication of two books: the first, *Seventh-day Adventists Answer Questions on Doctrine*; the second, *The Truth About Seventh-day Adventism*. The first is a definitive statement of contemporary Adventist belief ... The second work, by Walter R. Martin, a leading expert on American cults, defines and examines Seventh-day Adventist doctrines, using

the first work as source and authority. In his book Martin removed the Seventh-day Adventist Church from his list of non-Christian cults and acknowledged that all whose beliefs followed the *Questions on Doctrine* should be counted members of the Body of Christ (the Christian church in the Evangelical definition) and therefore his brethren.[2]

These conferences and the resulting book, *Questions on Doctrine*, compromised the SDA position which they had held on the atonement. Specifically, the SDA denied their understanding of the dual atonement and relegated Christ's high priestly ministry to nothing more than a series of meaningless motions. This chapter will document the denial that occurred at the time of *Questions on Doctrine*, the continual denial, and God's response to that denial.

g) THE QUESTIONS ON DOCTRINAL DENIAL

On page 390 of *Questions on Doctrine* we read: "Adventists do not hold any theory of a dual atonement." Dr. Barnhouse, writing in reference to the great disappointment, called the doctrine of the investigative judgment "a human face-saving idea" and "that any effort to establish it is *stale, flat,* and *unprofitable!*"[1]

Later, he called it "unimportant and almost naive ..."[2]

He also wrote the impressions the SDA leaders conveyed to him of their understanding of the investigative judgment:

> It should also be realized that some uninformed Seventh-day Adventists took this idea and carried it to fantastic literalistic extremes. Mr. Martin and I heard the Adventist leaders say, flatly, that they repudiate all such extremes. This they have said in no uncertain terms. Further, they do not believe, as some of

their earlier teachers taught, that Jesus' atoning work was not completed on Calvary but instead that He was still carrying on a second ministering work since 1844. This idea is also totally repudiated.[3]

The SDA leaders repudiated the biblical teachings of James and Ellen White, Uriah Smith, etc. They also provided an answer to satisfy the evangelicals about the atonement Christ is now making in heaven. Unfortunately, it was not a biblical answer. The brethren in *Questions on Doctrine* stated:

> When, therefore, one hears an Adventist say, or reads in Adventist literature, even in the writings of Ellen G. White that Christ is making atonement now, it should be understood that we mean simply that Christ is now making application of the benefits of the sacrificial atonement He made on the cross; that He is making it efficacious for us individually, according to our needs and requests.[4]

This agrees with the position that Barnhouse understood the Adventist brethren to have taken, for he wrote: They believe that since His ascension Christ has been ministering the benefits of the atonement which was completed on Calvary."[5]

But what is meant when we read that Jesus is "making application of the benefits of the sacrificial atonement He made on the cross"? *Questions on Doctrine* gives the answer.

> How glorious is the thought that the King, who occupies the throne, is also our representative at the court of heaven! This becomes all the more meaningful when we realize that Jesus our surety entered the "holy places," and appeared in the presence of

God for us. But it was not with the *hope* of obtaining something for us at that time, or at some future time. No! He had already obtained it for us on the cross.[6]

h) PRESENT POSITION

Questions on Doctrine was published nearly forty-seven years ago. Upon what basis could we say that the views it contains would still be valid and representative? Walter Martin documented the position the church leadership held in 1983. He wrote:

> Since I have always stressed the importance of doctrinal integrity in my evaluations of religious movements, the doctrinal upheaval in Adventism is of special concern. Consequently, on February 16, 1983, I wrote the General Conference of Seventh-day Adventists (Washington, D.C.), calling for the Conference's public and official statement reaffirming or denying the authority of the Adventist book, *Questions on Doctrine*, which was the representative Adventist publication on which I based my earlier evaluation and book. On April 29, 1983, W. Richard Lesher, vice-president of the General Conference, responded in a personal letter. His reply read, in part: "You ask first if Seventh-day Adventists still stand behind the answers given to your questions in *Questions on Doctrine* as they did in 1957. The answer is yes. You have noted in your letter that some opposed the answers given then, and, to some extent, the same situation exists today. But certainly the great majority of Seventh-day Adventists are in harmony with the views expressed in *Questions on Doctrine*."[1]

On the basis of the above letter, dialog with several Adventist leaders, and the continuing state of flux within Adventism itself, I must for the time being, stand behind my original evaluation of Seventh-day Adventism as presented comprehensively in my first book on the subject and later in this volume.[2]

In 1983, it was considered that the church was still supporting the views held in *Questions on Doctrine*. That view was that Jesus obtains nothing for us in heaven; it had all been secured on the cross: No final atonement! The most current publication that claims to be representative of Seventh-day Adventist doctrine is the book *Seventh-day Adventists Believe....* This book claims to be "A Biblical Exposition of 27 Fundamental Doctrines." It was prepared in a manner similar to *Questions on Doctrine*; i.e., a single writer preparing the initial draft with a large group of ministers and scholars then giving input. Originally, the initial draft for *Seventh-day Adventists Believe...* was prepared by Norman Gulley. This draft was too far to the left for then-ministerial leader Bob Spangler. Spangler then requested P. G. Damsteegt to rewrite the initial draft of each chapter. On page *v* of the book we learn more of the input process:

> The church's ten world divisions selected a committee of 194 persons who went over each chapter, suggesting corrections, additions, and deletions. A smaller committee of 27 church leaders, theologians, and pastors met regularly with Damsteegt to give additional supervision to the preparation of this work.[3]

Among those who are credited as "sharing their counsel, checking sources, researching materials, rewriting, and editing" are Roy Adams, Duncan Eva, Samuele Bacchiocchi,

B. B. Beach, Norman Gulley, William Johnsson, and a host of other "new theology" proponents. While Damsteegt himself may be "historic" in his understanding of the atonement, the above-named rewriters and editors are not. Anyone familiar with the publishing process knows that many times the finished product is very different from what is submitted. While some sincere brethren have seen *Seventh-day Adventists Believe...* as "a courageous realignment with the historic faith of the Adventist pioneers and their church," the truth is that it teaches the same doctrine of the atonement as does *Questions on Doctrine*. The evangelicals clearly understand *Seventh-day Adventists Believe...* as setting forth the teachings of *Questions on Doctrine*. I believe this difference of opinion does not lie with insincerity as much as with ignorance. Most of our brethren have not really examined the new book closely. Notice how closely the language of *Seventh-day Adventists Believe...* follows that of *Questions on Doctrine*:

> The once-for-all sacrifice has been offered (Hebrews 9:28); now He makes available to all the benefits of this atoning sacrifice.[4]

> Similarly, Christ, in the heavenly sanctuary, has been ministering the benefits of His completed atonement to His people; at His return He will redeem them and give them eternal life.[5]

> This is the very language of *Questions on Doctrine*. In chapter nine of *Seventh-day Adventists Believe...*, "The Life, Death, and Resurrection of Christ" we read: "There, as High Priest, He [Christ] applies the benefits of His complete and perfect atoning sacrifice to achieve the reconciliation of humans to God."[6]

Both *Questions on Doctrine* and *Seventh-day Adventists Believe...* carry statements which claim that *they are representative but not authoritative.* First we read in *Questions on Doctrine*:

> But because of the very nature of the Seventh-day Adventist Church organization no statement of Seventh-day Adventist belief can be considered official unless it is adopted by the General Conference in quadrennial session, when accredited delegates from the whole world field are present. The answers in this volume are an expansion of our doctrinal positions contained in the official statement of *Fundamental Beliefs* already referred to. Hence this volume can be viewed as truly representative of the faith and beliefs of the Seventh-day Adventist Church.[7]

Seventh-day Adventists Believe... holds to the same position of *Questions on Doctrine.* It claims to be a representative *Statement of Beliefs,* but not an official Statement of Beliefs because it was not voted on by a General Conference in session:

> While this volume is not an officially voted statement—only a General Conference in world session could provide that it may be viewed as representative of "the truth ... in Jesus" (Ephesians 4:21) that Seventh-day Adventists around the globe cherish and proclaim.[8]

Therefore, in both *Questions on Doctrine* and *Seventh-day Adventists Believe...* we find what is claimed to be a true and representative, but not official statement. To be official, a statement must be voted on by the General Conference. Such a statement does exist! When the church met in 1980 at Dallas for the General Conference Session, a Statement of Beliefs was voted on. That statement can be found in any church manual printed after 1980 and also in the book *Seventh-day Adventists Believe....* Belief #23 states in part:

> There is a sanctuary in heaven, the true tabernacle which the Lord set up and not man. In it Christ ministers on our behalf, making available to believers the benefits of His atoning sacrifice offered once for all on the cross.[2]

From 1872, when the first *Statement of Beliefs* was published, until 1980, no statement like this was presented. Where did this language come from? It came from *Questions on Doctrine*, page 355. There we read that "Christ is now making application of the benefits of the sacrificial atonement He made on the cross." What does this language mean? "... it was not with the *hope* of obtaining something for us at that time, or at some future time. No! He had already obtained it for us on the cross."[10]

This is an official denial of the final atonement!

In 2005, the SDA church may be on the verge of an undoing of that transformation, resulting in a reversal of all that the original *Questions on Doctrine* accomplished. Jan Paulsen, President of the worldwide Seventh-day Adventist Church, gave an address to church leaders in May 2002. His presentation, "The Theological Landscape," indicated much of what George Knight has written in the *Annotated Edition*. Paulsen makes these following statements:

... we are Christians of a very specific identity ... are we becoming more recognizable as "Christians" than we are as Seventh-day Adventist Christians? I'm speaking about our *readiness to protect our identity.*

Has our stand on ecumenism changed? ... The answer, emphatically, is no ... And we have stated openly our reasons ... There is no change in our being separate; neither do we need to change our basic prophetic scenario.

... I underscore again *that it is vital that we keep our separate identity.* ... And we continue to see ourselves *as the historical remnant gathering the faithful remnant* from any and all corners to the purpose of God.

Some would have us believe that there has been significant shifts in recent times in regard to doctrines that historically have been at the heart of Seventh-day Adventism.

Let no one think that there has been a change of position in regard to this unique historical SDA doctrines.[11]

Paulsen's address was difficult for many "evangelical" Adventists. It stated, in effect, that *the church is not an evangelical church.* George Knight's annotations in the republished *Questions on Doctrine,* supports Paulsen's idea of *separatism and uniqueness.*

George Knight has demonstrated several times that:

Ellen G. White is the final voice and authority in doctrinal matters. Without using those words, he and others in the church unabashedly refer to her for beliefs and *then attempt to find support for those beliefs from the Bible.*

The church leadership was never transparent nor straightforward and was definitely one-sided to appease the evangelicals. In a word, *they were deceptive.*

The original *Questions on Doctrine, cannot be trusted as an official doctrinal statement* from the Seventh-day Adventist Church.

The Annotated Edition published by a university as part of a collection of early "heritage" documents shows that the church has relegated this volume to the status of an historical relic.[12]

Knight made a strange statement about the wording of *Questions on Doctrine.* In his introduction; however, he has demonstrated that *Questions on Doctrine* was neither a *"clear restatement"* nor was it *"faithful to Adventist beliefs."* He uses history to counter his own statement as well as to provide insight into the doctrinal workings of this church.

To conclude, take a look at the seventeenth fundamental belief of the church. In part it reads:

> ... *her* [Ellen G. White's] *writings are a continuing and authoritative source of truth* which provide for the church comfort, guidance, instruction and correction.

For those familiar with the New Testament, this sounds eerily like a verse from the book of Timothy.

All scripture is inspired by God and profitable for teaching, for reproof, for correction, for training in righteousness ... (2 Timothy 3:16 NASB).

Adventists and evangelicals can be thankful that the *Annotated Edition of Questions on Doctrine* has been published. Rather than being confused by the deceptive leaders of the church in 1956, we can read Knight and be sure that *the church never really changed from its historical positions.* While there may be those Adventists who are trinitarian, *the church is a haven for works-orientated, anti-trinitarians* who make symbolic gestures to other Christian groups, but do not interact spirituality as members of the body of Christ.

5

ELLEN G. WHITE'S ABERRANT VIEWS OF JESUS AND GOD

Before the entrance of evil there was peace and joy throughout the universe. All was in perfect harmony with the Creator's will. Love for God was supreme, love for one another impartial. Christ the Word, the Only Begotten of God, was one with the eternal Father—one in nature, in character, and in purpose—the only being in all the universe that could enter into all the counsels and purposes of God. By Christ the Father wrought in the creation of all heavenly beings. "By Him were all things created, that are in heaven ... whether they be thrones, or dominions, or principalities, or powers" (Colossians 1:16); and to Christ, equally with the Father, all heaven gave allegiance.[1]

The Sovereign of the universe was not alone in His work of beneficence. He had *an associate—a co-worker* who could appreciate His purposes, and could share His joy in giving happiness to created beings. "In the beginning was the Word, and the Word was with God, and the Word was God. The same was in the beginning with God." John 1:1, 2. Christ, the Word, the only begotten of God, was one with the eternal Father—one in nature, in character, in purpose—the only being that could enter into all the counsels and purposes of God. "His name shall be called Wonderful, Counsellor, The mighty God, The everlasting Father, The Prince of Peace." Isaiah 9:6. His "goings forth have been from of old, from everlasting." Micah 5:2. And the Son of God declares concerning Himself: "The Lord possessed Me in the beginning of His way, before His works of old. I was set up from everlasting. ... When He appointed the foundations of the earth: then I was by Him, as one brought up with Him: and I was daily His delight, rejoicing always before Him." Proverbs 8:22-30. The Father wrought by His Son in the creation of all heavenly beings. "By Him were all things created ... whether they be thrones, or dominions, or principalities, or powers: all things were created by Him, and for Him." Colossians 1:16.[2]

There was one who perverted the freedom that God had granted to His creatures. Sin originated with him who, next to Christ, had been most honoured of God and was highest in power and glory among the inhabitants of heaven. Lucifer, "son of the morning," was first of the covering cherubs, holy and undefiled. He stood in the presence of the great Creator, and the ceaseless beams of glory enshrouding the eternal God rested upon him ... And coveting the glory with which the infinite Father had invested His Son, this prince of angels aspired to power that was the prerogative of Christ alone.³

In heavenly council the angels pleaded with Lucifer. The Son of God presented before him the greatness, the goodness, and the justice of the Creator, and the sacred, unchanging nature of His law. ... The King of the universe summoned the heavenly hosts before Him, that in their presence He might set forth the true position of His Son and show the relation He sustained to all created beings. The Son of God shared the Father's throne, and the glory of the eternal, self-existent One encircled both.⁴

Yet the Son of God was exalted above him, as one in power and authority with the Father. He shared the Father's counsels, while Lucifer did not thus enter into the purposes of God. "Why," questioned this mighty angel, "should Christ have the supremacy? Why is He honoured above Lucifer?"... Leaving his place in the immediate presence of the Father, Lucifer went forth to diffuse the spirit of discontent among the angels. He worked with mysterious secrecy, and for a time concealed his real purpose under an appearance of reverence for God. ... The *exaltation of the Son of God as equal with the Father was represented as an injustice to Lucifer,* who, it was claimed, was also entitled to reverence and honour.⁵

The great Creator assembled the heavenly host, that he might in the presence of all the angels confer special honour upon his Son. The Son was seated on the throne with the Father, and the heavenly throng of holy angels was gathered around them. The Father then made known that it was ordained by himself that

Christ, his Son, should be equal with himself; so that wherever was the presence of his Son, it was as his own presence. The word of the Son was to be obeyed as readily as the word of the Father. His Son he had invested with authority to command the heavenly host. Especially was his Son to work in union with himself in the anticipated creation of the earth and every living thing that should exist upon the earth. His Son would carry out his will and his purposes, but would do nothing of himself alone. The Father's will would be fulfilled in him.[6]

This angel was the angel of God's presence (Isaiah 63:9), the angel in whom was the name of the great Jehovah (Exodus 23:20-23). The expression can refer to no other than the Son of God ... He was revealed to them as the Angel of Jehovah, the Captain of the Lord's host, Michael, the Archangel.[7]

He rises above humanity, throws off the guise of sin and shame, and stands revealed, the Honoured of the angels, the Son of God, One with the Creator of the universe.[8]

The Apostle Paul, under inspiration, writes concerning Christ: "Who, being in the form of God, thought it not robbery to be equal with God: But made himself of no reputation, and took upon him the form of a servant, and was made in the likeness of men." (Philippians 2:6, 7) The original Greek in the first part of verse 7 is: αλλα εαυτον εκενωσε which literally translates to: "but himself emptied." Paul says that the One who was divine—"in the form of God," "emptied" Himself of that divine form. In other words, Christ emptied Himself of the divine attributes in the incarnation and accepted the essential attributes of a slave. Jesus laid aside His omnipotence. "The faithful and true witness" stated very clearly: "Verily, verily (truly, truly), I say unto you, The Son can do nothing of himself, but what he seeth the Father do: for what things so ever he doeth, these also doeth the Son likewise. ... I can of mine own self do nothing: as I hear, I judge: and my judgment is just; because I seek not mine own will, but the will of the Father which hath sent me." (John 5:19, 30) Ellen G. White wrote: "*All the miracles of Christ performed for the afflicted and suffering were, by the power of God, through the ministration of angels.*"[2]

Recounting her vision of December, 1844, Ellen speaks of her and Jesus as "In a moment we were *winging our way* upward..." Seeing this, in the light of her calling Him Michael the Archangel, in (*Desire of Ages,* p. 99, 379; *Spiritual Gifts,* Va, p. 158 and *Prophets & Kings,* p. 572), one is led to question if she did not, in fact, really view Him as just that—an angel! And if so, what about His deity and bodily resurrection?

As we consider the above quotes of Ellen G. White's writings, her view of who Jesus Christ is and who is the God of this universe, becomes unravelled. Upon examination, is this the orthodox view of Jesus and God, or is this another jesus spoken of in 2 Corinthians 11:4? We should also examine her view of God to see if the view stands up to biblical scrutiny. At first, Ellen describes Jesus as being one with the Father, having the same nature, character, and purpose. This sounds good. Then she states that Jesus was the only one who could enter into the counsels and purposes of God. Now wait a minute! How did this entrance in the counsels and purposes take place? Was it by invitation by God? Was this Jesus that Ellen is describing an exalted angel? Though this Jesus was one in nature, character, and purpose with God, was He not God that He didn't have to enter into the counsels and purposes of God? You see, when God decides on His purposes and counsels, He doesn't need to consult with outside sources. The difference being, when we speak of God, we refer to the Triune God. With her unorthodox view of God, Ellen mentions that Jesus was the only one to enter into the counsels and purposes of God. Where does this leave the Holy Spirit?

Ellen mentions that God had a co-worker, an associate to appreciate His purposes. What type of an associate, co-worker was this? Could it be possible that all things were created by two Gods working together or was this co-worker associate not God in order to be faithful to Isaiah 43:10? If that were the case, then how could this co-worker associate be one in nature, character, and purpose with God? With this dilemma, the false god of Ellen G. White is revealed! She cannot make her view of God harmonize with the Holy Scriptures.

Ellen sees Christ as God's most honoured creature, followed by Lucifer. Christ had the most power and glory amongst the inhabitants of heaven of which the Father had invested in Him. Because the Father had invested this power and glory in Christ, is Ellen suggesting that there was a time when Christ didn't have this power and glory? Is she implying that the Holy Spirit is the fourth highest in honour, power, and glory after Lucifer? How blasphemous!

By slight of hand, Ellen suggests that the angels of God were pleading with Lucifer. She goes on to say that the Son of God presented to him (Lucifer) the greatness, goodness, and justice of his Maker. Are we to understand that the Son of God is an angel? Referring to God, she calls Him the King of the universe. What kind of king is the Son of God? The true position of the Son of God is to share the glory of the eternal, self-existent One. Are we to understand from this statement that the Son of God is *not* eternal?

The god of Ellen G. White is not omniscience as is the God of the Holy Scriptures. She believed that Lucifer worked with mysterious secrecy and was able to conceal his real purposes under an appearance of reverence to God. The only ones that were fooled were Lucifer and Ellen G. White. Labelling the Son of God as the angel of Jehovah's presence and Michael, the Archangel, the Captain of the Lord's hosts, we see that Ellen did not consider the Son of God to be God Himself. Why would she say the Son of God was one with the Creator of the universe when it is Jesus who is the Creator?

> The Saviour gathered His disciples about Him, and said to them, "If any man desires to be first, the same shall be last of all, and servant of all." There was in these words a solemnity and impressiveness which the disciples were far from comprehending. That which Christ discerned they could not see. They did not understand the nature of Christ's kingdom, and this ignorance was the apparent cause of their contention. But the real cause lay deeper. By explaining the nature of the kingdom, Christ might for the time have quelled their strife; but this would not have touched the underlying cause. Even after they had received the fullest knowledge, any question of precedence might have renewed the trouble. Thus disaster would have been brought to the church after Christ's departure. The strife for the highest place was the outworking of that same spirit which was the beginning of the great controversy in the worlds above, and which had brought Christ from heaven to die. There rose up before Him a vision of Lucifer, the "son of the morning," in glory surpassing all the angels that

surround the throne, and united in closest ties to the Son of God. Lucifer had said, "I will be like the Most High" (Isaiah 14:12, 14); and the desire for self-exaltation had brought strife into the heavenly courts, and had banished a multitude of the hosts of God. Had Lucifer really desired to be like the Most High, he would never have deserted his appointed place in heaven; for the spirit of the Most High is manifested in unselfish ministry. Lucifer desired God's power, but not His character. He sought for himself the highest place, and every being who is actuated by his spirit will do the same. Thus alienation, discord, and strife will be inevitable. Dominion becomes the prize of the strongest. The kingdom of Satan is a kingdom of force; every individual regards every other as an obstacle in the way of his own advancement, or a steppingstone on which he himself may climb to a higher place.[10]

In Ellen G. White's opinion, Jesus Christ, the Son of God, was united in closest ties with Lucifer. Doesn't this sound a lot like Mormonism? Jesus Christ never was an angel nor ever will be, unlike Lucifer. The vast difference between the Son of God and Lucifer is that the Son of God is God and Creator, whereas Lucifer is a created angel. Ellen implies that Lucifer would have been like the Most High if he hadn't deserted his appointed place in heaven. There is no way that Satan could have ever been God, despite what Ellen said. She bought Lucifer's lie, "Did God really say?" Lucifer's problem resulted in his rebellion where he was trying to deify and exalt himself above God and God showed him who was in authority by casting him out of heaven. To say Lucifer deserted heaven seems to imply that this was Lucifer's choice, when we know God gave him no choice in this matter.

If Christ isn't God Himself, He would not have any glory, for God doesn't share His glory with another according to Isaiah 42:8 and 48:11. If Christ is only a god separate from God Almighty, this idea is refuted according to Isaiah 43:10; 44:6, 8; 45:6, 14, 18, 21-22 and 46:9. With this overwhelming evidence from the Holy Scriptures, Christ is God Almighty. With this distorted heretical view of the Son of God, Ellen G. White and the Seventh-day Adventist Church have removed themselves from the true Church of God that was redeemed by God's blood (Acts 20:28).

a) JESUS, AS AN ANGEL

> *Jesus, the Angel* who went before the Hebrews in the wilderness, would save them from destruction. Forgiveness is lingering for them. It is possible for them to find pardon. The vengeance of God has come very near, and appealed to them to repent. A special, irresistible interference from Heaven has arrested their presumptuous rebellion. Now, if they respond to the interposition of God's providence, they may be saved.[1]

> *This was no common angel. It was the Lord Jesus Christ*, he who had conducted the Hebrews through the wilderness, enshrouded in the pillar of fire by night, and a pillar of cloud by day. The place was made sacred by his presence; therefore Joshua was commanded to put off his shoes.[2]

When did Jesus change from being an angel to being God in Seventh-day Adventism? It is clear to see from this quote that the Ellen G. White/Seventh-day Adventist jesus isn't eternal. In Hebrews 1:5-8, to what angel did God ever call My Son, *none*. Did God tell Jesus to worship Himself in verse 6? *No.* And in verse 8, God the Father addresses the Son as God and states that His throne is forever and ever. Eternal God versus a created angel. Big contrast!

b) ARIAN AND SEMI-ARIAN VIEWS OF JESUS

SEVENTH-DAY ADVENTIST ANTI-TRINITARIANS

"Trinity?" (p. 5) tells that in recent years a number of anti-trinitarian publications have appeared in the SDA church, contending that "the church as a whole rejected the doctrine of the Trinity, and it was not until many years after the death of Ellen G. White that the Adventist Church changed their position in regards to the Trinity." By the evidence above it was at least fifteen years after she died before a Trinity statement of faith is seen. Yet the SDA denomination upholds Arian members, and has been heavily promoting their reversion to Arianism, by two means in these last two decades.

They've been strongly advocating Ellen White as their canonical and divinely inspired interpreter of the Bible. Thus, her views have become *more authoritative than Scripture* itself. This was more subtly affected in their 1958 *Bible Commentary* which upheld her positions and gave her quotes that established them. So they defended Jesus being Michael the Archangel, and upheld him as the angel of Revelation 1, 8, and 10, etc.

Also, their Clear Word Bible has been heavily promoted since 1994. In America today, nearly half of the Adventist homes are already using this so-called Bible for regular reading and Bible study—many for Sabbath school lesson study! The church has promoted this Bible because SDA's unorthodox positions have been translated right into the text, most of which came from Ellen White's endorsements. But the sweet scroll that becomes bitter in the stomach is that *this so-called Bible upholds and promotes her Arianism* as well:

Genesis 1:26; 3:22: God is speaking with His Son of making man; then of man's fall into sin

Genesis 1:28: "Then God and His Son blessed them and said "*We* have given you..."

Genesis 1:31: "Then God looked at everything He had created (following text added) through His Son

Revelation 10:1: "Next I saw a mighty angel come down from heaven... (following text added) Then I knew it was the Lord Jesus"

Revelation 10:5: "Then this mighty angel (adds) the Lord Jesus..."

Revelation 10:8-9: "...Go and take the little open book out of the hand of the mighty angel ... so I went up to the Son of God ..."

1 Thessalonians 4:16: "When Christ descends from heaven, (adds) He as Michael the Archangel will give a shout..."

Revelation 12:7: "... (adds) God's Son Michael and the loyal angels fought against the dragon..."

Jude 9: "... (adds) the Lord Jesus Christ, also called Michael the Archangel..."

John 8:58: "...before Abraham was I AM" changed to "I existed before Abraham was born"

Colossians 1:16: "...By Him all things were created" changed to "...through him the Father created"

Colossians 1:15: "He is the firstborn over all creation" changed to "He has the right to be placed over all creation"

Colossians 1:18: "that in all things He might have pre-eminence" changed to "...therefore He is worthy to be given first place"

Colossians 1:18: "He is the Beginning" changed to "He existed from the beginning"

Colossians 1:19: "The Father acknowledged Him as fully God, (adds) in spite of his human nature"

Hebrews 1:10: "You, O Yhwh, in the beginning laid the foundations of the earth..." is changed to "You existed before the beginning of time. You carried out our plan and created..."

John 20:28: "My Lord and My God" changed to "Lord, you're alive! They were right! I believe! You are the Son of God."

Acts 2:25: "I foresaw Yhwh always before my face" is changed to "I have seen the presence of God in all my life."

Titus 1:3-4; 2:13; 3:4-6; 2 Peter 1:1: Takes identity of God from Jesus Christ, sometimes gives it to the Father!

John 10:30: "I and My Father are One" changed to "I and my Father are so close we're One."

Revelation 3:14: "...the beginning [source] of the creation of God" changed to "who is in charge of God's creation"

Romans 10:9-10 omits "that Jesus is LORD (Yhwh)"; "you shall be saved" changed to: "you have the relation you need"

With SDA heavily promoting Ellen's infallible and canonical interpretive gift, and such a gross perversion of the Bible, that so freely and heavily rewrites it to include Ellen's unorthodox views, including her denial of Jesus' absolute deity and the Trinity, and with SDAs yet upholding as members those denying these essential articles from their statement of faith, actively destroying them, to support Ellen's false views, it is only a matter of time before the whole denomination will revert to the Christ-debasing positions they once held for sixty years!

c) JESUS' SINFUL FALLEN HUMAN NATURE

So, while *SDA Believe* says He had a sinless and unfallen nature "with no evil propensities, or inclinations, or even sinful passions," then why does SDA believe teach He had a "sinful nature" and "fallen nature" with "all its liabilities, including the possibility of yielding to temptation"? (p. 46-47). F. D. Nichol tells us in *Answers* (p. 391), "it agrees with revelation and reason." By *revelation* he means their "only pronouncement that is truly authoritative"—Ellen G. White.

Since they accept her as a prophet, then her views had to be upheld, though contrary to Scripture, Christ's deity, and the purpose of His virgin birth! Thus, they are left trying to reason her views into the Scriptures. So through false reasoning from several texts, they try to uphold Ellen's anti-Christian statements. Ridding ourselves of these revelations and reasonings, we'll avoid all the contrary double-talk seen in their *Questions on Doctrine* or *SDA Believe* (p. 46-52):

Page 46 says He was made in sinful human nature, or fallen human nature; but page 47 says it was not fallen because "He had no moral impurities." Page 49 says, "He took the nature of fallen man" and "He took our nature with all its infirmities"; yet it also says "He was free from hereditary corruption or depravity or actual sin" and "unlike fallen humanity He had no evil propensities," just the opposite of their interpretation of Hebrews 2:17. Page 52 says, "He exercised no power that humanity cannot exercise" in resisting sin—almost verbatim from Ellen White: "He exercised in His own behalf no power that is not freely offered to us. As a man he met temptation and overcame in strength given from God." But page 51 says, "Christ's humanity alone could never have endured the powerful deceptions of Satan. He was able to overcome sin because "in Him dwelt all the fullness of the Godhead bodily ... His Divine Power combined with humanity in behalf of man, infinite victory."

The sad end to which Ellen's statement (above) leads is shown on page 52, as we're told that because we also may be filled with the fullness of God, being partakers of the divine nature, then through Christ's divine power we have the same power to overcome sin as He did. But again this is false reasoning, for He was God by nature, and so immutable and infallible; but our being filled with the Holy Spirit does not make us God by nature, so we're still fallible and capable of sin. The phrase "partakers of the divine nature" means we feed and live on His divine nature—not that *we take part in His deity!*

Elder White wrote:

> ... Christ, enfeebled with our nature ... enfeebled by the seed of Abraham ... takes upon Himself the weakness of the seed of Abraham, that He might reach those who are enfeebled by transgression.[1]

d) WHO IS IN THE FULNESS OF DEITY BODILY?

WAS THE FATHER ALSO HUMAN?

This questions her 1905 "unambiguous" view of the Trinity, which "Trinity?" tells of.

It's also self-indicting, for she starts saying *"The Father is the fullness of the Godhead Bodily..."*[1]

Jesus said "God is Spirit" (John 4:24) and "a spirit does not have flesh and bone as you see I have" (Luke 24:39). So the Father cannot be the fullness of the Godhead bodily, which only Christ is, and Christ can't be an angel, for He's not a spirit, but "the man Christ Jesus" risen bodily.

Maybe Ellen was affected by both the Jehovah's Witnesses (who began as Adventists) and the Mormons who wrote and prophesied in her day. The JWs predicted Jesus' return in the early 1870s with the SDA, and then denied Jesus' bodily resurrection to allow his spiritual presence. Joseph Smith widely published his visitation, by God and Christ, where God was not a spirit being, but a person of flesh and bones, which was the basis of their progression of God doctrine so Adam became God and Jesus who was a man became God. In 1898, even SDA's Uriah Smith held a degree of this in his book *Looking Unto Jesus*, where he wrote "With the Son, the evolution of deity, as deity, ceased". From all the above, Ellen's view of God was unbiblical. It was a different Godhead with a different Jesus and a different Father from the real Jesus Christ and real Father, found in the Scriptures.

Worse yet, her calling Christ an angel, namely Michael the Archangel, and affirming his body dropped off at his ascension, denies He is returning in the flesh. The SDA *Commentary IV* (p. 860) and *VII* (p. 706), holds her view that He is the archangel who comes from heaven for his saints. Here we must note 2 John 7, "For many deceivers have gone out into the world, those who deny Christ is coming in the flesh, this is the deceiver and the antichrist." Scripture attests Jesus' bodily resurrection and ascension, that He'll return in like manner; He is the fullness of the Godhead bodily; He is the man Christ Jesus in heaven today; we are bone of His bone and flesh of His flesh; and when He returns we will be like Him; receiving glorified resurrection bodies. Ellen's making Him an angel, makes Him to be a spirit, and denies He's coming in the flesh, which makes her both a false prophet and anti Christ—against Christ Himself. Dr. Luke writes in Luke 24:39-40, "Behold My hands and My feet, that it is I Myself. Handle Me and see, for *a spirit does not have flesh and bones as you see I have.*" When He had said this, He showed them His hands and His feet."

Obviously, the light did not get brighter for Ellen. SDA largely took the Trinity doctrine because it was biblical, while suppressing Ellen's anti-trinitarian statements over the years. Yet, for almost 2,000 years the orthodox church has held to the Trinity, while combating heresies in every century—especially in this end of the church age, when apostasy is so rampant. The biblical view is so plain, that since 1931 it was the official position of the SDA, though the Arian views weren't expunged from their books, and Ellen's writings. Her vision that Satan was in full possession of the churches, all their prayers and professions are an abomination to God has been upheld, though *her words are a categorical indictment of the Trinity!*

e) ARE ELLEN G. WHITE AND THE SEVENTH-DAY ADVENTISTS GUILTY OF THE TRITHEISM HERESY?

TRITHEISM

The Father, the Son, and the Holy Spirit are three separate gods.

HERESY

Tritheism is the belief in three distinct and separate Gods. See Isaiah 43:10; 44:6, 8; 45:6, 14, 18, 21-22 and 46:9.

TRUTH

The three are one God, distinct but not separate. The clear Bible pronouncement is that there is one God (Deuteronomy 6:4; 1 Corinthians 8:4; 1 Timothy 2:5). There is certainly a Trinity: the Father, the Son, and the Holy Spirit, who are distinct yet never separate. The unique indivisible divine essence is fully resident in each of the three; hence, not one of Them is merely one-third of God. The Father is God, the

Son is God and the Holy Spirit is God—all distinct, co-equal and co-eternal—nevertheless, there are not three Gods, but one unique God. Isaiah 48:16: "Come near to Me, hear this: I have not spoken in secret from the beginning; from the time that it was, I was there. And now the Lord GOD and His Spirit have sent Me."

Several groups have gone on record as rejecting the leading of Adventist leaders in the early days of the Advent movement and have strongly supported the Trinity doctrine. A leader of an independent ministry supposedly threw his *Spirit of Prophecy* books into a trash can. Later, another pastor threw reprints of materials which the pioneers had written about the Godhead into a trash can and then proceeded to collect materials from his church members to throw in the trash can!

In response to materials sent, which clearly presented the historical position of the pioneers, one ministry sent out an *amazing* letter full of so-called facts:

a. Many of the pioneers were in error on several Bible teachings. We do not base our doctrines on what various pioneers believed, but rather, upon what the church decided.

b. The *Spirit of Prophecy* is clear that:

   i. Light is not revealed to a few[1]
   ii. Light is not given contrary to the established faith of the body[2]
   iii. Light should be submitted to the brethren and laid aside if they see no light in it.[3]

Like Froom and many other SDA ministries have accounted the first fifty years as "error" based on the Arian theology. While we agree that we should not accept any doctrine just because the pioneers believed it, we also believe that just because a church decides a certain doctrine is truth does not make it truth! The *Spirit of Prophecy* (Ellen G. White) references are excellent in revealing the original teachings of who the Adventist God was. The church didn't listen to that counsel when the Trinity doctrine was adopted!

a) The wonderful truth about God and His Son was not revealed to just a few! All the pioneers understood and believed it. The Trinity came into the church through the efforts of a few key men.
b) The Trinity was contrary to the "established faith of the body."
c) New light is to be submitted not just to the brethren, but "the brethren of experience."[4]

The "brethren of experience," especially those that Ellen White referred to, were those who went through the 1844 experience. They all rejected the Trinity, seeing no light in it. To avoid the connection the Trinity has to the papacy, some independent ministries have gone to the other extreme and accepted *tritheism, the belief in three gods*. Like Kellogg and Froom, they are quick to quote the *Testimonies* to prove their position.[5]

J. H. WAGGONER

Read Matthew 28:19. In this baptismal formula, it is notable that the word name is in the singular, but it is followed by the three names, Father, Son, and Holy Spirit.

The word persons must be understood in a theological sense. If we equate human personality with

God, we would say that three persons means three individuals. But then we would have *three Gods, or tritheism.* But historic Christianity has given to the word person, when used of God, a special meaning: a personal self-distinction, which gives distinctiveness in the Persons of the Godhead without destroying the concept of oneness. This idea is not easy to grasp—or to explain! It is part of the mystery of the Godhead.

WHAT HINTS OF A TRINITY DOES THE OLD TESTAMENT GIVE US? GENESIS 1:1-3.

The Hebrew word for God in this passage is Elohim, a plural form. Yet the verb bara, "created," is in the singular form. God speaks; that is, He uses the Word, in Creation. (See John 1:1.) And the Spirit of God "moved upon the face of the waters." Here there seems to be an indication of at least more than one person. Note also the use of us and our in this pronouncement, "Let us make man in our image" (Genesis 1:26). "The plural 'us' was regarded by the early church theologians almost unanimously as indicitive of the three persons of the Godhead."[6]

"There are *three living persons of the heavenly trio*; in the name of these *three great powers the Father, the Son, and the Holy Spirit*—those who receive Christ by living faith are baptized, and these powers will co-operate with the obedient subjects of heaven in their efforts to live the new life in Christ."[7]

Others, notably the Seventh-day Adventist Church, have concluded that the word, *God is a collective noun, which really refers to three Gods (!)* working together in unity. The SDA church will deny that it teaches or believes in three Gods. However, semantics will not deny the truth. *The SDA belief in three co-equal, co-eternal, co-omnipotent Beings who are not related to each other clearly teaches Tritheism, a doctrine of three Gods*, even though it is claimed that the three are one in the sense that they are united in character, goals and purposes.[8]

Is it not a mystery that, although borrowing the term from the Roman Catholics, *Seventh-day Adventists today subscribe to a definition of the Trinity* which is based on specific or generic unity which was *condemned by the Catholics as tritheism or polytheism*, and yet seem to be unaware of what the Catholics teach?

Is it not a mysterious irony that a church which has besmirched the credibility of its own Founding Fathers with the Arian label, has itself in the very process of doing so become sullied by that very heresy? *Through its denial that the Son of God was from the substance of the Father* and consequently its *teaching of three unrelated beings*, the first instance is, in fact, tacitly *lending support to the Arian declaration that Christ was from a different substance, and in the second instance, promoting tritheism or polytheism*.

The doctrine of the Trinity, as taught by the SDA church, *is in reality tritheism and hence polytheistic*. The claim to orthodoxy, as based on an acceptance of the Trinity, is therefore misleading since the doctrine of the Trinity, as taught by the SDA church, is inconsistent with the orthodox belief.[9]

Realizing that the Father, Son, and Spirit are one God annuls any need for spiritual legality concerning which of the three to address in prayer, into which One a believer is baptized, etc. The Trinity who has saved us, who indwells us, and who operates within us is the Three-One God—distinct but not separate, coexisting and coinhering eternally. Without a doubt, the greatest truth entrusted to the Christian is the truth concerning the Triune God. As to himself, he must know it and treasure it. As to others, he must defend it and proclaim it. As to God, he must honour it and experience it. A lucid understanding of the Triune God serves not only to fortify a believer against unscriptural teachings about God abounding in today's religious world, but also to increase his appreciation of God and benefit his personal spiritual experience. To a human being, there is indeed no undertaking greater, no calling nobler, than to know, love, experience, and preach the Triune God.

6

IS JESUS MICHAEL THE ARCHANGEL AS THE SDA TEACH?

Recounting her 'vision' of December 1844, Ellen speaks of her and Jesus as, "In a moment we were winging our way upward..." Seeing this, in the light of her calling Him Michael the Archangel,[1]

In *Desire of Ages*, one is led to question if she did not, in fact, really view Him as just that—*an angel!*

DENSE FOG.COVERING.THE "LIGHT"

Dr. Rea has shown many of the articles credited to Ellen were first written or assembled by her secretaries, as Fanny Boulton, or Marion Davis, who worked on *Desire of Ages*, using the work of other Christian writers as their sources. Thus, those statements may not accurately portray Ellen's own view of Christ. This becomes more apparent from some of her statements written in that time period:

> 1903: "The man Christ Jesus was not the Lord God Almighty"[2]
> 1904: "To Christ had been given an exalted position. He has been made equal with the Father"[3]
> 1900: "The mighty angel who instructed John (Revelation 1:1) was no less than the person of Christ"[4]
> 1905: "The instruction ... was so important that Christ came ... to give it to his servant..."[5] (Revelation 10:6). "In swearing by the creator, the angel who is Christ, swore by himself"[6] (Revelation 8:3). "The ministry of the angel at the altar of incense is representative of Christ's intercession..."[7]

These, and her 1844 vision of Jesus with wings, and her calling Him the archangel in *Desire of Ages*, etc., certainly befog her 1897-8 statements regarding Jesus' deity. In *Daniel and Revelation* (p. 341), Uriah Smith identified the angel of Revelation 1:1, etc., as Gabriel. But Ellen made it to be Jesus Himself! Her error is manifest in the context of Revelation 1:1; '*allos*' in 8:3, shows this angel the same kind as the seven angels of verse 2; and in Revelation 19 the angel rebukes John's attempt to worship him. "Trinity?" quotes W. W. Prescott "For a long time we believed ... that *Christ was created, in spite of what the Scripture says.*"[8]

D. Canright showed how Ellen synthesized the risen Jesus with her view of him as the angel Michael. In *Life of Mrs. E. G. White*, chapter 17, page 31, he tells of Dr. Kellogg's theory that the *dead body wouldn't be raised, but all that was left of a person at death was a record of his life kept in heaven, and a new body of new matter was raised* and made to think that it was the same person as the old one. When asked if she had light on this, Ellen declared the Lord shew her *not a particle of the old body would ever be raised, but a new body of new material would be formed.* Canright asked, "How about Christ's body which was raised?" She responded, *"He dropped it all when he ascended."* She failed to recognize him as the man Christ Jesus (1 Timothy 2:5 and Hebrews 7:24-25); and that in Him dwells all the fullness of the Godhead in bodily form (Colossians 2:9).

> Jude 1:9: Michael the Archangel ... said (to Satan) "The Lord rebuke thee."
> Romans 10:9: If you confess "Jesus is LORD"... you shall be saved.

Most Christians are amazed to learn that Seventh-day Adventism teaches that Jesus is Michael the Archangel, but Ellen White said He was Michael, so if they changed this, they'd need to reject her as the spirit of prophecy and they'd not be the remnant church! So now they hold He's both God the Son, and Michael. Dr. Kellogg and Ellen G. White both denied the future bodily resurrection of the saints when Jesus Christ comes again. Notice they said that the dead body would not be raised, but rather a new body of new material will be formed. *This is not a resurrection, but rather a re-creation.* This means that Seventh-day Adventists' only hope is to have a record of them infused into an entirely different body at the resurrection. This means that they themselves will *not* be at the resurrection or in heaven. This teaching is not only limited to Adventists, but was passed on to their offspring, the Jehovah's Witnesses through Charles Taze Russell. This doesn't reflect the true Christian's hope.

It makes a great difference who Jesus really is for 2 Corinthians 11:4 says there'll be those who teach another Jesus, preach a different gospel, and have another spirit.

These marks identify cults, who invariably attack the doctrine of Christ. Early SDA denied His deity saying He's the archangel. Their *Commentary* (Volume 5, page 1129) cites Ellen: "The man *Christ Jesus was not the Lord God Almighty.*" First Timothy 2:5; Hebrews 7:4; Revelation 15:3; 16:5-7; 17:14 shows He is Almighty God.

The real Jesus is the God-man Christ Jesus. He was never an archangel! He's not God-angel-man. So SDA has a different Jesus. But Ellen White said:

> Michael, or Christ, with the angels that buried Moses...[2]

> And before the context closed Christ Himself came to Gabriel's aid ... Gabriel declares 'But lo, Michael, one of the Chief Princes came to help me...'[10]

> There is none that holdeth with me in these things but Michael (Christ) your prince.[11]

> Moses passed under the dominion of death ... but Christ the Saviour brought him forth from the grave. Jude 9[12]

SDA use her so-called gift to prove He is Michael as seen from their *Commentary*, Volume 4, page 860 where they appeal to her writings as their final authority; and that Michael standing up in Daniel 12:1 is Jesus ending his mediation for us, quoting *Desire of Ages* page 379. In 1 Thessalonians 4:16 they reason as He's coming with the voice of the archangel, then He must be Michael! To allow this, they redefine what an archangel is, in Volume 7, page 706: "...Michael is one of the names of Christ ... not as the chief angel, but as the ruler over the angels." Here they say an archangel is not an angel, but is an archbishop, a bishop, or the chief of police, a police? Isaiah 8:20: "If they speak not according to this Word, there is no light in them."

We must show the Bible definition of this, to see how wrong their redefinition is. To evade this test of Scripture, SDA have made their own Clear Word Bible (1994), *adding E. G. White's interpretations into the text!*

> 1 Thessalonians 4:16: "When Christ descends from heaven, He, as the Archangel will..."
> Revelation 12:7: "...God's Son Michael and the loyal angels fought."
> Jude 9 "...the Lord Jesus Christ, also called Michael the Archangel..."
> Daniel 10:13: "then Michael, the prince of the Lord's host, came to help me..." While their commentary tried to accommodate Ellen by saying an archangel is not an angel, now their Clear Word Bible is actually making Christ into an angel!
> Revelation 10:1: "Next I saw a mighty Angel ... I knew it was the Lord Jesus."
> Revelation 10:5: "Then this mighty Angel, the Lord Jesus..."
> Revelation 10:8-9: (...take the book from the Mighty Angel...) "So I went up to the Son of God and asked..."

Thayer's *Greek-English Lexicon of the New Testament* shows the word archangel is from two words: *archay* meaning *chief* and *aggelos* meaning *angel*, defining *archangel* as "the chief of the angels," flatly confuting SDA's *Commentary's* words "not as chief of the angels."

The LXX, Daniel 10:13 shows he is "one of the Chiefs of the princes." Here the article is in plural spelling *twv* and *archay* is also plural *Archwvtwv* so it literally says "one of the *chiefs* of the *angels*." There are more archangels.

The Bible makes clear distinctions between Jesus and the angels:

a) Hebrews 1:14 says angels are all spirits but Jesus showed He was not a Spirit (Luke 24: 27-29). So to the SDA who made Him an angel in Revelation 10, He *is* a spirit, which denies His bodily resurrection, an anti-Christian deception (2 John 7), as well as denying He is the God-man (Colossians 2:9).
b) Angels are all created beings, while Jesus is their creator (John 1:1-3; Colossians 1:16-18) but not created!
c) Hebrews 1 and 2 tell of many ways Jesus is better (by nature) than the angels, emphasizing His true deity!

Gesenius' *Hebrew Chaldee Lexicon of the Old Testament* proves decisively that the chiefs of princes in Daniel 10 are the archangels. Of Michael, it says "One of the seven archangels who interceded for the people of Israel before God." *Strong's Exhaustive Concordance Dictionary* concurs, and Thayer's *Greek Lexicon* gives more insight regarding the seven archangels. In Luke 1:9 Gabriel says, "I am Gabriel, who stands in the presence of God." Revelation 1:4 speaks of the seven spirits (which angels are) who are before God's throne.

But Jesus is God on the throne (John 1:1; Mark 16:19; Acts 2:32-36). In Revelation 3:1 it is "He who has the seven spirits [angels] of God". In 15-16 these seven angels hold the seven vials with the last plagues for the earth. In Zechariah 3:9 Jesus is the Stone having seven eyes—the seven archangels before His throne.

As the Bible shows these seven spirits and the seven archangels are seven spirits, these are the seven archangels in Tobit (LXX), and so Michael the Archangel is one of the seven archangels. Jesus who is the fullness of deity bodily, is the man Christ Jesus, and *not* a Spirit, thus not the archangel, Michael.

Thayer's *Lexicon* also tells of more information in the *Jewish Encyclopedia* and the *Book of Enoch*. We know Enoch is quoted in Jude 14 (the same context as verse 9 about Michael). Here we learn who the archangels are, as the Jews knew about. "And then Michael, Uriel, Raphael and Gabriel looked down from heaven..." The footnote points to 40:2 where it explains the names of the seven archangels as being Michael, Uriel, Gabriel, Raphael, Raguel, Saraquel, and Remiel. The note continues to tell their ministry, sometimes expressed in their names.

But SDA defend their stance saying that since Jesus comes with the archangel's voice, and since He says all who are in their graves will hear His voice and be raised to life, then His voice is the archangel's voice, and He's the archangel! Looking carefully at these passages we see why they only allude to them. First Thessalonians says He's coming with the archangel's voice, and with the trump of God. *If His coming with the archangel's voice makes Him the archangel, then His coming with the trump of God also makes Him a trumpet!* The error is evident, yet it's deeper for it's the voice He's coming with. This reduces Him to merely a voice—not even an angel. But the preposition *with*, followed by an article *the* plus a noun, speaks of a separate entity, not the same entity.

The verse says, "The Lord Himself will descend from Heaven with a shout—a commanding call..." Jesus Himself is going to shout, and this is what He refers to in John 5, that those who are asleep in the dust of the earth will hear His voice—not an angel's when He comes. Since He says in Matthew 25 that He will come with all His angels, of course He will bring the seven archangels with Him. But in Matthew

24:31 He says He'll send them forth "with the great sound of a trumpet" while 1 Corinthians 15:52 says the "trumpet will sound and the dead will rise."

Since Jesus Christ brings all archangels at His second coming, there's no reason that the archangel in 1 Thessalonians is Michael. The odds are seven to one that it's a different one, especially as SDA teach, that God cast off Israel, and seeing that Michael is the archangel for the Jewish people, and Jesus is coming for His church, in contrast to Israel. Since Michael and his angels evicted Satan and his hosts from heaven in Revelation 12 (where Christ is God on the throne), and as Michael was dispensed with the prince of Persia in Daniel 10, it follows there would be a great spiritual battle taking place in conjunction with Armageddon, when Christ comes for His church.

In Daniel 10, Michael is not the one who spoke to Daniel, but the archangel who came to dispense with the prince of Persia. The *one* speaking to Daniel is described as "a man clothed in linen, whose waist was girded with gold of uphaz, His body was like beryl, His face like the appearance of lightning, His eyes were like torches of fire, His arms and feet like burnished bronze..." (vs. 5-6). We see this same *one* in Revelation 1:13-18 who is clothed in linen and His eyes, are like flame of fire, and His feet like fine brass, refined in fire. He is Jesus Christ. Thus Christ spoke to Daniel, and so He was not Michael, one of the chiefs of the angels!

A distinction between Jesus and Michael is seen by comparing Revelation 12 with the gospels, for when Michael cast Satan from heaven, Jesus said, "I beheld Satan as lightning fall from heaven," showing He was God on the throne as He watched Michael, with the division of angels at his command, casting Satan and his hosts from heaven. Jesus watched as Michael was fighting.

A similar distinction is seen comparing Jude 9 with Romans 10:9, cited in the heading of this article. Here

Michael did not dare accuse Satan, but said, "The LORD rebuke thee." Jesus, who is LORD over all, had no problems accusing Satan, declaring him a liar from the beginning and the father of lies. Romans 10:9 says we must confess that Jesus is Lord to be saved.

SDA argue that since the name Michael means *Who is like God*, then it must be Jesus who is God, for it would be desecration to apply such a name to an angel. This is only human logic, based on inadequate evidence and asks: "Why did Ellen apply it to Jesus before they accepted He was God, and while she denied He was Almighty God?" The name Michael means Who is like God? in a question, subjunctive mood. It's linguistic nonsense to apply this to Jesus, who *is* God. Since He is God, it would be against His divine nature to call Him a name saying He is *like* God, much less asking, "Is He like God?"

The Bible shows the names of all the other archangels were even given to men, as well as these angels, though and while each of these names describes some characteristic of Jesus as God. We illustrate these:

Gabriel: from El Gibbor (Mighty God). Ezra 2:20 a man is called Gibbar.

Raphael: from Jehovah Rapha (El heals) used for man in 1 Chronicles 8:2-37

Raguel: means friend or husband-lover (Songs), of Christ. The name Reu

(Genesis 11:18) is a short form of this, as also in Luke 3:35 (Greek #4466).

Saraquel: Sar (prince) and Raquel (wandering sheep). Jesus is Prince and the

Lamb who journeys (Mark 13:34). In Matthew 2:18 we see Rachel.

Remiel: (Ram Yah) is Jehovah raised God. It's used for men in Ezra 10:25

Uriel: is the flame of God, as in Deuteronomy 4:24; 2 Chronicles 13:2 etc. apply this to men.

Phanuel: (the face of God) in Deuteronomy 34:10 is applied to men in Luke 2:36 as Peniel; also 1 Chronicles 4:4 and 8:25.

Michael: Who is like God? Not applied to God, but nine men as 1 Chronicles 5:13-14.

NB: Uriel and Phanuel are two names for the same angel, the one earlier, the other later dating.

When other efforts to show Jesus is Michael fail, SDA pastors often turn to Zechariah 3:1-2, saying that the angel of the Lord often speaks of theophanies of the pre-advent Christ, so here the angel of the Lord who tells Satan, "The Lord rebuke thee..." is Jesus as Michael of Jude 9 who says these words to him.

This straw man assumes what it tries to prove. It assumes only one person can say "the Lord rebuke thee"; and each time we see the angel of the Lord it is Yhwh; and that as Yhwh the Son—not Yhwh the Father or Holy Spirit. It's error to use the Old Testament to define the New, and to use prophetic passages to overturn didactic Scripture and establish doctrine. And it's error to use the Hebrew Malach of *messenger* as equal to *archaggelos* in New Testament Greek, when in Daniel the Hebrew *Sar* (prince) is used for Michael—not *malach* as in Zechariah.

Here they limit the persons of Zechariah 3:2 to those in 3:1, when there's no reason there could not be four: the Lord's messenger, Joshua, Satan, and Yhwh Himself. The context of Zechariah 3 begins in Zechariah 1 where the Lord's angel (vs. 11) stands between the myrtle trees, talking to Yhwh (vs. 12) who answers the angel (vs. 13).

As the messenger *is* an angel, and not Yhwh in Zechariah 1, and this context leads us into Zechariah 3, then neither is the angel the Yhwh who tells Satan, "Yhwh rebuke thee"

(3:2); and there are four entities in 3:1-2 (as noted apparent, above).

That the *messenger* is not Yhwh is also seen from vs. 6 onward where the angel says, "Thus says Yhwh" and Yhwh says He'll send, "My Servant, the Branch." Yhwh's Servant, the Branch (Hebrew *netzer*) speaks of Jesus (Isaiah 42:1; 52:15) the Nazarene. Thus Jesus whom Yhwh would send, is not the Yhwh who speaks in Zechariah 3, and neither the messenger of Yhwh who as we've shown isn't Yhwh. So the Yhwh of this passage must be either Yhwh the Father or Yhwh the Holy Spirit. But since here in Zechariah 3:2 the Yhwh who spoke said, "Yhwh who chose Israel rebuke thee," and as Ephesians 1:2-3 says God the Father chose us in Christ; we deduce it was Yhwh the Holy Spirit who was speaking in Zechariah 3:2.

As Peter said, "Holy men of old spoke being impelled by the Holy Spirit," and since the Holy Spirit spoke through Isaiah (Acts 28:25), and as the Holy Spirit was the Yhwh who Israel tested in the wilderness (Hebrews 3:7; Exodus 17:2-7), so too here He was the Yhwh who was speaking in Zechariah 3:1-2 and verse 6.

Thus here in Zechariah 3, the angel (messenger) of Yhwh is not Yhwh, and neither is this angel the pre-incarnate Christ. The Yhwh who rebuked Satan was the Holy Spirit here, which is a very different scene in Jude 9 where Michael the Archangel did not dare to accuse Satan, while Jesus Himself both accused and rebuked Satan during His ministry saying, "Get behind me Satan," and "the devil was a liar and a murderer from the beginning." Here the SDA's misuse of Zechariah 3 has failed in every way. But they show they know their efforts were wrong:

To deny Jesus was first created by God (Proverbs 8:22) their commentary says:

There is an obvious parallel in this passage to the work of the Second Person of the Godhead. However, the passage is allegorical, and caution must be exercised not to press an allegory beyond what the original writer had in mind. Interpretations derived must always be in harmony with the analogy of Scripture.[13]

...Dogmatic conclusions from parabolic passages are unjustified ... verification of doctrinal beliefs should always be sought in the literal statements of the Bible.[14]

Since SDA know and use these principles in Proverbs 8, then it is conclusive they know it's wrong to violate these same principles in using Zechariah 3:1-2 to try and show Jesus is Michael the archangel, especially when they ignore the context of Zechariah 1:7 through 3:10, they use the Old Testament to define the New, begging the question on many assumptions, and assuming what they set out to prove.

Former SDA Dudly Canright, in his *Life of E. G. White*, on page 162 says Dr. Kellogg theorized *all that was left of a person at death was a record of his life kept in heaven, and at the resurrection a new body of new matter would be formed like the old one and made to think he was the same person.* James White who accepted this, also asked Ellen for her "light" on it. *She said God had shown this to her.* When Canright asked, "How about Christ's body which was raised?" she answered, *"He dropped it all when he ascended."* Here Jesus' dropping off His resurrected body allowed Him to be the Spirit-being, Michael the archangel, who Ellen G. White recorded as winging his way with her around in heaven, in *A Word to the Little Flock*, in 1847.

In 1878, Dr. Kellogg advocated the theory that the dead body would never be raised, but all that was left of a person at death was a record of his life kept in heaven. At the resurrection an entirely new body of new matter would be formed like the old one, and made to think that he was the same person as the old one! Dr. Kellogg influenced Elder James White to advocate this new view. Kellogg presented his new theory before the General Conference on October 8, 1878, and later published it in a book called *Soul Resurrection*. It met with strong opposition; but Elder White used all his influence for it. He invited Elder J. N. Andrews to a private conference with himself and wife, hoping to win him to his side. But he failed to answer any objections. Then he asked his wife is she had any light on the subject. *She promptly declared that the Lord had showed her that not a particle of the old body would ever be raised, but that a new body of new material would be formed. Ellen was asked how Christ's body was raised. She said he dropped it all when he ascended. As the Lord had settled it,* no one dared say any more, though not convinced. Then she went before the conference and made the same positive statements as to what the Lord had "shown" her.

A young minister asked her how she reconciled her present statement with what she had written previously about angel's "watching the precious dust of William Miller." Of course, she could not answer. Instead, she denounced the minister as a little upstart, and set him down summarily. The rest of the people kept still.

Here we see how she was influenced by Dr. Kellogg and her husband to confirm what they wished. It illustrates how easily she was influenced, how readily she adopted any new or wild theory advocated by her associates, and how prompt she was to put upon it the stamp and sanction of divine inspiration and approval.

7

DID JESUS HAVE A SINFUL FALLEN HUMAN NATURE?

For the sake of Christians confronted with this question or Adventist brethren who've only seen their own view, we will address this briefly, hopefully with enough Scripture to establish them in the truth:

> SINFUL means full of sin; having a propensity to sin and having evil desires. It refers to one having inherited Adamic sinfulness (Romans 3:23; 5:12).
>
> FALLEN describes one's spiritual condition after having yielded to sin, so having become actively depraved by his own sinning (as in Adam's case); or, being born in this depraved state that Adam passed to all (Psalm 51:5; Jeremiah 17:9; Ephesians 2:3; Romans 3:10-18).

SINFUL NATURE speaks of the state of one's inner man (soul/spirit) in having evil lusts and desires, also called the carnal man or the flesh or sinful flesh (Romans 7:14-24; 8:3-8).

FALLEN NATURE describes the separated-from-God state which the depraved soul inherited from birth, and continually activates by yielding to sin, with its consequences of death and eternal damnation in the lake of fire (Matthew 25:41-46; Romans 1:18-32; 2:1-5; 5:12-14; 6:23; Revelation 19:20; 20:10)

We recall Adam was created perfect, having a sinless and righteous nature. But when he rebelled, he acquired both a sinful and a fallen nature. He passed this sinful and fallen nature to the whole human race, bar none—except for Christ, who through His virgin birth, bypassed this fallen sinful human nature. He didn't inherit Adamic sin, and thus wasn't born in sin and shaped in iniquity as was everyone else. Neither did He commit any sin, whereby He would obtain a fallen sinful nature.

A critical facet of the doctrine of Christ is His dual nature, that when He became flesh, He continued to be entirely divine and full deity by nature (Philippians 2:6-8; John 1:1-3, 14; Hebrews 1:8-10). So He was and is both man of man and God of God. Colossians 2:9 says, "In Him is dwelling all the fullness of deity in bodily form." This doesn't admit a human side and a divine side, rather it insists He was fully human and fully deity simultaneously. Being fullness of deity, he possesses all the attributes of God by nature: omnipotent, omniscient, omnipresent, eternal, creative, immutable, and infallible. He cannot and does not change, sin, lie, err, or alter His word. For example: (James 1:3), "God cannot be tempted by evil." (Malachi 3:6), "I am Yahweh, I change not" (Hebrews 6:17-18), "Immutability of His counsel ...

two immutable things" (His oath and Promise). (Titus 1:2), "God who cannot lie." (Hebrews 6:18), "It was impossible for God to lie." (John 1:14-15), "We beheld His glory, as the glory of the Father, the fullness of grace and truth." (1 John 2:21), "No lie is of the truth." (Hebrews 13:8), "Jesus Christ is the same, yesterday, today, and forever."

Since Jesus as God by nature is immutable, infallible, never changing, nor sinning; and since coming in bodily form He still maintained the fullness of deity, it was impossible for Him to sin or even alter His divine nature, and yet continue to remain true deity by nature. Fully recognizing this, *SDA Believe* also says:

> Jesus had no evil propensities or inclinations, or even sinful passions ... unlike fallen humanity Jesus' spiritual nature is pure and holy, free from every taint of sin ... nor should we think of Him as a man with propensities of sin ... Never was there in Him an evil propensity.[1]

Here's a perfect definition of sinless nature, yet the very opposite from the quotes of the same book!

James 1:14 says, "Each one is tempted when he is drawn away by his own lusts ... and lust when it is conceived, brings forth sin." Since Jesus had no evil lusts, He could not be tempted to sin (James 1:13). As He had no such desires and neither was prone to them, this proves His sinless nature. And how different He was from us with our own fallen sinful natures! The Bible shows this comparative:

MANKIND	JESUS—SON OF MAN
In sin did my mother conceive me	He knew no sin

born in sin and shaped in iniquity	In Him ...no sin; "He is righteous"
There is none righteous, no, not one	He is Christ the Righteous Judge
In me there dwells no good	Holy, undefiled and separate from sinners
I acknowledge my sins of sin?"	He said, "Who convicts Me "Satan has nothing in Me"
My heart is ... desperately wicked	No deceit was found in His mouth
All have sinned and fallen	His glory was *as the glory of the Father*

Indeed, He was *without sin, without spot, without blemish!* How well these seven comparisons contrast our fallen sinful nature with His unfallen sinless nature, being full deity in unfallen humanity. God foretold, "He will not fail" and when Christ ascended to the Father, He said, "You loved righteousness and hated iniquity" as fulfillment of this prophecy. What a marvellous array of Scriptures; there are more which attest to His sinless and unfallen nature! Being full deity in unfallen humanity, He could not sin, nor did He have any evil lusts to draw Him into sin!

How different from Paul, in Romans 7 who though being born again, filled with the Spirit, and having the gifts of the Spirit found his sinful flesh causing him to do the very things he hated, although he desired to serve God alone, yet he continued stumbling in the flesh! John, likewise born again, full of the Spirit says, "If we say we have no sin, we deceive ourselves." But Jesus could say He had no sin, and affirmed His sinless nature. So while we were all as sheep gone astray, He is the great shepherd and bishop of our souls.

WHY CONTRADICTORY SDA VIEWS

So, while *SDA Believe* says He had a sinless and unfallen nature "with no evil propensities, or inclinations, or even sinful passions," why does *SDA Believe* teach He had a sinful nature and fallen nature with all its liabilities, including the possibility of yielding to temptation? (p. 46-47). F. D. Nichol tells us in "Answers" (p. 391), "It agrees with revelation and reason." By revelation he means their "only pronouncement that is truly authoritative"—Ellen G. White.

Since they accept her as a prophet, her views had to be upheld, though contrary to Scripture, Christ's deity, and the purpose of His Virgin Birth! Thus they're left trying to reason her views into the Scriptures. So through false reasoning from several texts, they try to uphold Ellen's anti-Christian statements. Here we'll survey these texts:

As Romans 8:3 says, He was made in likeness of sinful flesh; they say He had sinful flesh or a sinful human nature or fallen human nature (*SDA Believe*, p.46... ; *Bible Readings*, p. 174; and *Answers*, p. 391). However, when God made man in the likeness of God, this didn't mean He made man in the nature of God. So too, because Christ took our likeness (by taking a body of flesh), he did not Himself become sinful flesh. A statement of similarity does not show equality, but infers inequality, even though similarity exists. Thus, made in likeness of sinful flesh doesn't mean born in sinful flesh.

Hebrews 2:17 says that in all things He was made like His brethren. Here SDA contend that all things includes a sinful human nature. But if so, then He must also have been a sinner to be like us in all things. But *things* speak of tangibles, of concrete substance, of physical attributes.

It doesn't describe intangibles or abstracts as one's state of being or condition of sinful or fallen spiritual nature. Jesus was not like us in His state of being, for He was sinless, not fallen, even as SDA *Believe* says, "Nor should we think of Him as a man with the propensities of sin ... never an evil propensity."

So too, Hebrews 2:14 in saying, "He partook of flesh and blood" is adduced to mean He had a sinful human nature. But it only means He became *one* of humanity, having our material substance of flesh and blood. It does not mean or imply a fleshly carnal nature!

A greater misunderstanding occurs because of the KJV of Hebrews 4:15, "He was tempted in all points as we are, yet without sin." Regardless of *SDA Believe* saying He had no evil propensities, or inclinations, or fleshly lusts to draw Him into sin; and regardless of the many above texts showing He was full deity and so incapable of sin, not even begin tempted to sin; yet for the SDA this verse becomes a grid to filter out the whole of our study thus far! The problem is the translation of the KJV, not contradictory Scriptures!

> In the Greek text, it is properly rendered "He was tested in all points as we are, apart from sin." Here 'tested' means 'He was proved'—it doesn't mean 'tempted to sin' for God cannot be tempted to sin! So the verse shows that sin is exempted, by saying 'apart from sin'. Here *Vine's Expository Dictionary* tells us the Greek 'peirazo' means 'to test, prove, in a good sense, said of Christ and of believers, Hebrews 2:18 where the context shows that the temptation was the cause of suffering to him, and only suffering, not a drawing away to sin, so that believers have the sympathy of Christ as their High Priest in the suffering which sin occasions to those who are in enjoyment of communion with God; so in the similar

passage in 4:15; in all the temptations which Christ endured, there was nothing in Him that answered to sin. There was no sinful infirmity in Him. While He was truly man, and His Divine nature was not in any way inconsistent with His manhood, there was nothing in Him such as is produced in us by the sinful nature which belongs to us.[2]

Vine also says that the Greek *choris* rendered *without sin* means *apart from*, frequently used as a preposition, especially in Hebrews 4:15 (p. 1236). Thus Jesus was tested or proven, even as we believers are, but except or apart from sin, in that He had nothing within Him to draw Him into sin such as we have with our own fallen sinful human natures, which He didn't have!

Christ had a sinless, unfallen human nature, while we don't, which put Him on an infinite vantage ground. His deity with His sinless and un-fallen nature even gave Him advantage over Adam, who *had no divine nature,* and so was still able to be tempted, and to sin. But Jesus' deity was *God's surety that "He will not fail or be discouraged"* in His mission.

Now, to make their "Christ's example of overcoming sin in a sinful fallen nature" seem biblical, the SDA Clear Word Bible has added these thoughts to Romans 8:1-4. After adding *sinful nature* to verses 1-2, they make verse 3 to say, "Jesus took on human nature and demonstrated by the power of the Holy Spirit that sin can be overcome" (v. 4). "This disproved any notion that there is no out for human beings except to be slaves to their own sinful natures. The Lord Jesus did this to give us an example that we can do it, too, when we are not controlled by our sinning, but by the Holy Spirit." Verses 5-6 again have "sinful human nature" by its inclusion four times, and by His equation with us who have such, and saying that Jesus took on human nature in verse 3, no other conclusion could be logically deduced.

The nature of man is necessary because Christ was both God and man; thus we must know how to define His death, and the biblical definition of a sinful fallen nature, which if Christ had, as many SDA uphold, and *then He too needed a Saviour from sin.* As well, there needs be a biblical definition of what happens at one's rebirth.

Only the infinite One, in His infinite holiness, sinlessness and purity, could substitute for us whose inherent sinfulness and whose sins against God were infinite! Only His infinite holiness could bridge the infinite gap separating us from God, because of our inherited Adamic sin, as well as our own iniquities and vileness of heart! How wonderful that God accounts and imputes to us that infinite holiness of Christ. Only by virtue of His sinless, unfallen nature could He be the perfect and complete Saviour, which we as fallen humanity so desperately needed!

8

WILL THE REAL JESUS PLEASE STAND UP?

One of the real problems besetting modern Adventists is their differing views of Jesus Christ, which they've received through their prophet Ellen G. White, who at times spoke differently from Scripture as we've come to understand it today.

This is so well illustrated in that SDA today hold the true deity of Christ, in their statement of faith (*SDA Believe #4*), yet in 1903 Ellen said, "The man *Christ Jesus was not the Lord God Almighty*.[1]

As Hebrews 13:8 says, "Jesus Christ the same, yesterday, today and forever," and since He as the man Christ Jesus is our mediator in heaven today (1 Timothy 2:5) then He has always been the Lord God Almighty, for it's impossible for Almighty God to ever lay aside His full deity! So Paul says of Christ, "In Him is dwelling all the fullness of deity, bodily" (Colossians 2:9).

Yet Ellen White contended that Jesus was Michael, one of the archangels. The SDA *Bible Commentary*, Volume IV, page 860, appeals to her writings as their final authority that Jesus is Michael the archangel who stands up in Daniel 12:1, which signifies Jesus ending His mediation for us. They quote *Desire of Ages* (p. 379) to prove this, while she also identifies Jesus as Michael on page 99; and in *Prophets and Kings* (p. 572) as well as *Spiritual Gifts IV*, page 158.

> To make these aberrant views appear as Biblical, the SDA's 1994 Clear Word Bible has changed the text to make Jesus Michael the Archangel in 1 Thessalonians 4:16; Revelation 12:7 and Jude 9; and to make Him to a mighty angel in Revelation 10:1, 5, 8 & 10. This is because in her comments on Revelation 10, as in Revelation 8—even Revelation 1, Ellen White identified these angels as also being Jesus Christ![2]

Yet Ellen's making Jesus to be Michael creates added problems for their Clear Word Bible, requiring even more changes, for Daniel 12:1 says that after Michael stands up there'll be a time of trouble such as never was (Greek *thlipsis*). In Matthew 24:15-21 Jesus says the abomination of desolation introduces this tribulation (*thlipsis*), as in Daniel 12. Then in verse 29 Jesus says immediately after this thlipsis there will be signs in the heavens, and Jesus returns with His angels to gather his saints. Here comes the problem: E. G. White said this great tribulation was 1260 years of papal supremacy from AD 538 to 1798.[3] Conflicto de los Siglos p. 492.

Also, Michael standing up (Daniel 12:1) is when Jesus ceases His intercession and says, "It is done" of Revelation 22:11 (ibid, 613). Since this great tribulation begins after Michael stands up (Daniel 12), her interpretation of this tribulation beginning in AD 538 requires that Jesus as Michael stood up and ended His intercession in AD 538.

So to evade this contradiction Ellen White also says that the time of trouble such as never was has not yet come, and Michael has not yet stood up![4]

In keeping with her creating another "time of trouble such as never was" the SDA's Clear Word Bible alters Daniel 12:1 to say "but *before* that there will be tribulation..." as well as changing Matthew 24:29 from "immediately after" to *during*.

All this to ensure that Jesus as Michael has not yet stood up! But this brings a worse problem.

Scripture is abundant in stressing that Jesus, as our mediator, finished His work when He offered His blood to the Father through the Spirit (Hebrews 9:14) so that He sat down at the right hand of God, until His enemies are made his footstool (Acts 2:34-35; Mark 16:19-20; Hebrews 1:4, 13; 10:11-14).

In the Old Testament, priests stood up to minister (Hebrews 10:11). In concord with the Old Testament priestly ministry, standing before the altar, Ellen tells of Jesus as our High Priest, since 1844: "Then *Jesus rose up* from the throne ... as He *left the throne*... There I beheld Jesus as He was standing before the Father, a great High Priest..."[5]

WHO IS STANDING.WHEN?

The Lord has shown me in vision, that *Jesus rose up*, and shut the door, and entered the Holy of Holies, at the 7th month 1844; but *Michael's standing up* (Daniel 12:1) to deliver his people, *is in the future*.[6]

This, will not take place, until Jesus has finished his priestly office in the Heavenly Sanctuary, and lays off his priestly attire, and puts on his most kingly robes, and crown, to ride forth on the cloudy chariot, to "thresh the heathen in anger," and deliver his people.[2]

If Jesus and Michael are one and the same person as Ellen G. White and the Seventh-day Adventist Church say they are, why would the Lord show Ellen in a vision Jesus rising up to shut the door and enter the Holy of Holies in July 1844 while Michael doesn't stand up to deliver his people until sometime in the future? Is it possible that they are two different identities? Absolutely! Jesus, the Lord God Almighty the Creator versus Michael, a created archangel.

So Seventh-day Adventists have Jesus who is Almighty God, yet Ellen taught He was not Almighty God, which they hold to. They have Jesus who is the fullness of deity, bodily, yet Ellen says He's an angel—which they uphold. She says that Jesus as Michael has *not yet stood up*, which they endorse! Yet she says that Jesus as our great High Priest *has stood up* and left God's throne, contrary to many Scriptures saying He is seated at the Father's right hand until His enemies are his footstool. Who is right?

9

FINALLY BRETHREN...

Upon analysis of Ellen G. White's and the Seventh-day Adventism's view of who Jesus Christ is, it is very evident that the evangelical Christian has nothing in common with them and they can not be considered as another denomination. It is Jesus Christ who started His church based on His person and ministry and this is the true and only basis for the redeemed evangelical Christian. The Ellen G. White and Seventh-day Adventist faith is based on an entirely different jesus (a created archangel) and a different ministry described in 2 Corinthians 11:3-4:

> But I'm afraid, lest as the serpent deceived Eve by his craftiness, your minds should be led astray from the simplicity and purity devotion to Christ. For if one comes and *preaches another Jesus, whom we have not preached*, or you receive a different spirit which you have not received, or a different gospel which you have not accepted, you bear this beautifully.

There is only one true gospel. The gospel of Jesus: the God-man who liberates the sinner by granting him eternal life, whereas the false gospel of any other, places the sinner into an even greater bondage. To illustrate what the hope is for the Seventh-day Adventists, consider the following references:

> Christ desires His hearers to understand that it is impossible for men to secure the salvation of the soul after death. "Son, " Abraham is represented as answering, "remember that thou in thy lifetime receivedst thy good things, and likewise Lazarus evil things; but now he is comforted, and thou art tormented. And beside all this, between us and you there is a great gulf fixed; so that they which would pass from hence to you can not; neither can they pass to us, that would come from thence." Thus Christ represented the *hopelessness of looking for a second probation*. This life is the only time given to man in which to prepare for eternity.[1]

> Death entered the world because of transgression. But Christ gave his life that man should have another trial. He did not die on the cross to abolish the law of God, *but to secure for man a second probation*. He did not die to make sin an immortal attribute: he died to secure the right to destroy him that had the power of death, that is, the devil. He suffered the full penalty of a broken law for the whole world. This he did, not that men might continue in transgression, but that they might return to their loyalty and keep God's commandments, and his law as the apple of their eye.[2]

It is because He [Christ] has borne the punishment in His own body on the cross that *man has a second probation*. He may, if he will, return this loyalty. But, if he refuses to obey the commands of God, if he rejects the warnings and messages God sends, choosing rather the words of fallacy spoken by those who echo the word of the Deceiver, he is willingly ignorant, and the condemnation of God is upon him. He chooses disobedience because obedience means lifting the cross and practicing self-denial, and following Christ in the path of obedience.[3]

"But He who came to our world to seek and to save that which was lost has pledged His own life that *men might have a second probation*. He has pity, and compassion, and love that are without a parallel; and He has made every provision in behalf of men that none need perish. The divine Son of God came into our world, its Light and Life, to encompass the whole world and to attract and unite to Himself every human being who is under Satan's discipline and rule. He invites them, "Come unto me, all ye that labour and are heavy laden and I will give you rest. Take my yoke upon you, and learn of me; for I am meek and lowly in heart: and ye shall find rest unto your souls" (Matthew 11:28, 29). Thus He unites with Himself by a new inspiration of grace all who will come unto Him. He puts upon them His seal, His sign of obedience and loyalty to His holy Sabbath.[4]

God's Word declares, "The soul that sinneth, it shall die." But God does not desire the death of any one. When Adam's sin had forfeited eternal life, at infinite cost God *provided for the race a second probation*. He "so loved the world, that He gave His only begotten

Son, that whosoever believeth in Him should not perish, but have everlasting life." Should not those to whom the light of truth for this time has come, place themselves in close connection with God, using their capabilities to advance the work of soul-saving? Should not the one who possesses an understanding of the Scriptures impart the knowledge given him to those who know not the truth? Upon every believer in present truth rests the responsibility of working for sinners. God points them to their special work—the proclamation of the Third Angel's Message. They are to show their appreciation of God's great gift by consecrating themselves to the work for which Christ gave His life. They are to be stewards of the grace of God, dispensing to others the blessings bestowed on them. He who has found comfort in the Word of God is to share this comfort with others. Thus only can be continue to receive comfort.[5]

We can understand the value of the human soul only as we realize the greatness of the sacrifice made for its redemption. The word of God declares that we are not our own, that we are bought with a price. It is at an immense cost that we have been placed upon vantage ground, where we can find liberty from the bondage of sin wrought by the fall in Eden. Adam's sin plunged the race into hopeless misery; but by the sacrifice of the Son of God, *a second probation was granted to man.* In the plan of redemption a way of escape is provided for all who will avail themselves of it. God knew that it was impossible for man to overcome in his own strength, and he has provided help for him. How thankful we should be that a way is open for us, by which we can have access to the Father; that the gates are left ajar, so that beams of light from the glory within may shine upon those who will receive them![6]

At an infinite cost to *heaven we have been given a second probation.* Then should not God be in all our thoughts? Should not His will control our actions?[7]

He who does nothing until he feels especially compelled to do something for God, will never do anything, God has given his word, and is this not sufficient? Can you not hear his voice in his word? If you will use God's appointed means, and diligently search the Scriptures, having a determined purpose to obey the truth, you will know the doctrine whether it be of God; but God will never work a miracle to compel you to see his truth. God, in giving his only begotten Son to die on Calvary's cross, has made it possible for all men to be saved. Christ died for a ruined world, and through the merit of Christ, God has elected that *man should have a second trial, a second probation, a second test as to whether he will keep the commandments of God,* or walk in the path of transgression, as did Adam. Through an infinite sacrifice, God has made it possible that men shall practise holiness in this life. Those who would ascertain their election for the future life may ascertain it by their attitude of obedience to the commandments of God. Strong emotions, strong impulses, or desires, for heaven, when listening to a description of the charms of a future life, will not prove that you are elected to sit down with Jesus Christ upon his throne. If you would know the mystery of godliness, you should follow that which has been revealed. The conditions of eternal life have been plainly stated. Jesus says: "If ye love me, keep my commandments.

... He that hath my commandments, and keepeth them, he it is that loveth me: and he that loveth me shall be loved of my Father, and I will love him, and will manifest myself to him. ... If a man love me, he will keep my words: and my Father will love him, and we will come unto him, and make our abode with him. He that loveth me not keepeth not my sayings: and the word which ye hear is not mine, but the Father's which sent me." Here are the conditions upon which every soul may be elected to eternal life. Your obedience to God's commandments will prove that you are predestinated to a glorious inheritance. You are elected to be labourers together with God, to work in harmony with Christ, to wear his yoke, to lift his burden, and to follow in his footsteps. You have been provided with means whereby you may ascertain what to do to make your calling and election sure. Search the Scriptures, and you will find that not a son or daughter of Adam is elected to be saved in disobedience to God's commandments.[8]

Christ declared, "I am the way, the truth, and the life; no man cometh unto the Father, but by me." Christ alone can bridge the gulf that sin has made between earth and heaven, and make it possible to reach fallen man with the overtures of mercy. But through the merits of Christ, *man has been given a second probation,* that he may be tested and proved by another trial to see whether he will be obedient to all the commandments of God, and be brought back in freedom from sin, with his loyalty proved, to have a right to the tree of life, and to enter in through the gates into the city.[9]

Christ became our substitute and surety. He took the case of fallen man upon himself. He became the Redeemer, the Intercessor. When death was proclaimed as the penalty of sin, he offered to give his life for the life of the world, in order that *man might have a second probation*, and that individually he might enjoy the privileges that would come to us through this divine provision, and receive power to form a character after the divine image. But God has a day in which he will judge the world by that Man whom he hath ordained. All judgment is given into the hands of the Son. Christ has engaged to become the sinner's surety, but he does not engage to lessen or detract from the obligation to the divine law. Should Christ change the law in any particular, the demands of Satan would be fulfilled, and God and Christ and the universe would be brought under bondage to his claims. Christ is the star of hope. He is the one to contest the claims of Satan; he is the seed of the woman that shall bruise the serpent's head. He overcome Satan in heaven, and cast him out because of his rebellion and apostasy.[10]

I have a message for your daughters: You are not feeding upon the bread which came down from heaven, but upon husks. All the praise and glory you receive from human beings is of no value. Repent ye, for the kingdom of heaven is at hand. Christ, the Sent of God, gave His life a sacrifice that the *world might have a second probation in which to return to their loyalty to God*. When Christ was threatened by His foes, He said, "My kingdom is not of this world" (John 18:36). "It is not My mission to recognize caste and human theories, or to establish political interests. My kingdom is not to be set up by the power of human armies or the sword. If My kingdom were of this world, then would My soldiers fight. No human power can weaken or overthrow My kingdom through the enemies of God."[11]

There is not the least excuse for the church to be dwarfed and crippled. Our religious experience needs to be of a higher order, that we may see the greatness of the hope presented to us in the gospel. Christ offered Himself as a willing sacrifice in our behalf. He stooped from His high command in heaven to rescue man from the slavery of sin. The Son of God gave up His honour and glory and tasted the bitterness of death that man might be a partaker of the divine nature. He died that *everyone might have a second probation, another chance to choose God as their Leader.* He has made every provision that men and women may have an experimental knowledge of the character and work of their Redeemer.[12]

For our sakes He became poor, that we through His poverty might become rich. What kind of riches? It was not the riches of this earth, but it was the eternal riches, the knowledge of God communicated through Jesus Christ. He consents to become man's substitute and surety; He engages to bear the penalty of the debt which man had incurred by transgression. It is He that loved us, and so loved us that He offered His life as a living sacrifice to bear the sins of a guilty world, that *man should have a second probation, that man should be tested and proved* and tried to see whether he will stand under the blood-stained banner of Prince Emmanuel or whether he will choose to stand under the banner of the prince of darkness.[13]

This was the position of the human race after man divorced himself from God by transgression. Then he was no longer entitled to a breath of air, a ray of sunshine, or a particle of food. And the reason why man was not annihilated was because God so loved him that He made the gift of His dear Son that He should suffer the penalty of his transgression. Christ proposed to become man's surety and substitute, *that man, through matchless grace, should have another trial—a second probation—having the experience of Adam and Eve as a warning not to transgress God's law as they did.* And inasmuch as man enjoys the blessings of God in the gift of the sunshine and the gift of food, there must be on the part of man a bowing before God in thankful acknowledgement that all things come of God. Whatever is rendered back to Him is only His own who has given it.[14]

Christ gave His life to redeem humanity, and He calls upon men and women to make every sacrifice in their power to glorify God by placing light in contrast with darkness. Christ gave His life as a sacrifice, not to destroy God's law, not to create a lower standard, but to maintain justice, *and to give man a second probation.* No one can keep God's commandments except in Christ's power. He bore in His body the sins of all mankind, and He imputes His righteousness to every believing child.[15]

The apostle Paul looking down to our day, declares, "It is high time to awake out of sleep; for now is our salvation nearer than when we believed." And again, "The night is far spent, the day is at hand. Let us therefore cast off the works of darkness, and let us put on the armour of light. Let us walk honestly, as in the day; not in rioting, and drunkenness, not in chambering and wantonness, not in strife and envying; but put ye on the Lord Jesus Christ, and make not provision for the flesh, to fulfill the lusts thereof." These words plainly set forth our duty. *Every year is shortening our probation,* and bringing us nearer the coming of our Lord. We should now put forth every energy to prepare for the great event. This life at the longest is represented as a vapour, which soon passes away. Its treasures, its honours, and its joys are transitory and uncertain. If we live for God and the immortal future, we shall secure all that is worth the having.[16]

As the reader can see from the sixteen references, this is the hope and gift (if you can call it that) that Ellen G. White and Seventh-day Adventists have in receiving a second probation from the work that Jesus Christ did on the cross. Is this what He died for? The true Christian church knows nothing of a second probation (conditional), but rather a pardon (free) unto eternal life. The difference is, one still speaks of continual bondage, while the other speaks of instant liberty! See John 8:31-36; Romans 8:2; Galatians 4:22-31; 5:1.

For the Seventh-day Adventist, what is done in us is as integral to salvation as what was done for us. However, in Protestant evangelicalism, what is done for us is salvation. What is done in us is the lifetime work of the Holy Spirit. Nothing done in us is an integral part of salvation. For Protestants, it is a benefit of having been completely saved by the blood of Jesus Christ.

Galatians 1:6-9: I am amazed that you are so quickly deserting Him who called you by the grace of Christ, *for a different gospel*; which is really not another; only there are some who are disturbing you, and want to distort the gospel of Christ. But even though we, or an angel from heaven, *should preach to you a gospel contrary to that which we have preached to you, let him be accursed.* As we have said before, so I say again now, *if any man is preaching to you a gospel contrary to that which you received, let him be accursed.*

To teach and receive a false gospel is a destructive consequence of alienation from the promises of God for both the hearer and teacher. Let us pay extra attention to our message when sharing the gospel with people so we will not convey false doctrine even in the slightest sense leaving the hearer with a false hope.

> Ephesians 1:13-14: In Him, you also, after listening to the message of truth, the gospel of your salvation—*having also believed, you were sealed in Him with the Holy Spirit of promise, who is given as a pledge of our inheritance, with a view to the redemption of God's own possession, to the praise of His glory.*

The message of the gospel in based on truth including the truth of who Jesus Christ is, because He is the truth. If we preach a message of another jesus, there is no truth or hope in that false belief.

> Jeremiah 14:14: Then the LORD said to me, "The prophets are *prophesying falsehood in My name.* I have neither sent them nor commanded them nor spoken to them; *they are prophesying to you a false vision, divination, futility and the deception of their own minds."*

Jeremiah 23:28-32: "The prophet who has a dream may relate his dream, but let him who has My word speak My word in truth. What does straw have in common with grain?" declares the LORD. "Is not My word like fire?" declares the LORD, "and like a hammer which shatters a rock? Therefore behold, I am against the prophets," declares the LORD, "who steal My words from each other. Behold, I am against the prophets," declares the LORD, "who use their tongues and declare, 'The Lord declares.' Behold, *I am against those who have prophesied false dreams,*" declares the LORD, "and related them, and *led My people astray by their falsehoods* and reckless boasting; yet I did not send them or command them, nor do they furnish this people the slightest benefit," declares the LORD.

Ezekiel 13:6-9: "They see *falsehood and lying divination who are saying, 'The LORD declares,' when the LORD has not sent them*; yet they hope for the fulfillment of their word. "Did you not see a false vision and speak a lying divination when you said, 'The LORD declares,' but it is not I who have spoken?" Therefore, thus says the Lord GOD, "Because you have spoken falsehood and seen a lie, therefore behold, I am against you," declares the Lord GOD. "So My hand *will be against the prophets who see false visions and utter lying divinations.* They will have no place in the council of My people, nor will they be written down in the register of the house of Israel, nor will they enter the land of Israel, that you may know that I am the Lord GOD."

Matthew 7:15: *Beware of the false prophets*, who come to you in sheep's clothing, but inwardly are ravenous wolves.

2 Peter 2:1-3: But false prophets also arose among the people, just as *there will also be false teachers among you, who will secretly introduce destructive heresies, even denying the Master* who bought them, bringing swift destruction upon themselves. And many will follow their sensuality, and *because of them the way of the truth will be maligned; and in their greed they will exploit you with false words;* their judgment from long ago is not idle, and their destruction is not asleep.

Just like the times during the Old Testament period, we have had throughout history, including today, prophets (prophetesses) who prophesy falsely in God's name. They will claim visions, dreams, and divination and pass them off as new revelations from God, but when they are tested under the microscope of God's Word, we see the deception of their propaganda. Tragically, they are able to deceive a lot of people and lead them away from God's Word. Who are we going to trust—the false dreams and visions of fallible people or the trustworthiness of God through His Word?

1 John 4:1-3: Beloved, *do not believe every spirit, but test the spirits to see whether they are from God*; because many false prophets have gone out into the world. By this you know the Spirit of God: every spirit that confesses that Jesus Christ has come in the flesh is from God; and every spirit that does not confess Jesus is not from God; and this is the spirit of the antichrist, of which you have heard that it is coming, and now it is already in the world.

According to the Holy Scriptures, we are not to believe everything, but must test everything as to whether they are from God and in accordance with His holy Scriptures. <u>The jesus of Ellen G. White and the Seventh-day Adventist is not in the flesh, but ceased to exist after His death on the cross in keeping with their soul sleep doctrine.</u> *Their jesus is not a bodily resurrected, but rather re-created, making him a different jesus from the biblical Jesus.* <u>According to Dr. Kellogg, James and Ellen G. White, all that is left of a person at death is a record of his life kept in heaven. At the resurrection an entirely new body of new matter will be formed like the old one, and made to think that he is the same person as the old one. This false doctrine is also true for the Jehovah's Witnesses, Christadelpians, and other Arian cults. When Ellen G. White was asked what happened to Christ's body when it was raised, she said he dropped it all when he ascended into heaven. The Seventh-day Adventist does not have a resurrection hope, but rather a re-creation hope that they will be copied into another body. The original person will not be there at the resurrection. Tragic!</u>

> These asserted that the *human soul, as long as the present state of the world existed, perished at death and died with the body*, but that it would be raised again with the body at the time of resurrection.[17]

> It will be seen that these heretics held the same doctrine as the Adventists. They were set down in those early days as "the propagators of false opinions," the same as now. "For the Sadducees say that there is no resurrection, neither angel, nor spirit: but the Pharisees confess both." Acts 23:6-8. The Pharisees believed in the resurrection, in angels and in spirits, and so did Paul. Adventists believe the first two and deny the third.[18]

Our personal identity is preserved in the resurrection, though not the same particles of matter or material substance as went into the grave. ... In the resurrection every man will have his own character. God in His own time will call forth the dead, giving again the breath of life, and bidding the dry bones live.[19]

Ephesians 4:11-15: And He gave some as apostles, and some as prophets, and some as evangelists, and some as pastors and teachers, for the equipping of the saints for the work of service, to the building up of the body of Christ; until we all attain to the unity of the faith, and of the knowledge of the Son of God, to a mature man, to the measure of the stature which belongs to the fullness of Christ. As a result, we are no longer to be children, *tossed here and there by waves, and carried about by every wind of doctrine, by the trickery of men, by craftiness in deceitful scheming; but speaking the truth in love*, we are to grow up in all aspects into Him, who is the head, even Christ.

The purpose for the Christian is to know Jesus Christ personally and grow in the grace and knowledge of Him. If we have a false and inaccurate knowledge, we are subject to being tossed here and there by every wind of doctrine engineered by the craftiness and trickery of men. With Jesus Christ being the nucleus of Christianity, His identity is of vital importance and has to be in accordance and established by the Holy Scriptures so we can worship the true and not false Jesus.

1 Timothy 4:6-7: In pointing out these things to the brethren, you will be a good servant of Christ Jesus, constantly nourished on the words of the faith and of the sound doctrine which you have been following.

But have nothing to do with worldly fables fit only for old women. On the other hand, discipline yourself for the purpose of godliness;

1 Timothy 6:1-5: Let all who are under the yoke as slaves regard their own masters as worthy of all honor so that the name of God and our doctrine may not be spoken against. And let those who have believers as their masters not be disrespectful to them because they are brethren, but let them serve them all the more, because those who partake of the benefit are believers and beloved. Teach and preach these principles. If anyone advocates a different doctrine, and does not agree with sound words, those of our Lord Jesus Christ, and with the doctrine conforming to godliness, he is conceited and understands nothing; but he has a morbid interest in controversial questions and disputes about words, out of which arise envy, strife, abusive language, evil suspicions, and constant friction between men of depraved mind and deprived of the truth, who suppose that godliness is a means of gain.

2 Timothy 4:1-4: I solemnly charge you in the presence of God and of Christ Jesus, who is to judge the living and the dead, and by His appearing and His kingdom: preach the word; be ready in season and out of season; reprove, rebuke, exhort, with great patience and instruction. For the time will come *when they will not endure sound doctrine*; but wanting to have their ears tickled, they will accumulate for themselves teachers in accordance to their own desires; and *will turn away their ears from the truth, and will turn aside to myths.*

Titus 1:7-11: For the overseer must be above reproach as God's steward, not self-willed, not quick-tempered, not addicted to wine, not pugnacious, not fond of sordid gain, but hospitable, loving what is good, sensible, just, devout, self-controlled, *holding fast the faithful word which is in accordance with the teaching, that he may be able both to exhort in sound doctrine and to refute those who contradict.* For there are many rebellious men, empty talkers and deceivers, especially those of the circumcision, who must be silenced because they are upsetting whole families, teaching things they should not teach, for the sake of sordid gain.

Titus 2:1: But as for you, speak *the things which are fitting for sound doctrine.*

Titus 2:7-8: In all things show yourself to be an example of good deeds, *with purity in doctrine, dignified, sound in speech* which is beyond reproach, in order that the opponent may be put to shame, having nothing bad to say about us.

Titus 2:10-15: ...not pilfering, but showing all good faith that they may adorn the doctrine of God our Savior in every respect. For the grace of God has appeared, bringing salvation to all men, instructing us to deny ungodliness and worldly desires and to live sensibly, righteously and godly in the present age, looking for the blessed hope and the appearing of the glory of our great God and Savior, Christ Jesus; who gave Himself for us, that He might redeem us from every lawless deed and purify for Himself a people for His own possession, zealous for good deeds.

> These things speak and exhort and reprove with all authority. Let no one disregard you.

As we have seen in the preceding Scripture references, sound doctrine is essential for the Christian to have a healthy spiritual life. Not only is this essential for the Christian, but also for the people who will hear the Christian proclaim Jesus' gospel so that they can have a faith based on truth and the irrefutable facts about Jesus Christ.

> Acts 17:10-11: And the brethren immediately sent Paul and Silas away by night to Berea; and when they arrived, they went into the synagogue of the Jews. Now these were more noble-minded than those in Thessalonica, for they received the word with great eagerness, *examining the Scriptures daily, to see whether these things were so.*

Lastly and probably the most important, let us all be as noble-minded as the Bereans in Acts 17:11, checking out every speaker and writer's message in light of the Holy Scriptures regardless of the person's stature. Given Paul's stature, spiritually speaking, who wrote half the New Testament under the inspiration of the Holy Spirit, was subject to examination of his messages by the Bereans to see if what Paul preached was in accordance with the Scriptures. We know that God's Word is faithful, being the Supreme Court by which we must determine all things pertaining to life and godliness.

APPENDIX

1

JESUS CHRIST AS GOD IN THE BIBLE

Due to the fact that the Bible is God's Word, there are no contradictions and thus it is important that we allow the Holy Scriptures to interpret themselves. Since the New Testament defines the Old, and the Old must be understood in the light of the New, we'll see by comparing the Scriptures, that Jesus of the New Testament is also Jehovah God of the Old, also called *the Word*.

O THEOS—"GOD" BY IDENTITY
Matthew 1:23; 4:7-10 (compare with Hebrews 1:6); 19:17; Mark 2:7; 10:6 (compare with Colossians 1:16); 10:9-27; 13:19; Luke 1:47; Luke 2:13 (compare with Hebrews 1:6); Luke 4:8-12; 5:21; 7:16; 11:20; 18:7; John 2:18-22; 5:22-27; 20:28; Acts 7:57-60; 20:28; Romans 9:5; 1 Corinthians 1:2; 10:40; Ephesians 5:5; 2 Thessalonians 1:12; 1 Timothy 1:17; 2:3; Titus 1:3-4; 2:13; 3:4-6; Hebrews 1:8; 2 Peter 1:1; 1 John 5:20.

THEOS — GOD BY NATURE
John 1:1; 5:18; 10:33.

EQUAL WITH GOD
John 5:18 (as Son of God); 10:30-31; Philippians 2:6 (before incarnation); Colossians 2:9 "all the fullness of deity in bodily form"; 1 Timothy 3:16; Hebrews 1:5, 8-10; Son of God 110 times.

CREATOR
JESUS IN NEW TESTAMENT
Matthew 19:4-6; John 1:3, 10; Acts 3:15; 17:24-28; Ephesians 3:9; Colossians 1:12-17; 1 Corinthians 8:6; 1 Timothy 2:13-14; Hebrews 1:2, 8-12; Revelation 3:14; 4:8-11; 7:17; 10:6; 14:6-7; 21:5-7; 22:3.
JEHOVAH IN OLD TESTAMENT
Genesis 1:1, 31; 2:4, 7; 5:1-2; Job 19:26; 26:7; 33:4; Proverbs 3:19; 8:22-30; 30:4; Psalm 8:69; 33:6-9; 89:37; 96:10; 102:25-27; 104:30; Isaiah 40:28; 41:4; 42:5; 43:10-11, 13-15; 44:24; 45:5-18; 48:12-13, 16; Zechariah 12:1; Malachi 2:10.

FIRST AND LAST
JESUS IN NEW TESTAMENT
Revelation 1:8-17; 22:13.
JEHOVAH IN OLD TESTAMENT
Isaiah 41:4; 43:10-11; 44:6, 8.

SAVIOUR AND REDEEMER
JESUS IN NEW TESTAMENT
Luke 2:10-11; 24:21-29; John 3:16-18; 4:40-42; Acts 20:28; Romans 3:24; Galatians 3:13; Ephesians 1:7; Philippians 3:20; Colossians 1:14; 2 Thessalonians 1:12; 1 Timothy 1:1-3; 2:3; 4:10; Titus 1:3-4; 2:13; 3:4-6; Hebrews 9:12-15;

1 Peter 1:10-11; 1:18-20; 2:20-24; 3:2, 18; 2 Peter 1:1;
1 John 4:14; Jude 25; Revelation 5:9.
JEHOVAH IN OLD TESTAMENT
2 Samuel 22:3; 2 Kings 13:5; Job 19:25; Proverbs 23:11;
Psalm 19:14; 78:35; 106:21; Isaiah 41:14; 43:3-14; 44:6-24; 45:15-21; 47:4; 48:17; 49:7-26; 54:5, 8; 59:20; 60:16;
Jeremiah 50:34; Hosea 13:4.

I AM (ABSOLUTES—EGO EIMI WITHOUT SUBSTANTIVES)
JESUS IN NEW TESTAMENT
Mark 13:16; 14:61-62; Luke 21:8; John 7:28; 8:24, 28, 58; 13:19 (compare with Isaiah 43:10; 46:10); John 18:5-8.
JEHOVAH IN OLD TESTAMENT Exodus 3:14; Deuteronomy 32:39; Isaiah 41:4; 43:13; 43:25; 46:4.

I AM (EMPHATIC—EGO EIMI WITHOUT SUBSTANTIVES):
JESUS IN NEW TESTAMENT
Matthew 16:13-15; 27:43; Mark 8:27, 29; Luke 22:70; John 6:35, 41, 48, 51; 9:5; 10:7, 9, 11, 14, 36; 11:25; 15:1-5; 19:21; 11:25; Revelation 1:8, 11, 17-18; 2:23; 3:21; 21:6; 22:13-16.
JEHOVAH IN OLD TESTAMENT
Isaiah 42:8; 43:10-11, 15, 25; 46:9-10.

STONE OF STUMBLING
JESUS IN NEW TESTAMENT
Acts 4:10-12; Romans 9:32-33; 11:9-11; 1 Corinthians 1:23; 1 Peter 2:4-8.
JEHOVAH IN OLD TESTAMENT
Psalm 118:22; Isaiah 8:13-15; 28:16; etc., also called Jehovah of Armies.

THE KING
JESUS IN NEW TESTAMENT
Matthew 25:34; 1 Timothy 1:17; 6:15; Hebrews 7:1-2; Revelation 15:3-4; 17:14.
JEHOVAH IN OLD TESTAMENT
Psalm 5:2; 10:16; 44:4; 45:11; 47:2-7; 68:24; 74:12; 98:6; 147:5; 149:2; Isaiah 51:22.

ALMIGHTY GOD
JESUS IN NEW TESTAMENT
Revelation 1:8; 4:8; 11:17; 15:3-4; 16:5-7 (John 5:22-27).
JEHOVAH IN OLD TESTAMENT
Genesis 17:1; 35:11; 43:14; 48:3; 49:25; Exodus 6:3; (compare with 3:14; John 8:58); Numbers 24:4-16.

MIGHTY GOD (EL GIBBOR)
JESUS IN OLD TESTAMENT
Isaiah 9:6; 10:21; 30:29.
JEHOVAH IN OLD TESTAMENT
Isaiah 49:26; 60:16; Jeremiah 20:11; 32:18.

HA ADON (THE LORD, FOR "LORD OF LORDS")
JESUS IN NEW TESTAMENT
Acts 2:25-34; Romans 10:9; Revelation 17:14; 19:16.
JEHOVAH IN OLD TESTAMENT
Deuteronomy 10:17; Psalm 110:1; 136:3; Isaiah 1:24; 3:1; 10:16; 10:33; 19:4; Malachi 3:1.

THE ROCK
JESUS IN NEW TESTAMENT
Matthew 7:24-25; 16:18; Luke 6:48; Corinthians 10:4; Ephesians 2:20-22; 1 Peter 2:6-8.
JEHOVAH IN OLD TESTAMENT
Exodus 12:6; Deuteronomy 32:1-4, 15, 30-31; 1 Samuel 2:2; 2 Samuel 22:2, 32, 47; 23:3; Psalm 18:2, 31-46; 28:1;

31:2-3; 42:9; 61:2; 71:3; 78:34-35; 89:26; 92:15; 94:22; 95:1; Isaiah 17:10-11.

LORD OF HOSTS
JESUS IN NEW TESTAMENT
Romans 9:29; James 5:4.
JEHOVAH IN OLD TESTAMENT
1 Samuel 1:3-11; 2 Samuel 5:10; Psalm 84:1, 3, 8, 12; Isaiah 10:23; 24:23; 37:16; Jeremiah 9:7, 15, 17; Amos 3:13. etc. (273 times total).

SHEPHERD
JESUS IN NEW TESTAMENT
John 10:11, 14, 16; Hebrews 13:20; 1 Peter 2:21-25; 5:4.
JEHOVAH IN OLD TESTAMENT
Psalm 23:1; 80:1; Isaiah 40:10-11; 63:11; Jeremiah 31:10; Ezekiel 34:23; 37:24; Zechariah 11:16.

BEGINNING AND ENDING
JESUS IN NEW TESTAMENT
Colossians 1:18; Hebrews 1:10; 12:2; Revelation 1:8; 3:14; 22:3.
JEHOVAH IN OLD TESTAMENT
Psalm 102:25-27; 111:10.

LIVES FOREVER
JESUS IN NEW TESTAMENT
Romans 1:20; 16:26; Revelation 1:17-18; 5:14.
YHWH IN OLD TESTAMENT
Deuteronomy 33:27; Micah 5:4.

KURIOS (LORD)
JESUS IN NEW TESTAMENT
John 20:28; Acts 2:21-25; 1 Timothy 2:5; Hebrews 1:10; Revelation 15:3-4; 16:5-7.

JEHOVAH AS LORD IN OLD TESTAMENT
Psalm 16:8-11; 102:25-27; 110:1; Joel 2:32 (compare with Acts 2:21; Romans 10:9) etc. (7000 times).

OUR STRENGTH
JESUS IN NEW TESTAMENT
Philippians 4:13.
JEHOVAH IN OLD TESTAMENT
Isaiah 26:4.

ALWAYS PRESENT
JESUS IN NEW TESTAMENT
Matthew 18:20; 28:20.
JEHOVAH IN OLD TESTAMENT
Jeremiah 23:24.

THE ONE PIERCED
JESUS IN NEW TESTAMENT
John 19:34-37; 20:27-28; Revelation 1:7.
YHWH IN OLD TESTAMENT
Psalm 22:16; Zechariah 12:10; 13:6.

REWARDER
JESUS IN NEW TESTAMENT
Titus 2:13-14; Revelation 2:23; 22:12.
YHWH IN OLD TESTAMENT
Isaiah 40:10; Jeremiah 17:10.

JUDGE
JESUS IN NEW TESTAMENT
Matthew 25:31-46; John 5:22-27; Revelation 16:7; 19:11.
YHWH IN OLD TESTAMENT
Deuteronomy 32:36; Psalm 94:2; 96:13.

LIGHT OF LIFE
JESUS IN NEW TESTAMENT
John 1:4-7; Acts 26:23; Revelation 21:23.
YHWH IN OLD TESTAMENT
Isaiah 60:19; Zechariah 2:5.

COMING WITH SAINTS
JESUS IN NEW TESTAMENT
Colossians 4:4; 1 Thessalonians 3:13; Jude 14.
YHWH IN OLD TESTAMENT
Daniel 7:10; Zechariah 14:5.

BELIEVED IN FOR SALVATION
JESUS IN NEW TESTAMENT
Matthew 3:13; John 3:16; Acts 16:31; Romans 10:9-13.
YHWH IN OLD TESTAMENT
Exodus 6:3; Isaiah 40:3; Joel 2:32.

SUSTAINS THE UNIVERSE
JESUS IN NEW TESTAMENT
Colossians 1:15-17; Hebrews 1:3; 2 Peter 3:7.
JEHOVAH IN OLD TESTAMENT
Genesis 1:3; Psalm 33:9.

HOPE FOR MANKIND
JESUS IN NEW TESTAMENT
1 Timothy 1:1; Titus 2:13.
JEHOVAH IN OLD TESTAMENT
Isaiah 30:18; Jeremiah 17:7-13.

CREATOR (EX NIHILO) OF UNIVERSE
JESUS IN NEW TESTAMENT
Colossians 1:16; Hebrews 1:10; 3:4; Revelation 3:14.

YAHWEH IN OLD TESTAMENT
Proverbs 8:22-30 (compare with Hebrews 1:10); Psalm 102:25; Isaiah 9:7; Zechariah 12:1.

THE SAME FOREVER
JESUS IN NEW TESTAMENT
Hebrews 1:12; 13:8-9.
JEHOVAH IN OLD TESTAMENT
Psalm 102:27; Micah 3:6.

FORGIVER OF SINS
JESUS IN NEW TESTAMENT
Luke 7:38-49.
YHWH IN OLD TESTAMENT
Exodus 34:7; Psalm 103:1-3; Isaiah 43:25.

HOLY ONE
JESUS IN NEW TESTAMENT
Acts 3:14; Revelation 4:8-11.
JEHOVAH IN OLD TESTAMENT
Psalm 71:22; Isaiah 41:14.

LIGHT OF THE WORLD
JESUS IN NEW TESTAMENT
Luke 2:32; John 1:4-5; 8:12
YHWH IN OLD TESTAMENT
Psalm 27:1; Isaiah 9:2; 42:6.

LORD OF GLORY
JESUS IN NEW TESTAMENT
John 16:14; 17:5; 1 Corinthians 2:8; 2 Peter 1:17.
YHWH IN OLD TESTAMENT
Exodus 33:18; Psalm 24:7-10.

OUR HIDING PLACE
JESUS IN NEW TESTAMENT
Colossians 3:3.
JEHOVAH IN OLD TESTAMENT
Exodus 15:1; Psalm 9:9; 32:7; Isaiah 32:2.

GIVES LIVING WATER
JESUS IN NEW TESTAMENT
John 4:14; 7:38-39.
JEHOVAH IN OLD TESTAMENT
Isaiah 32:1-15; 44:3; Jeremiah 17:13.

WORSHIPPED BY ANGELS
JESUS IN NEW TESTAMENT
Hebrews 1:6; Revelation 4:8-11.
JEHOVAH IN OLD TESTAMENT
Nehemiah 9:6; Isaiah 6:2-3.

GIVES SIGHT
JESUS IN NEW TESTAMENT
Luke 9:26; John 17:24; James 2:1; 2 Peter 3:18; Revelation 1:6.
YHWH IN OLD TESTAMENT
Psalm 29:1-3; 115:1; Isaiah 42:8; Jeremiah 13:16.

COMING WITH REWARDS
JESUS IN NEW TESTAMENT
Matthew 25:31-46; 1 Corinthians 15:24-25; Revelation 11:15; 19:16; 22:12-13.
JEHOVAH IN OLD TESTAMENT
Psalm 45:6; 47:7-8; Isaiah 40:9-10.

HIS WITNESSES
JESUS IN NEW TESTAMENT
Acts 1:8; 22:15; Revelation 11:3; 20:4.

YHWH IN OLD TESTAMENT
Isaiah 43:10-12; 44:8.

AT GOD'S RIGHT HAND
JESUS IN NEW TESTAMENT
Mark 16:19; Acts 2:25, 34-36.
JEHOVAH IN OLD TESTAMENT
Psalm 16:8-11; 110:1.

DECLARES END FROM BEGINNING
JESUS IN NEW TESTAMENT
Matthew 24; Mark 13; Luke 21; John 13:19; 14:29; 16:4; Revelation 1:1-2.
JEHOVAH IN OLD TESTAMENT
Isaiah 41:22; 43:9; 45:21; 46:9-10; 48:3.

O ZWN (THE LIFE SOURCE)
JESUS IN NEW TESTAMENT
John 6:51; Revelation 1:17-18.
JEHOVAH IN OLD TESTAMENT
Jeremiah 2:13; 17:3.

LORD OVER SABBATH
JESUS IN NEW TESTAMENT
Matthew 12:8; Luke 6:5.
JEHOVAH IN OLD TESTAMENT
Exodus 20:8-11; Deuteronomy 5:12-13; Nehemiah 9:6-14.

These forty New Testament to Old Testament comparisons conclusively show Jesus of the New Testament was Jehovah of the Old Testament, before His incarnation. Do these references identify your Jesus? Is it enough that Jesus is called God? In the following chapter, we will establish that not only is Jesus called God, but He is also God by nature.

2

JESUS CHRIST BIBLICALLY SHOWN AS GOD BY NATURE

In Galatians 4:8 Paul tells us that false gods are not God by nature. Thus, being God by nature is what makes the true God be God! To be true deity requires having the traits and qualities which made God be God. Thus, He must be eternal, omnipotent, omniscient, immutable, omnipresent, and creative. In our "Jesus Christ as God in the Bible" we showed hundreds of Bible texts that identified Jesus in the New Testament as being Jehovah God from the Old. Yet we must do more than show He is called God; we must also show that He is God—God by nature. There are a number of different ways the Scriptures show this conclusively:

In Hebrews 1:1-3, Paul introduces Jesus' deity with many evidences.

    a) "His Son" speaks of Christ as The *Son* of God. Just as every human's son is human by nature, so then the Son of God must also be God by nature.

b) "Heir of all things" shows Jesus is the *sole owner* of everything in the universe.
c) "Through whom He made the worlds" shows Jesus as the creative agent of deity. He was creation's active cause.
d) "Upholding all things by the word of His power" proves Jesus is the sustainer of the universe, so He must be God.
e) "Brightness of His (the Father's) glory" shows He has equal glory with the Father. Compare John 17:5 with Isaiah 42:8.
f) "Express image of His person." Christ is in every way the same and equal with the Father.
g) "By Himself purged our sins." He alone is responsible for our salvation. He's not a mere tool in the Father's hands.
h) "Sat down at the right hand of the Majesty on high" tells He has God's seat of authority. Matthew 28:18.

Hebrews 1:4-14: Paul continues to show *why* Christ is so much *better* than the angels:

a) verse 4. He has a more excellent name. ("Yeshuah" means *Yahweh is salvation*). "Your name, you gave Me" (John 17:11-12).
b) verse 5. Called Son, therefore equal to God by nature. (John 5:16-18: "making Himself equal with God.")
c) verse 6. All angels are told to worship Jesus.
d) verse 7 addressing the angels, they are told "Who makes His angels spirits and His ministers a flame of fire."
e) verse 8 God the Father speaks to the Son, "Your throne, O God, is forever and over;…"

f) verse 9 God the Father anoints God the Son.
g) verse 10 God the Father addresses Jesus as the "Lord" who laid the foundation of the earth and the heavens are the works of Jesus' hands.
h) verse 11 Jesus is unperishable
i) verse 12 Jesus is eternally unchanging
j) verse 13 Jesus, not being an angel, is the unique One to sit at God's right hand.
k) verse 14 the role of angels is to minister to those who will inherit salvation.

By investigating the nature of Jesus Christ, the evidence overwhelming reveals that He is God by nature. This is one of the essential elements of determining the genuine Jesus. Having established that Jesus is called God and is God by nature; often, the Holy Spirit is delegated to being something lesser than God like an active force or some other distorted explanation.

3

THE PERSON AND DEITY OF THE HOLY SPIRIT

Like Thomas who did not believe in the risen Christ until seeing Him, so many refuse to believe in the Holy Spirit, because they don't see Him. Jesus predicted this "...even the Spirit of Truth whom the world cannot receive, because it sees Him not" (John 14:16-17; 20:25). Men today try to reason away the person of the Holy Spirit, affirming He is merely God's influence or power. (As in 1 Corinthians 2:14 and Genesis 1:2 *New World Translation*.) But John 4:24 says God is spirit.

a. Qualifications of Personality. *Person* doesn't always mean a human being. Though all humans are persons, so also are angels and God and Christ. The Holy Spirit likewise has three qualifications of personality:

1. *Mind.* He has His own mind. (Romans 8:27; 1 Corinthians 2:11; Isaiah 40:13-14)

2. *Will.* He has His own will. (1 Corinthians 12:11, distributes gifts as He wills; John 3:8 Greek: "The Spirit Himself He breathes upon whom He wills..." *New International Version Interlinear*, Alford; *Yeager's Renaissance New Testament.*)
3. *Emotions.* He has personal emotions. (Romans 15:30; Ephesians 4:30; Isaiah 63:10.) Grieve, vex, love, joy, etc. Since He has His own mind, will and emotions, He is a separate person from the Father and from Jesus.

b. Personal pronouns are often used such as he, him, his, who, whom, etc for the Holy Spirit (Isaiah 40:13-14, John 14:16-17; 16:7, 13-14) To arbitrarily assert this is personification, a figure of speech is inadequate, since these are in direct discourse.

c. Important Greek personal pronouns used of the Holy Spirit (which cannot be figurative):

1. *Ekeinos*: demonstrative pronoun pointing out an individual "that one; masculine" (John 16:13).
2. *Eautos*—emphatic reflexive pronoun, "He Himself" "His Very Own Person," masculine (1 Corinthians 2:14-16).
3. *To En To Auto*—"The One and Self Same" shows He has His very own being (1 Corinthians 12:11).
4. *EI* suffix adds male person to the verb. For example: *lalesei* means *He will speak*. In Greek the true gender is shown by the verb as over the noun. So Spirit, which is neuter, is shown to be masculine by the verb.

d. Another Comforter. Jesus called the Holy Spirit another comforter (Greek: *parakletos*—mediator). Just as Jesus Himself is our mediator between man and God, so also the Holy Spirit is another parakletos. Here He uses the word *allos* as another of the same kind, not *heteros*—a different kind. Thus as Jesus is a person of deity as parakletos, then the Holy Spirit is another person of deity as parakletos. (So we come to God through Christ; but God speaks and deals with us through the Holy Spirit, our other mediator). It is He who regenerates us, witnesses and seals our sonship, leads us in repentance, worship, prayer, ministry, etc.!

e. Jesus identifies Himself as the One who gives living water upon request. Jesus goes on to elaborate that those who believe in Him would have rivers of living water flow from their hearts in John 4:10-11 and 7:37-39.

f. The Holy Spirit's own testimony. He calls Himself I, Me, My, numerous times, proving He exists! Acts 13:2: "Separate unto Me Barnabas and Saul, for the work to which I have called them." In Hebrews 3:7-11 and 4:3-5, He uses I, Me, and My about ten times. In Hebrews 10:15-17, He uses I and My five times. In these He is the Jehovah who is talking (see Psalm 95:7>; Jeremiah 31:22 with I, Me, My, etc.). Thus, just as the Father is Yahweh Elohim and Jesus Christ is Yahweh Elohim, so also is the Holy Spirit Yahweh Elohim (Exodus 17).

g. The Holy Spirit is called God by name (Acts 5:3-4). "You lied to the Holy Spirit ... you lied to God."

h. The Holy Spirit seen by men. He is called Jehovah the Spirit in 1 Corinthians 3:18 in the Jehovah's Witnesses' *New World Translation*! Acts 28:25> shows that the Holy

Spirit is the Jehovah whom Isaiah saw in Isaiah 6:9>. In Exodus 17 He is the Jehovah whom Israel tested in the wilderness, which Hebrews 3:7-11 refers to. In Exodus 17 He says, "I will stand on the Rock and you shall smite the Rock." When they saw Him stand on the rock, Moses smote the Rock, bringing forth living water! First Corinthians 10 says that rock was Christ. In Acts 10, He was the messenger whom Cornelius saw (vs. 3) for He said to Peter, "Three men seek thee ... I have sent them" (vs. 19-20). Other similar theophanies of the Holy Spirit occur in the Bible.

The "Holy Spirit" is spoken of under various titles in the New Testament. ("Spirit" and "Ghost" are renderings of the same word, pneuma; the advantage of the rendering "Spirit" is that it can always be used, whereas "Ghost" always requires the word "Holy" prefixed.) In the following list the omission of the definite article marks its omission in the original (concerning this see below):

Spirit, Matthew 22:43; Eternal Spirit, Hebrews 9:14; the Spirit, Matthew 4:1; Holy Spirit, Matthew 1:18; the Holy Spirit, Matthew 28:19; the Spirit, the Holy, Matthew 12:32; the Spirit of promise, the Holy, Ephesians 1:13; Spirit of God, Romans 8:9; Spirit of (the) living God, 2 Corinthians 3:3; the Spirit of God, 1 Corinthians 2:11; the Spirit of our God, 1 Corinthians 6:11; the Spirit of God, the Holy, and Ephesians 4:30; the Spirit of glory and of God, 1 Peter 4:14; the Spirit of Him that raised up Jesus from the dead (i. e., God), Romans 8:11; the Spirit of your Father, Matthew 10:20; the Spirit of His Son, Galatians 4:6; Spirit of (the) Lord, Acts 8:39; the Spirit of (the) Lord, Acts 5:9; (the) Lord, (the) Spirit, 2 Corinthians 3:18; the Spirit of Jesus, Acts 16:7; Spirit of Christ, Romans 8:9; the Spirit of Jesus

Christ, Philippians 1:19; Spirit of adoption, Romans 8:15; the Spirit of truth, John 14:17; the Spirit of life, Romans 8:2; the Spirit of grace, Hebrews 10:29.[1]

The use or absence of the article in the original where the "Holy Spirit" is spoken of cannot always be decided by neither grammatical rules, nor can the presence or absence of the article alone determines whether the reference is to the "Holy Spirit." Examples where the Person is meant when the article is absent are Matthew 22:43 (the article is used in Mark 12:36); Acts 4:25, Revised Version (absent in some texts); 19:2, 6; Romans 14:17; 1 Corinthians 2:4; Galatians 5:25 (twice); 1 Peter 1:2. Sometimes the absence is to be accounted for by the fact that Pneuma (like Theos) is substantially a proper name, e. g., in John 7:39. As a general rule the article is present where the subject of the teaching is the Personality of the Holy Spirit, e. g., John 14:26, where He is spoken of in distinction from the Father and the Son. See also 15:26 and compare with Luke 3:22.

In Galatians 3:3, in the phrase "having begun in the Spirit," it is difficult to say whether the reference is to the "Holy Spirit" or to the quickened spirit of the believer; that it possibly refers to the latter is not to be determined by the absence of the article, but by the contrast with "the flesh"; on the other hand, the contrast may be between the "Holy Spirit" who in the believer sets His seal on the perfect work of Christ, and the flesh which seeks to better itself by works of its own. There is no preposition before either noun, and if the reference is to the quickened spirit it cannot be dissociated from the operation of the "Holy Spirit". In Galatians 4:29 the phrase "after the

Spirit" signifies "by supernatural power," in contrast to "after the flesh," i. e., "by natural power," and the reference must be to the "Holy Spirit"; so in 5:17.

The full title with the article before both pneuma and hagios (the "resumptive" use of the article), literal, "the Spirit the Holy," stresses the character of the Person, e. g., Matthew 12:32; Mark 3:29; 12:36; 13:11; Luke 2:26; 10:21; John 14:26; Acts 1:16; 5:3; 7:51; 10:44, 47; 13:2; 15:28; 19:6; 20:23, 28; 21:11; 28:25; Ephesians 4:30; Hebrews 3:7; 9:8; 10:15.

The Personality of the Spirit is emphasized at the expense of strict grammatical procedure in John 14:26; 15:26; 16:8, 13, 14, where the emphatic pronoun ekeinos, "He," is used of Him in the masculine, whereas the noun pneuma is neuter in Greek, while the corresponding word in Aramaic, the language in which our Lord probably spoke, is feminine (rucha, compare with Hebrew ruach). The rendering "itself" in Romans 8:16, 26, due to the Greek gender, is corrected to "Himself" in the Revised Version.

The subject of the "Holy Spirit" in the New Testament may be considered as to His divine attributes; His distinct Personality in the Godhead; His operation in connection with the Lord Jesus in His birth, His life, His baptism, His death; His operations in the world; in the church; His having been sent at Pentecost by the Father and by Christ; His operations in the individual believer; in local churches; His operations in the production of Holy Scripture; His work in the world, etc.[2]

The third person of the Trinity, the Holy Spirit possesses co-equal power to the Father and the Son, exercised His creative power with the Father and the Son in creation and redemption. The three persons of the Godhead never contradict each other in word or in deed, but operate in unison to achieve God's eternal purposes. Because the Holy Spirit is the power by which believers come to Christ and see with new eyes of faith, He is closer to us than we are to ourselves. Like the eyes of the body through which we see physical things, He is seldom in focus to be seen directly because He is the one through whom all else is seen in a new light. This explains why the relationship of the Father and the Son is more prominent in the gospels, because it is through the eyes of the Holy Spirit that the Father-Son relationship is viewed.

The Holy Spirit appears in the Gospel of John as the power by which Christians are brought to faith and helped to understand their walk with God. He brings a person to new birth: "That which is born of the flesh is flesh, and that which is born of the Spirit is spirit": John 3:6; "It is the Spirit who gives life": John 6:63. The Holy Spirit is the paraclete, or helper, whom Jesus promised to the disciples after His ascension. The triune family of Father, Son, and Holy Spirit are unified in ministering to believers: John 14:16, 26. It is through the Holy Spirit that Father and Son abide with the disciples: John 15:26.

This unified ministry of the Trinity is also seen as the Spirit brings the world under conviction of sin, righteousness, and judgment. He guides believers into all truth with what He hears from the Father and the Son: John 15:26. It is a remarkable fact that each of the persons of the trinitarian family serves the others as all defer to one another: The Son says what He hears from the Father: John 12:49-50; the Father witnesses to and glorifies the Son: John 8:16-18, 50, 54; the Father and Son honor the Holy Spirit by commissioning Him to speak in their name: John 14:16, 26; the Holy Spirit honors the Father and Son by helping the community of believers.

Like Father and Son, the Holy Spirit is at the disposal of the other persons of the triune family, and all three are one in graciously being at the disposal of the redeemed family of believers. The Holy Spirit's attitude and ministry are marked by generosity; His chief function is to illumine Jesus' teaching, to glorify His person, and to work in the life of the individual believer and the church.

This quality of generosity is prominent in the Gospels of Matthew, Mark, and Luke, where the Holy Spirit prepares the way for the births of John the Baptist and Jesus the Son: Matthew 1:20; Luke 1:15, 35, 41. At the baptism of Jesus, the Spirit of God is present in the form of a dove. This completes the presence of the triune family at the inauguration of the Son's ministry: Matthew 3:16-17; Mark 1:9-11; Luke 3:21-22; John 1:33. Jesus is also filled with the Holy Spirit as He is led into the wilderness to be tempted: Luke 4:1. He claims to be anointed by the Spirit of the Lord in fulfillment of Old Testament prophecy: Isaiah 61:1; Luke 4:18-19>.

During His ministry, Jesus refers to the Spirit of God: Matthew 12:28-29; Luke 11:20 as the power by which He is casting out demons, thereby invading the stronghold of Beelzebub and freeing those held captive. Accordingly, the Spirit works with the Father and Son in realizing the redeeming power of the kingdom of God. God's kingdom is not only the reign of the Son but also the reign of the Spirit, as all share in the reign of the Father.

The person and ministry of the Holy Spirit in the gospels are confirmed by His work in the early church. The baptism with the Holy Spirit: Acts 1:5 is the pouring out of the Spirit's power in missions and evangelism: Acts 1:8. This prophecy of Jesus (and of Joel 2:28-32) begins on Pentecost: Acts 2:1-18. Many of those who hear of the finished work of God in

Jesus' death and resurrection: Acts 2:32-38 repent of their sins. In this act of repentance, they receive the gift of the Holy Spirit: Acts 2:38, becoming witnesses of God's grace through the Holy Spirit.

Paul's teaching about the Holy Spirit harmonizes with the accounts of the Spirit's activity in the gospels and Acts. According to Paul, it is by the Holy Spirit that one confesses that Jesus is Lord: 1 Corinthians 12:3. Through the same Spirit, varieties of gifts are given to the body of Christ to ensure its richness and unity: 1 Corinthians 12:4-27. The Holy Spirit is the way to Jesus Christ the Son: Romans 8:11 and to the Father: Romans 8:14-15. He is the person who bears witness to us that we are children of God: Romans 8:16-17. He "makes intercession for us with groanings which cannot be uttered": Romans 8:26-27.

The Holy Spirit also reveals to Christians the deep things of God: 1 Corinthians 2:10-12 and the mystery of Christ: Ephesians 3:3-5. The Holy Spirit acts with God and Christ as the pledge or guarantee by which believers are sealed for the day of salvation: 2 Corinthians 1:21-22, and by which they walk and live: Romans 8:3-6 and abound in hope with power: Romans 15:13. Against the lust and enmity of the flesh Paul contrasts the fruit of the Spirit: "Love, joy, peace, longsuffering, kindness, goodness, faithfulness, gentleness, self-control": Galatians 5:22-23.

Since the Holy Spirit is the expressed power of the triune family, it is imperative that one not grieve the Spirit, since no further appeal to the Father and the Son on the day of redemption is available: Ephesians 4:30. Jesus made this clear in His dispute with the religious authorities, who attributed His ministry to Satan rather than the Spirit and committed the unforgivable sin: Matthew 12:22-32; John 8:37-59.

In Paul's letters, Christian liberty stems from the work of the Holy Spirit: "Where the Spirit of the Lord is, there is liberty": 2 Corinthians 3:17. This is a process of "beholding as in a mirror the glory of the Lord," and "being transformed into the same image from glory to glory, just as by the Spirit of the Lord": 2 Corinthians 3:18. The personal work of the Holy Spirit is accordingly one with that of the Father and the Son, so Paul can relate the grace, love, and communion of the triune family in a trinitarian benediction: "The grace of the Lord Jesus Christ, and the love of God, and the communion of the Holy Spirit be with you all. Amen": 2 Corinthians 13:14.

Among the other New Testament writings the Spirit's ministry is evident in the profound teaching of Hebrews 9:14, which shows the relationship of God, Christ, and the eternal Spirit. The Holy Spirit's work in the Old Testament in preparation for the coming of Christ is explained in this and other passages in Hebrews 3:7; 9:8; 10:15-17.

This leads us to consider the working of the Spirit in the Old Testament in light of His ministry in the New Testament. The Spirit is the energy of God in creation: Genesis 1:2; Job 26:13; Isaiah 32:15. God endows man with personal life by breathing into his nostrils the breath of life: Genesis 2:7. The Spirit strives with fallen man: Genesis 6:3, and comes upon certain judges and warriors with charismatic power (Joshua: Numbers 27:18; Othniel: Judges 3:10; Gideon: Judges 6:34; Samson: Judges 13:25; 14:6). However, the Spirit departed from Saul because of his disobedience: 1 Samuel 16:14.

In the long span of Old Testament prophecy the Spirit plays a prominent role. David declared, "The Spirit of the Lord spoke by me, and His word was on my tongue": 2 Samuel 23:2. Ezekiel claimed that "the Spirit entered me when He spoke to me": Ezekiel 2:2. The Spirit also inspired holiness in the Old Testament believer: Psalm 143:10. He also promised to give a new heart to God's people: "I will put My Spirit within you, and cause you to walk in My statutes": Ezekiel. 36:27.

This anticipates the crucial work of the Spirit in the ministry of the Messiah. The prophecy of Isaiah 11:1-5 is a trinitarian preview of the working of the Father, the Spirit, and the Son, who is the branch of Jesse. Looking forward to the ministry of Jesus Christ, the Holy Spirit inspired Isaiah to prophesy: "The Spirit of the Lord shall rest upon Him": Isaiah 11:2. The Holy Spirit inspired Jesus with wisdom, understanding, counsel, might, knowledge, fear of the Lord, righteousness, and faithfulness. Thus we come full cycle to the New Testament where Jesus claims the fulfillment of this prophecy in Himself: Isaiah 61:1-2; Luke 4:18-19.

Isaiah 42:1-9 summarizes the redeeming work of the Father, Son, and Spirit in the salvation of the lost, as God spoke through the prophet: "Behold! My Servant whom I uphold, My Elect One in whom My soul delights! I have put My Spirit upon Him; He will bring forth justice to the Gentiles": Isaiah 42:1. No clearer reflection of the intimate interworking of the triune family and the Spirit's powerful role can be found in the Old Testament than in this prophecy. It ties together God's grace in Old and New in remarkable harmony.

In the above we have numerous irrefutable proofs that the Holy Spirit is a person of deity!

4

BIBLICAL EVIDENCE FOR THE TRINITY

Definition: Within the nature of the one true God there simultaneously exists three eternal persons: The Father, the Son and the Holy Spirit, who are co-equal in nature and attributes, and co-eternal.

ONLY GOD
Deuteronomy 6:4-13; 10:20-21; Isaiah 6:1; 44:6-8; 45:5; 46:9; Malachi 1:6; 2:10; Matthew 4:10; 22:29-38; Mark 12:28-34; 1 Corinthians 8:4-6; Ephesians 4:5-6; 1 Timothy 2:5; James 2:19; Revelation 4:2-3; 22:1-3.

THE FATHER
Matthew 6:9; 26:39; Mark 8:38; 15:34; Luke 11:2; 23:34-36; John 10:15; 1 Peter 1:3; 2 Peter 1:17; Revelation 1:6.
HE'S GOD
Romans 1:7; 1 Corinthians 1:3; 2 Corinthians 1:3; Colossians 1:2-3; 2 Peter 1:17.

THE SON
Matthew 3:17; Luke 22:67-71; John 3:16-17; 5:17-18, 22-27; Acts 13:33; Hebrews 1:5-6, 8-10; 2 John 9.
HE'S GOD
Matthew 1:23; John 1:1; 20:28; 5:17-18; Titus 1:3; 2:10-13; 3:4; Revelation 1:8; 15:3; 16:5-7.

THE HOLY SPIRIT
John 14:16-26; 16:7, 13-15; Acts 13:1-2; 28:25-27; 1 Corinthians 3:18; 12:4-13; Hebrews 3:7-11; 10:15-17.
HE'S GOD
Exodus 17; 2 Samuel 23:2-3; Psalm 95:7>; 139:7-13; Isaiah 6:1-10; Acts 5:3-4; 10:19-20, 34.

Each has God's attributes: a. omnipresent, b. omniscient, c. omnipotent, d. eternal, e. creative, f. immutable.

a. OMNIPRESENT
FATHER 1 Kings 8:27; 2 Chronicles 2:5-6; Psalm 139:15-16; Jeremiah 23:24; Acts 7:49; fills all heaven; dwells in believers.
SON Matthew 18:20; 28:18-20; Mark 16:19-20; John 1:1-3; 17:5; Hebrews 13:8; in all heaven; indwells believers.
HOLY SPIRIT Psalm 139:7-10; Isaiah 66:1-2; 6:1-10; Acts 2:37-39; 1 Corinthians 6:19; in all heaven and in believers.

b. OMNISCIENT
FATHER Job 42:2; Psalm 139:15-16; 147:5; Isaiah 40:28; Daniel 2:20-22; Romans 8:29; 1 Peter 1:2, 20; Revelation 1:1.
SON Isaiah 40:13-14; Matthew 24; Mark 2:8; 3; Luke 5:22; John 1:47-50; 2:24; 11:14; 13:19; 16:30; 21:17.

HOLY SPIRIT Isaiah 40:13-14; John 14:26; 16:12-13; Romans 8:26-27; 1 Corinthians 2:10-11; 1 John 2:20-27.

c. OMNIPOTENT
FATHER Genesis 18:14; Job 42:1-2; Jeremiah 10:12; 32:17; Matthew 19:26; Romans 1:20; Ephesians 1:7-10; Revelation 19:6.
SON Isaiah 9:6; Matthew 28:18; Mark 2:10; John 1:12; 2:18-22; 5:24-29; 14:13-14; Revelation 1:8; 15:3-4; 16:5-7.
HOLY SPIRIT Micah 3:8; Job 26:13; 33:4; Luke 1:35; Romans 8:11; 15:13-19; Hebrews 2:3-4; 1 Peter 3:18.

d. ETERNAL
FATHER Genesis 21:33; Deuteronomy 33:27; John 1:1-2; 17:5; Romans 1:20; 16:26; Ephesians 1:4-5; 1 Peter 1:17-21.
SON Isaiah 9:6; Micah 5:2; John 1:1-3; 8:24, 28, 58; 13:19; 17:5; 18:5-6; Hebrews 1:10-12; 13:8; Revelation 21:6.
HOLY SPIRIT Genesis 1:2; Job 26:13; 33:4; John 1:12; 3:7-8; Romans 1:20; Titus 3:5-6; Hebrews 9:14.

e. CREATIVE
FATHER Genesis 1:1; Zechariah 12:1-2; John 1:1-3; Hebrews 1:1-4; Revelation 4:10-11.
SON Psalm 102:25-27; Isaiah 9:6; John 1:1-3; Acts 3:15; Colossians 1:16-18; Hebrews 1:10-11; Revelation 3:14.
HOLY SPIRIT Genesis 1:2; Job 26:13; . Matthew 1:20-23; Luke 1:35.

f. IMMUTABLE
FATHER Malachi 3:6; Romans 3:5-7; Titus 1:2; Hebrews 6:17-18; James 1:3; 1 John 2:21.
SON Malachi 3:6; John 1:1-3, 14-15; 17:5; 2 Timothy 4:8; Hebrews 13:8; 1 John 2:1; Revelation 16:5-7; 19:2.

HOLY SPIRIT Malachi 3:6; Acts 5:3-4; Titus 1:2; Hebrews 6:18; James 1:3; 1 Peter 1:21.

The Son is neither the Father nor the Spirit: Matthew 1:20-23; Luke 4:18; John 4:23-24. The Spirit is neither the Father nor the Son: John 14:16, 26; Romans 8:11; Hebrews 9:14; 1 Peter 3:18.

The unity and plurality of God is clearly shown in Scripture: Genesis 1:26-27; 3:22; 11:6-7; 18-19; Deuteronomy 6:4; Psalm 16:8-11; 110:1; Isaiah 6:8; 8:13-14; 28:16; Matthew 28:19; Acts 2:25-34; Hebrews 9:14; 1 John 5:7-10.

5

THE BIBLICAL VIEW OF MAN'S NATURE

a. Before addressing this we should review some essentials of Bible interpretation.

    i) The Bible alone is the Christian rule of faith and practice.
    ii) Biblical interpretation is not limited to man's reasoning capabilities.
    iii) The New Testament must define the Old.
    iv) Observe the contexts: what, when, where, who, how, why, etc.
    v) We must use many Scriptures—not a few vague proof texts.
    vi) Figures of speech must be recognized, defined, and rightly interpreted. Direct discourse takes precedent over poetic lingo.
    vii) Original languages must be correctly translated.

viii) Antitheses must be presented and resolved, to keep the unity of Scripture.

b. The Bible shows that man has two parts:

An inward man (called the soul or spirit); an outward man (the body).

> James 4:5: The Spirit, who dwells in us, yearns to envy.
> Ephesians 3:16: That ... you ...be strengthened in the inner man.
> Zechariah 12:1: Thus says Yhwh, who forms man's spirit within him. Thus God is called "the Father of Spirits" (Hebrews 12:9).
> Job 32:8: There is a Spirit in man, and the Almighty gives it inspiration.
> Acts 17:16: His Spirit was provoked within Him.
> Daniel 7:15: I was grieved in my spirit within my body.
> Job 14:22: His soul within him shall mourn.
> Psalm 42:6: My soul was cast down within me.
> 2 Peter 2:8: Lot tormented his righteous soul day by day.
> Ezekiel 11:19: I will put a renewed spirit within you.
> Ephesians 4:23: Being renewed in the spirit of our mind.
> Ezekiel 36:26: I will put a renewed spirit within you.
> Psalm 103:1: Bless the Lord, O my soul, all my innermost being, praise His holy name!
> 2 Corinthians 4:16-18: ... though our outward man is perishing, yet our inward man is being renewed day by day ... for the things that are seen outward man are temporary, but the unseen inward man is eternal.

c. One's inward man (his soul, or spirit) is his real being (person), having the essential attributes of personality (mind, will, emotions); it communicates, and has its own shape or form.

MIND
Ephesians 4:23 the spirit of our mind.
Psalm 139:14 My soul knows very well.
Proverbs 19:2 It is not good for a soul to be without knowledge.
Job 32:8 there is a Spirit in man ... the Almighty gives it understanding.
As the Holy Spirit has His mind, so too man's spirit must also have a mind, being made in God's image.

WILL
Psalm 34:1 I will bless the Lord ... My soul will make its boast in Thee. Here, *I* is *my soul*; *will* proves it has a will.
Matthew 26:38-39 My soul is exceedingly sorrowful ... Not My will, but thine be done. Mark 14:34-36: Not My will, but thine be done (His soul willed to escape crucifixion).

EMOTIONS
Genesis 35:3 cleaves
Genesis 34:8 longs for
Genesis 42:21 anguish
Leviticus 26:11 abhors
Numbers 11:6 feels dried up
Deuteronomy 4:9; 6:5; 10:12; 11:13 loves God
Deuteronomy 12:15 desires, lusts for
Judges 10:16 is grieved
Judges 16:16 vexed (tormented)

1Samuel 18:1 loves fellowman and self
Job 14:22 mourns

COMMUNICATES
Romans 8:16 The Spirit Himself bears witness with our spirit.
Proverbs 20:27 The spirit of man is the lamp of the Lord.
Job 32:8 There is a spirit in man, and the Spirit of the Almighty gives him understanding (Matthew 17, Mark 9, Luke 9). Moses' and Elijah's spirits from heaven were communicating with Christ!

SHAPE OR FORM
Zechariah 12:1 Yhwh forms the spirit of man within him. (Same word as Genesis 2:8). Matthew 17:3: Moses and Elijah appeared to the disciples, recognizing their form or shape. Mark 9:4: And Elijah appeared to them with Moses ... talking to Jesus.
Luke 9:32 They saw His glory and the two men stood with Him.
1 Samuel 28:11-16 When the woman saw Samuel ... she said to Saul, "I saw a spirit ascending out of the earth." So he said, "What is his form?" Because one's spirit has a form, it communicates, and has a mind, will, and emotions. It is therefore the real person, which dwells within his body, called a house of clay (flesh).

d. God is spirit (no body) and has a soul. Isaiah 1:14; Leviticus 26:11; Jeremiah 4:31; 5:9; 6:8; 9:9; 14:19; Zechariah 11:8; Matthew 12:18; Hebrews 10:38.

e. The body (outward man) and soul (inward man) are not the same.

> Matthew 10:28 Do not fear those who kill the body, but cannot kill the soul ... fear Him who can destroy both body and soul in hell.
> Luke 12:5 ... who after He has killed the body, has the power to cast [the soul] into hell. Micah 6:7: Shall I give my firstborn ... the fruit of my body for the sin of my soul?

f. Therefore man's spirit is his inward man, which at death leaves the body, and goes to be with Christ.

> James 2:26 The body without the spirit is dead.
> Luke 8:55 Then her spirit returned, and she arose immediately...
> Ecclesiastes 8:5 No one has power to retain his spirit in the day of death.
> 1 Kings 17:17 No spirit left in him ... Let this child's soul comes back to him ... the soul of the child returned to him and he revived...
> Hebrews 11:35 Women received their dead raised to life again...
> Genesis 35:18 ...as her soul was departing (for she died)...
> Ecclesiastes 3:20-21 [the body] the dust returns to the dust ... the spirit of the sons of men goeth upward...
> Ecclesiastes 12:5-7 The dust returns to the earth ... the spirit returns to God who gave it...
> Psalm 31:5 Into your hands I commit My Spirit.
> Acts 7:59 "Lord Jesus receive my spirit."
> Luke 23:46 Father into Your hands I commit My Spirit.
>   (Matthew 27:50 "He dismissed His Spirit")

Psalm 90:10 The years of our days are 70 or 80 years ... Soon they are cut off, and we fly away!

Matthew 22:32; Mark 12:27; Luke 20:38 I am the God of Abraham ... Isaac ... Jacob. God is not the God of the dead, but the living. (Though their bodies were dead, yet their spirits were alive! "The inward man is eternal" (2 Corinthians 4:16-18).

Matthew 17; Mark 9; Luke 9 The spirits of Moses and Elijah were in God's care, and alive!

Hebrews 12:22 & 23 But you have come to Mount Zion and to the city of the living God, the heavenly Jerusalem, to an innumerable company of angels, to the general assembly and church of the firstborn who are registered in heaven, to God the Judge of all, to the spirits of just men made perfect,

Philippians 1:21-24: We depart and go to be with Christ, which is far better!

2 Corinthians 5:8 We are confident, yes well pleased rather to be absent from the body, and to be present with the Lord.

Luke 23:43 Assuredly I say to you, today you shall be with Me in Paradise.

Luke 16:22 Angels carry Lazarus into Abraham's presence (bosom means presence, John 1:18). Revelation 6:9-11 under the altar, the souls of those who were slain for the Word of God, cry out for God to recompense their death. Revelation 15:1-3 in heaven are those who got the victory over the beast (yet this is before Christ comes (Revelation 16:12-18).

g. The souls of those who've died and are with Christ in heaven will return with Him for their resurrected bodies (1 Thessalonians 4:14). Even so God will bring with Him those who sleep in Jesus (1 Thessalonians 3:13) at the coming of our Lord Jesus Christ, with all His saints. (Greek. *haggios* means men, rather than angels (*aggelos*) (Colossians 3:4). When Christ appears, you also will appear together with Him in glory (Zechariah 14:5). The Lord my God will come and all the saints with You ... (Jude 14) Behold the Lord cometh with ten thousands of His saints (1 Thessalonians 4:13-18) God will bring with Him those who sleep in Jesus ... For the Lord will descend from heaven with a shout ... and the dead in Christ will rise first (1 Corinthians 15:35-58). How are the dead raised up? With what body ... The body is sown in corruption, it is raised in incorruption, it is sown in dishonour, it is raised in glory, it is sown in weakness, it is raised in power. It is sown a natural body, it is raised a spiritual body ... the dead will be raised incorruptible, we shall be changed ... incorruptible, mortal will put on immortality!

OUTWARD MAN	TEXT	INWARD MAN
Perishing, which is seen, temporary	2 Corinthians 4:16-18	Renewed day by day, unseen, eternal,
	Ephesians 3:16	Strengthened by the Holy Spirit
Earthly house, tent, is destroyed	2 Corinthians 5:1-8	Building from God, eternal in heaven
PHYSICAL LIFE		**PHYSICAL DEATH**
Home in the body, absent from the Lord	2 Corinthians 5:1-8	Absent from the body, present with the Lord

I live in the flesh	Philippians 1:21-24	Depart and be with Christ which is far better
Remain in the flesh	2 Timothy 4:6	My departure is at hand
I am in this tent	2 Peter 1:13>	I must put off this tent, My departure
You guide Me with your counsel	Psalm 73:24	afterward, You receive Me to glory
The days of our years are 70 or 80	Psalm 90:10>	Silver cord breaks, it is cut off, we fly away
	Ecclesiastes 7:1	The day of one's death is better than one's birth
	Revelation 14:13	Blessed are the dead in the Lord ... they rest from their labours

h. **ANSWERS TO ANTITHESES** raised by the cults.

   i) Genesis 2:7 shows that dust + breath = living soul. Thus body − breath = dead soul.
ANSWER
The correct translation is, "God breathed into man the living spirit, and man became a living creature." (Spirit of Life means living spirit; Nephesh means creature).

   ii) Ezekiel 18 says, "The soul that sins shall die." Since the body dies, it's the soul.
ANSWER
   a. Soul is the inner man where *sin* occurs (Micah 6:7).

b. Matthew 10:28 and Luke 12:4-5 also show this, and the death of the soul is being eternally separated from God in hell (Revelation 20:10).
c. One who's born again has eternal life (of soul), though the body dies (John 3:16-17; 5:24; 11:25-26).

iii) Ecclesiastes 9:5 says the dead don't know anything. Thus they're unconscious.
ANSWER
a. Context speaks of *under the sun* (Ecclesiastes 8:9; 8:15, 15, 17; 9:3; 6, 9, 13) which is "On the face of the earth" (Ecclesiastes 8:9, 14, 16; 10:7; 11:2). So the dead know nothing of what is happening on the face of the earth. (Rule of Context).
b. This verse also says, "Neither have they any more reward." Taking this out of context, as above, it denies any resurrection and rewards (Revelation 22:13). But as in the above (a.), it means no reward under the sun.

iv) Ecclesiastes 9:5 says the dead have no more memory. Thus they're unconscious.
ANSWER
It says the remembrance of them is forgotten (They won't be remembered) or loved, or hated any more — not that they won't remember anything (Revelation 6:9-11).

v) Psalm 146:4 says their thoughts perish, proving the soul is unconscious.
ANSWER
This is rightly translated as "their plans perish." The Hebrew *eshtonaw* means plans, counsels (*Gesenius' Hebrew Lexicon*). NB. C, D, and E show weakness of

using poetic literature to overturn the direct discourse of many texts!

vi) Psalm 49:19 says, "You will redeem My Soul from the Grave" proving the body is the soul.

ANSWER

Here the Hebrew Sheol is equivalent for Greek Hades speaking of hell inside the earth. It is not the literal grave, for which *qeborrah* is used. Comparing this text with Acts 2:31-32 shows Jesus' *soul* was not left in hell (Hades)—again not the grave—which is the Greek *mnameon*. In this we see that Hades is mistranslated in 1 Corinthians 15:54. Here new text reads "*ho thanatos* (O death) where is your victory?"

vii) Acts 2:29-34 says David has not gone to heaven, but is still dead!

ANSWER

a. The context is speaking of David's body which was still in the sepulcher (mnameon). His body was not resurrected or ascended to heaven, as he foretold Jesus' body would be. But this text does not speak of David's soul, which *is in* heaven (Ephesians 4:8; Psalm 68:18; Hebrews 12:24; and other texts shown above). John 11:11-14, and several other texts speak of death as sleep, so the dead are unconscious.

b. The dead body is spoken of as asleep, but the soul is not. Yet here sleep is used as a figure of speech. The body is not literally asleep; it's dead and decaying as in John 11:39: "By this time there is a stench" the right interpretation of this figure.[1]

6

CONCLUSION

Jesus Christ is the author and the pivotal figure of historical Christianity. It is His person and His ministry that separates Him from all other religious leaders. His identity is of prime importance as the object of our faith. John 8:24, "Therefore I said to you that you will die in your sins; *for if you do not believe that I am He (Yahweh), you will die in your sins.*" For everyone who doesn't believe in Jesus: the God/man which means He is God Almighty in human flesh, has a false saviour and will die in their sins bound for the eternal fire of hell. We've concluded that Jesus is the God of the Holy Scriptures by His nature and deeds. We have also established that the Holy Spirit is the third person of the Triune Godhead and He is fully God. While the word *trinity* does not appear in the Bible, by an inductive study of the Holy Scriptures, there is an abundance of evidence for the doctrine of the Trinity which reveals the biblical God and His attributes. We have also discussed the nature of man—defining the body, soul, and spirit and their respective roles. I trust that through the mercy and grace of our Triune God that I have shed some light on the heresies that Seventh-day Adventism has embraced from its beginning to our present day. They are precious souls who have been deceived, but nevertheless need to hear about the real Jesus Christ who can grant them the gift of eternal life if they will only place their faith on Him alone. It was my desire to, not only point out the essential false doctrines of Seventh-day Adventism, but to provide an answer for the dilemma that they and others like them are in. It is my hope that they could be delivered into the freedom that Jesus Christ accomplished on Calvary 2000 years ago. May our blessed God and Saviour Jesus Christ be glorified for His purposes!

INDEX

Adventist Review............ 62, 69, 77, 344, 355, 366
A. J. Dennis............... xiv, 86, 113, 114, 145, 334, 337, 355
A. J. Morton.................... xvi, 195
A. T. Jones................xiv, xv, 127, 128, 147, 172, 177, 329–331, 339, 340, 344, 355, 356, 369
A. T. Robinson.......... xv, 87, 132, 340, 356
Archangel... vi, xi, xvi, 22, 76, 77, 218, 219, 221, 224,225, 229, 237–245, 247–249,260, 262, 263, 349
Arian......... v, vi, vii, xiii, xiv, xvi, 27–34, 61, 74, 76, 83, 89,91, 94, 98, 101–103, 122, 123,127, 135, 139, 140, 145–150,165–167, 202, 224, 225, 230,234, 276, 327–329, 333, 336,337, 346, 362, 363, 372
Austin P. Cooke......... xv, 142, 149

Authoritative source of truth.. 213
Bible........ vi, vii, ix, xiii, xvii, 23, 40, 46, 48–50, 63, 66, 67,74–76, 78, 80, 89, 90, 92, 95,105, 108, 113, 114, 119, 124,125, 135, 136, 138, 144, 147–149, 153, 160, 162,163, 169–172, 174, 196, 203, 213, 224–226, 231, 241–243, 245, 248,253, 255, 257, 260, 261, 283,293, 300, 313, 314, 323, 326,330, 331, 334, 339, 340, 342–346, 348–352, 356–359, 361,362, 365, 366, 370, 374–376
Born again....................... 76, 154
Clear Word Bible ...... vii, 74, 224, 241, 257, 260, 261, 357
C. P. Bollman .... xiv, 121, 338, 357
C. W. Stone .... xv, 174, 363
Dialogue Magazine 144, 341, 366

D. M. Canright 52, 111–113, 122, 145, 146, 238, 239, 248, 337, 351, 357, 361, 362
Donald Grey Barnhouse.... 21, 51, 53, 54, 77, 204–206, 331, 357, 358
Dr. Kellogg.... 150, 232, 238, 239, 248, 249, 276
D. T. Bordeau .... xiv, 124, 140, 339, 358
D. W. Hull .....xiv, xv, 90–93, 103, 145, 146, 186, 334, 358
E. Goodrich.... xiv, 107, 108, 336, 358
E. J. Waggoner .... xiv, xv, xvi, 122, 123, 195, 329, 330, 338, 339, 358
Ellen G. White....... vi, vii, xiv, xv, xvi, 40, 41, 49, 50, 54, 57, 58, 61–63, 66, 67, 69, 74–80, 102, 134, 135, 141, 147–150, 160, 166, 167, 188, 202, 203, 206, 212, 213, 219–225, 227, 228, 230, 232, 238–241, 248, 255, 259–263, 272, 276, 336, 337, 340, 341, 346, 348, 350–352, 361, 363, 372–374
Erwin R. Gane.......... 99, 140, 336, 337, 363
Evangelical Conferences.........xiii, 51, 52, 56, 57, 60, 69
Father .... xv, xvi, xviii, 23, 25, 27–33, 36, 37, 41–43, 45, 84, 85, 87–93, 95–104, 106, 107, 109, 111–114, 116, 117, 119–128, 131, 132, 134, 135, 138–147, 149, 151–163, 165–176, 178–190, 193–196, 198, 201–203, 215–220, 224–226, 228–231, 233–235, 238, 246, 247, 253, 254, 261, 262, 266, 268, 294, 298–307, 309–312, 314, 317, 327, 328, 333, 339, 344, 358
– the fullness of Godhead bodily 228, 229,
Frances D. Nichol 77, 79, 227, 255, 331, 340, 355, 359, 376
G. C. Tenney .... xiv, 115, 330, 338, 359
George R. Knight 68, 211-214
Gina Foster..................... 144, 145
G. W. Amadon......... xv, 186, 345, 369
G. W. Morse ... xiv, 120, 123, 338, 361
Heresy .... xvi, 27, 30, 32, 36, 65, 76, 129, 149, 166, 230, 234, 348
Holy Spirit..........xvi, xviii, 25, 65, 67, 94–98, 103, 105, 107, 108, 112–116, 121, 122, 124, 125, 127, 128, 131, 142, 145, 147, 149, 151–155, 157–160, 162, 165, 166, 191–195, 197–203, 220, 228, 230, 231, 233, 234, 246, 247, 257, 272, 273, 280, 295, 297–307, 309–311, 315, 319, 323, 325, 334, 337, 339, 345, 352, 356, 357, 364

- deity..... xviii, 98, 116, 121, 131, 193, 297, 299, 307, 352
James White .... xiv, xv, xvi, 83, 86, 87, 103, 113, 140, 141,165, 168, 173, 198, 248, 249,333, 334, 344, 359, 363, 369
Jan Paulsen 211, 212
J. B. Frisbie .... xv, 138
Jehovah's Witnesses .... v, ix, 27, 34, 201, 229, 239, 276, 299
Jesus Christ .... v, vi, ix, xi, xii, xvii, xviii, 22–24, 27, 34,36–38, 41–44, 48, 49, 61, 67,73, 85, 88, 111, 121, 122, 124,142, 149, 162, 165, 168, 170–172, 174, 177, 180, 185, 187,190–194, 198, 201, 219, 222,223, 225, 226, 229, 239, 241,244, 253, 259, 260, 263, 267,269, 270, 272, 273, 275, 277,278, 280, 283, 293, 294, 299,301, 305–307, 318, 323, 324,331, 337, 357
– a co-worker 220
– an associate 215, 220
– deity .... v, vi, vii, xvi, 29, 34, 36, 41, 68, 69, 73, 76, 103,122, 134, 141, 145, 167–169,175, 188, 189, 202, 203, 219, 226– 229, 237, 238, 240, 242,243, 252–255, 257, 259, 262,284, 293, 294, 299, 346
– God by nature .... xvii, xviii, 228, 252, 253, 284, 292–294

– like essence 33
– Michael, the archangel 218, 221
– not God Almighty 188, 191, 223, 238, 240, 259
– sinful fallen nature 47, 50, 58, 61, 257, 258
– the angel 218, 221, 223,224, 238, 246, 247
J. E. Swift .... xiv, 114, 338, 359
J. H. Waggoner .... xvi, 117, 134, 139, 140, 146, 165, 336, 338, 341, 360
J. M. Hopkins .... xiv, 114, 337, 360
J. M. Stephenson .... xiv, 89, 334, 345
J. N. Andrews .... xv, 165, 249
J. N. Loughborough .... xiv, xvi, 104, 105, 336, 360
John Matteson .... xv, 184, 369
J. S. Washburn .... xv, 133–135, 340, 343, 360, 368
Joseph Bates .... xiv, xv, 69, 84, 85, 92, 93, 140, 145, 146,186, 333, 345, 360, 363
Leroy Edwin Froom 51, 56, 59
M. C. Wilcox .... xiv, xvi, 47, 74–77, 131, 132, 192, 331,340, 346, 361, 371
Michael .... vi, xvi, 76, 77, 218, 219, 221, 224, 225, 229,237–249, 260–262, 349
Monarchianism 85, 92, 93, 126, 135, 145

Norman R. Gulley .... xiii, 62 64, 67, 70–73, 208, 209, 332, 333, 361

Pacific Press 49, 117, 125, 330, 331, 332, 334, 336, 338, 339, 346, 356, 358, 360, 366, 367, 368, 372

Polytheism 32, 169, 234, 235

Questions on Doctrine .... xiii, xvi, 52, 56, 57, 59, 64–66, 68, 69, 74, 77–80, 204–214, 227, 347, 362, 368

Raoul Dederen 149, 344, 366

Resurrection 129, 134, 135, 141, 155, 159, 184, 189, 209, 219, 229, 237, 239, 242, 248, 249, 276, 277, 305, 321

Review and Herald .... 86, 89, 90, 95–98, 102, 103, 108, 110, 111, 114, 120, 124, 128, 132, 141, 331, 333 - 346, 353, 356–361, 363–365, 368–370, 372

R. F. Cottrell .... xv, 136, 183, 341, 362

Roy A. Anderson 49, 50, 51, 54, 57, 204, 331, 362

Sabbath .... xviii, 45, 55, 63, 89, 138, 143, 162, 164, 224, 265, 291, 330–333, 349, 351, 358, 366, 367, 370

Samuel T. Spears .... xiv, 125

S. B. Whitney .... xiv, 108, 109, 110, 145–147, 337

Second Probation 264–272

Self-existent 90, 99, 100, 114, 117, 149, 171, 175, 189, 217, 221

Semi-Arian ..... xiii, 29, 32, 33, 74, 150, 165, 166, 224, 327, 329

Seventh-day Adventist .... xi, xii, xiii, xvi, 21, 25, 35, 36, 37, 46, 47, 51–54, 65, 66, 68, 73, 74, 83–85, 100, 108, 110, 111, 117, 121–123, 139, 143, 145, 146, 148–150, 163–166, 201, 204, 205, 207, 208, 210–213, 223, 224, 230, 234, 239, 262–264, 272, 276, 329, 331, 333, 335–337, 341, 348, 357, 359, 373,

Seventh-day Adventists Believe .... xiv, 64, 66, 67, 208–211, 332, 347, 370

Son .... xv, xviii, 23, 25, 27–30, 32, 33, 37, 44–46, 49, 55, 78, 80, 84, 85, 88–98, 100–104, 107, 111–114, 116, 118–121, 123–127, 131, 132, 134, 135, 138, 139, 143, 149, 151–176, 178–190, 193, 195, 196, 198, 202, 203, 216–223, 225, 226, 229–235, 239, 241, 246, 253, 264, 265, 266, 267, 269, 270, 271, 277, 284, 293, 294, 300, 301, 303–307, 309–312, 327–329, 337, 339, 344, 357, 358

Sound doctrine 278–280

Three great powers......... 152–159, 166, 234
Trinity............ v, vi, xiv, xvi, xviii, 68, 69, 83, 84, 85, 88, 89, 94, 98, 104, 105, 106, 107, 108, 109, 113, 116, 117, 118, 119, 120, 125, 129, 130, 131, 133, 135, 136, 137, 138, 142, 143, 150, 152, 161, 163, 164, 165, 166, 167, 170, 173, 174, 183, 186, 201, 202, 203, 204, 224, 226, 228, 229, 230, 231, 232, 233, 234, 235, 238, 303, 309, 323, 333, 338, 339, 340, 341, 346, 349, 355, 356, 360, 363
Tritheism .... xvi, 31, 106, 145, 149, 150, 160, 163, 166, 230, 232–235, 348
T. R. Williamson .... xiv, 124, 125, 339, 364
Two Gods 32, 114, 220
Uriah Smith .... xiv, xv, xvi, 76, 94–99, 101–103, 108, 122, 123, 128, 139–141, 146, 165, 184, 195, 206, 229, 238, 335, 336, 339, 341, 345, 361, 362, 364
V. R. Christensen ..... xv, 143, 149, 363
Walter Martin .... ix, 21, 51–54, 57, 59–62, 64 - 66, 73–75, 77–81, 204, 205, 207, 331, 332, 347, 360, 363, 365, 368
Walter Rea .... v, vi, 203

William Johnsson .... xiii, 62, 66, 209
William Miller .... xiv, 83, 84, 86, 249, 333, 359, 363
W. W. Prescott .... v, xiii, xv, 39, 40, 76, 133 - 135, 176, 203, 238, 330, 365, 369

The Bible text designated (NKJ) is from The New Kings James Version, © 1982, Thomas Nelson, Inc. All Rights Reserved.

The Bible text designated (NASB) is from The New American Standard Bible, © 1960, 1962, 1963, 1968, 1971, 1972, 1973, 1975, 1977, 1988, 1995 The Lockman Foundation.

WHO Is The Adventist Jesus?

1) INTRODUCTION

2) ANALYSIS OF THE ARIAN AND SEMI-ARIAN HERESIES
   1 Πρ ο χρο ϛνων κα ι̅ αιφω͡νων.
   2 Θεο͡ϖ, λο͡γο͡ϖ, σοφι͡ϖα.
   3 Ποι͡ϖημα, κτι͡ϖσμα εφξ ουφκ ο[ντων. Hence the name Exukontians
   4 ϑΑρχη;ν ε[χει – υφκ η ∴ ν πρι;ν γεννηθη/⊥, η[τοι κτισθη/⊥ / η ∴ ν ποτε ο[τε ουφφκ η ∴ ν.
   5 ϑΑναλλοι͡ϖωτο͡ϖ, α[τρεπτο͡ϖ ουϑ υιϑο͡ϖ͡ϖ.
   6 €-Τρεπτο;͡ϖ φυ͡ϖσει ωϑσ τα; κρι͡ϖσματα.
   7 ουφσι͡ϖα
   8 ϑΕτεροου͡ϖσιο͡ϖ τω/⊥ πατρι͡ϖ.
   9 €Ανο͡ϖμοιο͡ϖ κατα; ουφσι͡ϖαν. Hence the name φΑνο͡ϖμοιοι, Anomoeans.
   10 Ανο͡ϖμοιο͡ϖ κατα; πα͡ϖντα/.
   11 Such as Prov. viii. 22-25 (Comp. Sir. i. 4; xxiv. 8f.), where personified Wisdom, *i.e.*, the Logos, says (according to the Septuagint): Κυ͡ϖριο͡ϖ ε[κτισε͡ϖν με [Heb. Vulg. possedit me] αφρχη;ν οϑδω⊥ ν αυφτου⊥ ειφ͡ϖ ε[ργα αυφτου⊥ προ; του⊥ αιφω⊥ νο͡ϖ εφθεμελι͡ϖωσε͡ϖν με, κ.τ.λ. This passage seemed clearly to prove the two propositions of Arius, that the Father created the Son, and that he created him for the purpose of creating the world through him (ειφσ ε[ργα αυφτου⊥). Acts ii. 36: Οτι και; κυ͡ϖριον αυφτο;ν και; Χριστο;ν εφποι͡ϖησεν οϑ θεο͡ϖ͡ϖ. Heb. i. 4: Κρει͡ϖττων γενο͡ϖμενο͡ϖ τφω⊥ ν αφγγε͡ϖλων. Heb. iii. 2: Πιστο;ν ο[ντα τω⊥/ ποιη͡ϖσαντι αυφτο͡ϖν. John i 14: ϑΟ λο͡ϖγο͡ϖ σα͡ϖρξ εφγε͡ϖνετο. Phil. ii. 7-9. The last two passages are of course wholly inapposite, as they treat of the incarnation of the Son of God, not of his pre-temporal existence and essence. Heb. i. 4 refers to the exaltation of the God-Man. Most plausible of all is the famous passage: πρωτο͡ϖτοκο͡ϖ πα͡ϖση͡ϖ κτι͡ϖσεω͡ϖ, Col.

i. 15, from which the Arians inferred that Christ himself is a κτισισ of God, to wit, the first creature of all. But πρωτοτοκοσ is not equivalent to πρωτοκτιστοσ or πρωτοπλαστοσ: on the contrary, Christ is by this very term distinguished from the creation, and described as the Author, Upholder, and End of the creation. A creature cannot possibly be the source of life for all creatures. The meaning of the expression, therefore, is: born before every creature, *i.e.*, before anything was made. The text indicates the distinction between the eternal generation of the Son from the essence of the Father, and the temporal creation of the world out of nothing by the Son. Yet there is a difference between μονογενησ and πρωτοτοκοσ, which Athanasius himself makes: the former referring to the relation of the Son to the Father, the latter, to his relation to the world.

12 Such as Luke ii. 52; Heb. v. 8, 9; John xii. 27, 28; Matt. xxvi. 39; Mark xii. 52; &c.

13 E.g., John xiv. 28: ϑΟ πατηρ μειζων μου εστιν.. This passage also refers not to the pre-existent state of Christ, but to the state of humiliation of the God-Man.

14 The ε[κτισε and εφθεμελιωσε in Prov. viii. 22 ff., on which the Arians laid special stress, and of which Athanasius treats quite at large in his second oration against the Arians, he refers not to the essence of the Logos (with whom the σοφια was by both parties identified), but to the incarnation of the Logos and to the renovation of our race through him: appealing to Eph. ii. 10: "We are his workmanship, created in Christ Jesus unto good works." As to the far more important passage in Col. i. 15, Athanasius gives substantially the correct interpretation in his Expositio fidei, cap. 3 (ed. Bened. tom. i. 101), where he says: πρωτοτοκον ειπων [Παυλοσ] δηλοι μη; ει∴ναι αυτο;ν κτισμα, αφλλα; γεννημα του πατροσ · ξενον

γαῶρ εφπι; τη⊥ῶ θεοῶτητοῶ αυφτου⊥ το; λεῶγεσθαι κτιῶσμα. Τα; γα;ρ παῶντα εφκτιῶσθησαν υϑπο; του⊥ πατρο;ῶ δια; του⊥ υιϑου⊥, οϑ δε; υιϑο;ῶ μοῶνοῶ εφκ του⊥ πατρο;ῶ αφι>διῶωῶ εφγεννηῶθη· διο; πρωτοῶτοκοῶῶ εφστι παῶσηῶ κτιῶσεωῶ οϑ Θεο;ῶ λοῶγοῶ ·, α[τρεπτοῶ εφξ αφτρεῶπτου.

15 Comp. on Marcellus of Ancyra below, § 126.
16 Mundus non factus est *in* tempore, sed *cum* tempore, says Augustine, although I cannot just now lay my hand on the passage. Time is the successional form of existence of all created things. Now Arius might indeed have said: Time arose with the Son as the first creature. This, however, he did not say, but put a time before the Son.
17 Of less weight is the objection, which was raised by Alexander of Alexandria: Since the Son is the Logos, the Arian God must have been, until the creation of the Son, α[λογοῶ, a being without reason.
18 Comp. the second Oration against the Arians, cap. 69 ff.
19 ϑΗμιαῶρειοι.
20 ϑΟμοιουσιαστοιῶ. The name *Eusebians* is used of the Arians and Semi-Arians, who both for a time made common cause, as a political party under the lead of Eusebius of Nicomedia (not of Caesarea), against the Athanasians and Nicenes.

Source: http://www.ccel.org/s/schaff/history/3_ch09.htm

3) THE NATURE OF THE SEVENTH-DAY ADVENTIST'S CHRIST IN QUESTION

1. E. J. Waggoner. General Conference Bulletin, 1891
2. A.T. Jones, General Conference-Bulletin 1893
3. S. H. Haskell Bible Echo, March 15, 1889

4. G. C. Tenney, editorial, Bible Echo, April 15, 1889
5. Stephen Haskell, Bible Echo, February 15, 1892
6. A. W. Semmens, Bible Echo, April 15, 1892
7. A. T. Jones, General Conference Bulletin, 1895
8. A. T. Jones, Review, February 18, 1896
9. W. W. Prescott, Bible Echo, January 6, 1896
10. Stephen Haskell, Signs, April 2, 1896
11. E. Farnsworth, Signs, May 6, 1897
12. E. J. Waggoner, General Conference Bulletin, 1897
13. S. N. Haskell, Signs, January 17, 1900
14. A. T. Jones, Consecrated Way to Christian Perfection
15. E. J. Waggoner, Christ and His Righteousness, 27
16. W. W. Prescott, Sermon October 31, 1895; printed in Bible Echo, January 6, 13, 1896
17. A. T. Jones, General Conference Bulletin, 1895
18. E. J. Waggoner. Christ and His Righteousness. 27-28 (1890)
19. (Series by E. J. Waggoner. No.4. Lincoln. Nebraska, 1897), 45
20. Op. cit., 31
21. Op. cit., 46
22. International Sabbath School Quarterly, "The Spirit of Sacrifice" a special testimony (Senior Division, No. 41, Third Quarter, 1905, Oakland: Pacific Press Publishing Association), 8-9
23. International Sabbath School Quarterly. "Baptism and Temptation of Jesus," Senior Division, No.56, Second Quarter, 1909, Pacific Press, 20
24. International Sabbath School Quarterly, "The Incarnation and the Priesthood" (Senior Division, No. 71, First Quarter. 1913. Pacific Press), 15
25. International Sabbath School Quarterly, "The Flesh and the Spirit" (Senior Division, No. 75. First Quarter, 1914, Pacific Press), 16

26. International Sabbath School Quarterly. "The Purpose of the Incarnation" (Senior Division. No.103. First Quarter. 1921), 248-249
27. International Sabbath School Quarterly, "The Last Adam" (Senior Division. No.105. Third Quarter. 1921. Pacific Press)
28. International Sabbath School Quarterly, "The Godly Life" (Senior Division, No. 112, Second Quarter, 1923, Pacific Press), 22
29. Llewellen Wilcox, Signs of the Times, March, 1927
30. Ibid. Like A. T. Jones and others, even while expressing this view of Christ's humanity, Elder Wilcox believed in the perfect sinlessness of Jesus Christ. (See Walter R Martin The Truth about Seventh-day Adventists [Grand Rapids Zondervan Publishing House, 1960], 86-87
31. Frances D. Nichol, Answers to Objections, Review and Herald, 1952, 389
32. Op. cit., 392
33. Ibid., 393
34. Bible Readings (Washington, D.C. Review and Herald Publishing Association, 1949), 143
35. Ibid.
36. (Ministry, September 1956, 12-14)
37. L. E. Froom, Movement of Destiny, 477
38. E. B. Jones. Op. cit., 479
39. Donald Grey Barnhouse, "Are Seventh-day Adventists Christians? A New Look at Seventh-day Adventists, Eternity magazine. September. 1956
40. Roy A. Anderson, "Human. Not Carnal." Ministry magazine, September 1956
41. R. A. Anderson, "God With Us." Ministry. April, 1957
42. R.A. Anderson. "Human, Not Carnal." Ibid.
43. R. A. Anderson. "God with Us,"Ibid.

44. Catholic Belief, 208
45. International Sabbath School Quarterly, "God Manifested in the Flesh" (Senior Division, No.72, Second Quarter, Oakland: Pacific Press Publishing Association, 1913), 26
46. International Sabbath School Quarterly, "The Incarnation and the Priesthood" (Senior Division, No.71 First Quarter, Oakland: Pacific Press Publishing Association, 1913), 14
47. Earnest W. Cox. "The Immaculate Christ," Ministry, December, 1957, 10
48. L. E. Froom, Movement of Destiny, 489
49. Op. cit., 59-60
50. Op. cit., 61-62
51. Op. cit., 383
52. L.E. Froom, Movement of Destiny, 466
53. Op. cit., 473
54. Walter Martin quoted in L.E. Froom, Movement of Destiny, 475
55. Ralph Larson, Documentary Fraud, FF-26. p.2, now in Doctrinal History Tract book
56. N.R. Gulley, Christ Our Substitute, 33
57. Op. cit., 38
58. Op. cit., 52
59. Op. cit., 53
60. The Beginning of the End, Part 18, and Doctrinal History Tract book
61. Seventh-day Adventists Believe. 49/1:4 (page 49, column 1, paragraph 4)
62. Op. cit., 46/1:3
63. Op. cit., 47/1:4-47/ 2:0
64. Op. cit., 49/ 1:1-2
65. Issues, 16
66. Issues, 47
67. Op. cit., 46-47

68. Norman Gulley, ': Jesus Our Example," Review February 1, 1990, 19, quoted in Issues, 120
69. Ibid.
70. Op. cit., 120-121
71. Op. cit., 121
72. Ibid.
73. Op. cit., 122
74. Op. cit., 122
75. Ibid.
76. Ibid.

Source: John Martin alt.religion.christian.adventist Newsgroup Article John@UponRequest.com

4) EARLY ADVENTISTS AS ARIANS
a) CONCERNING.THE TRINITY

1. Sketches of The Christian Life and Public Labours of William Miller
2. James White, Sketches of the Christian Life and Public Labours of William Miller (Battle Creek, Mich.: Steam Press of the Seventh-day Adventist Publishing Association, 1875), p. 59
3. Ibid
4. Joseph Bates, The Autobiography of Elder Joseph Bates (Battle Creek, Mich.: Steam Press of the Seventh-day Adventist Publishing Association, 1868). p. 205
5. James White, "Life Incidents," The Advent Review and Sabbath Herald, XXXI (February 18, 1868), 147. (Hereafter referred to as Review and Herald).
6. Ibid., p. 146
7. Ibid. The Christian Church referred to is generally understood to have been the Christian Connection. See L.E. Froom, The Prophetic Faith of Our Fathers

(Washington, D. C.: Review and Herald Publishing Association, 1954), IV 1057

8. James White, "Life Incidents," Review and Herald, XXXI (February 18, 1868), 147
9. A. J. Dennis, "One God," The Signs of the Times, V (May 22, 1879), 162
10. James White, Christ in the Old Testament (Oakland, Cal.: Pacific Press Publishing Association, 1877), p. 11
11. C. M. Taylor, "The Personality of the Holy Spirit," (unpublished Master's dissertation, James White Memorial Library, Andrews University, 1953), pp. 7, 8
12. (Letter in The Day-Star, IX – January 24, 1846)
13. (James White, August 5, 1852, Review & Herald, vol. 3, no. 7, page 52, par. 42)
14. (James White, December 11, 1855, Review & Herald, vol. 7, no. 11, page 85, par. 16)
15. (James White, February 7, 1856, Review & Herald, vol. 7, no. 19, page 148, par. 26)
16. J. M. Stephenson, "The Atonement," Review and Herald, VI (November 14, 1854), 128
17. Ibid
18. Ibid., p. 131
19. Ibid
20. Ibid., p. 133
21. D. W. Hull, "Bible Doctrine of Divinity," Review and Herald (November 10, 1859), 93
22. Ibid
23. Ibid
24. Ibid
25. Ibid., 194
26. D. W. Hull, "Bible Doctrine of the Divinity of Christ," Review and Herald, XIV (November 17, 1859), 201

27. Ibid
28. Review and Herald, Nov.10, 1859
29. Uriah Smith, "The Spirit of God," Review and Herald, XIII (February 17, 1859); 100
30. Ibid
31. Uriah Smith, "In the Question Chair," Review and Herald, LXVII (October 28, 1890), 664
32. Ibid
33. Uriah Smith, "The Spirit of Prophecy and Our Relation To It," The General Conference Bulletin, IV (March 18, 1891), 146
34. Ibid
35. Uriah Smith, "In the Question Chair," Review and Herald, LXVIII (November 10, 1891), 697
36. Uriah Smith, ibid., LXIX (September 6, 1892), 568
37. Uriah Smith, ibid., LXXIII (October 27, 1896), 685
38. Ibid
39. Ibid., LXXIV (March 23, 1897), 188
40. Uriah Smith, Thoughts Critical and Practical on the Book of Revelation (Battle Creek, Mich.: Steam Press of the Seventh-day Adventist Publishing Association, 1865), p. 59
41. Uriah Smith, Thoughts on the Book of Daniel and the Revelation (Battle Creek, Mich.: Review and Herald Publishing Association, 1882), p.487
42. Ibid., 1899, p. 371
43. Uriah Smith, Daniel and the Revelation (Nashville, Tenn.: Southern Publishing Association, 1941), p. 400
44. "Fundamental Beliefs of Seventh-day Adventists," Seventh-day Adventist Yearbook, (Washington, D. C.: Review and Herald Publishing Association, 1931), p. 377

45. Uriah Smith, op. cit., (Washington, D. C.: Review and Herald Publishing Association, 1944), p. 391
46. Uriah Smith, Thoughts Critical and Practical on the Book of Daniel and the Revelation (Battle Creek, Mich.: Review and Herald Publishing Association, 1882), p. 430
47. Ibid., p. 431
48. Ibid., p. 817
49. Uriah Smith, Looking Unto Jesus, (Battle Creek, Mich.: Review and Herald Publishing Company, 1898), p. 10
50. Ibid., p. 13
51. Ibid., p. 23
52. J. N. Loughborough, "Questions for Bro. Loughborough," Review and Herald, XVIII (November 5, 1861), 184
53. Ibid
54. J. N. Loughborough, "Questions for Bro. Loughborough," Review and Herald, XVIII (November 5, 1861), 184
55. Ibid
56. J. N. Loughborough, "The Spirit of God," Review and Herald, LXXV (September 20, 1898), 600
57. Review and Herald, Nov. 5, 1861
58. Gib. vol. iv, pp. 114, 345; Milner, vol. i, p. 519." RH-Nov. 5, 1861
59. Antiquities, book 11, chap. 3 & 4
60. Thoughts on Baptism, 1878
61. J. H. Waggoner, The Atonement (Oakland, Cal.: Pacific Press, 1884), p. 174
62. E. Goodrich, "No Spirit," Review and Herald, XIX (January 28, 1862), 68
63. Ibid
64. Compare with ante., p. 18. ; The Arian or Anti-Trinitarian Views Presented in Seventh-day

Adventist Literature and the Ellen G. White Answer, Erwin R. Gane, M.Div., M.Th

65. S. B. Whitney, "Both Sides," Review and Herald, XIX (March 4, 1862), 109
66. Ibid
67. Ibid
68. Ibid., 110
69. Ibid., 109. ; The Arian or Anti-Trinitarian Views Presented in Seventh-day Adventist Literature and the Ellen G. White Answer, Erwin R. Gane, M.Div., M. Th
70. D. M. Canright, "Jesus Christ the Son of God," Review and Herald, III (June 18, 1867), 1
71. Ibid
72. D. M. Canright, "The Personality of God," Review and Herald, III (August 29, 1878), 73
73. Ibid., Sept. 5, 1878, 81
74. Ibid., Sept. 19, 1878, 97
75. Ibid
76. D. M. Canright, "The Holy Spirit not a Person, but an Influence Proceeding from God," The Signs of the Times, IV (July 25, 1878), 218
77. Ibid
78. The Arian or Anti-Trinitarian Views Presented in Seventh-day Adventist Literature and the Ellen G. White Answer, Erwin R. Gane, M.Div., M. Th
79. A. J. Dennis, "One God," The Signs of the Times, V (May 22, 1879), 162
80. Ibid. ; The Arian or Anti-Trinitarian Views Presented in Seventh-day Adventist Literature and the Ellen G. White Answer, Erwin R. Gane, M.Div., M. Th
81. J. M. Hopkins, "Grieve Not The Spirit," Review and Herald, LX (July 3, 1883), 417

82. The Arian or Anti-Trinitarian Views Presented in Seventh-day Adventist Literature and the Ellen G. White Answer, Erwin R. Gane, M.Div., M. Th
83. J. E. Swift, "Our Companion," Review and Herald, LX (July 3, 1883), 421
84. G. C. Tenney, "The Comforter," Review and Herald, LX (October 30, 1883), 673
85. G. C. Tenney, "To Correspondents," Review and Herald, LXXIII (June 9, 1896), 362
86. Ibid
87. Ibid
88. J. H. Waggoner, The Atonement (Oakland, Cal.: Pacific Press, 1884), p. 174
89. Ibid., p.176
90. Ibid., p. 153
91. (J. H. Waggoner, The Atonement, 1872 ed, chapter 4, "Doctrine Of A Trinity Subversive Of The Atonement" p. 165.; 1884, The Atonement In The Light Of Nature And Revelation, page 173) (This is also found in Review & Herald, November 10, 1863, vol. 22, page 189)
92. The Atonement In the Light of Nature and Revelation p. 167-169
93. G. W. Morse, "How Many Eternal Thrones," Review and Herald LXIII (October 12, 1886), 634
94. G. W. Morse, "The Great God," Review and Herald, LXIII (May 11, 1886), 299
95. C. P. Bollman, "The Spirit of God," The Signs of the Times, XV (November 4, 1889), 663
96. Ibid
97. "Fundamental Principles of Seventh-day Adventists," Seventh-day Adventist Yearbook (Battle Creek, Mich.: Review and Herald Publishing Company, 1889), p. 147

98. E. J. Waggoner, Christ and His Righteousness (Oakland, Cal.: Pacific Press Publishing Co., 1890), p. 9, cf. 19, 21, 22
99. Ibid., p. 12
100. E. J. Waggoner, The Glad Tidings (Oakland, Cal.: Pacific Press Publishing Co., 1900), p. 13
101. Uriah Smith, Looking Unto Jesus (Battle Creek, Mich.: Review and Herald Publishing Co., 1989), p. 11
102. E. J. Waggoner, Confession of Faith ([n.p.], 1916), p. 8
103. compare with. ante, p. 42
104. D. T. Bordeau, "We May Partake of the Fullness of the Father and the Son," Review and Herald, LXVII (November 18, 1890), 707
105. T. R. Williamson, "The Holy Spirit—Is It a Person?" Review and Herald, LXVIII (October 13, 1891), 627
106. Ibid
107. Ibid
108. Samuel T. Spear, "The Bible Doctrine of the Trinity," The Bible Students' Library, No. 90, (March, 1892), 3-14. (Reprint from New York Independent, November 14, 1889)
109. Ibid., p. 9
110. Ibid., p. 3
111. Ibid., p. 7
112. Ibid
113. Ibid, p. 8
114. Ibid., pp. 11, 12
115. A. T. Jones, "Holy Spirit the Presence of Christ," The General Conference Bulletin, I (February 25, 1895), 329
116. Ibid

117. A. T. Jones (ed.), "The Faith of Jesus," Review and Herald, LXXVII (December 18, 1900), 808
118. A. T. Jones, The Consecrated Way to Christian Perfection (Mountain View, Cal.: Pacific Press Publishing Co., 1905), p. 129
119. A. T. Jones (ed.), "The Faith of Jesus," Review and Herald, LXXVII (December 25, 1900), 824
120. M. C. Wilcox, "The Spirit—Impersonal and Personal," The Signs of the Times, XXIV (August 18, 1898), 518
121. Ibid
122. M. C. Wilcox, "The Divine Unity," The Signs of the Times, XXIV (December 22, 1898), 816
123. Ibid
124. A. T. Robinson, "One God and One Mediator," Review and Herald, CVI (October 31, 1929), 6
125. Ibid
126. J. S. Washburn, "The Trinity." (Paper filed in Office of the Dean, Andrews University, Theological Seminary. [n.p., n.d.]), p. 2. (Mimeographed)
127. Ibid., p. 1
128. Ibid
129. Ibid., p. 2
130. Ibid., p.5
131. Ellen G. White, Letter 280, 1904, The Seventh-day Adventist Bible Commentary, ed. Francis D. Nichol, V (1956), 1113
132. Washburn, op. cit., p. 6
133. Ellen G. White, The Spirit of Prophecy, Vol. III (Battle Creek, Mich.: Steam Press of the Seventh-day Adventist Publishing Association, 1878), pp. 203, 204
134. Washburn, loc. cit.
135. Ibid., p. 8
136. Review and Herald, June 1, 1869

137. (R. F. Cottrell, November 19, 1857, Review & Herald, vol. 11, no. 2, page 13, par. 13)
138. Review and Herald, July 6, 1869
139. Review and Herald, Feb. 28, 1854, The Sunday God, p.50. [emphasis supplied]
140. "Uriah Smith's Restricted View Of The Atonement" (Paper supplied by L. E. Froom, General Conference of Seventh-day Adventists, [n.p., n.d.]), p.1. (Mimeographed)
141. "J. H. Waggoner's Position On The Atonement" (Paper supplied by L. E. Froom, General Conference of Seventh-day Adventists, [n.p., n.d.]), p.1. (Mimeographed)
142. Ibid
143. Ibid
144. E. G. White, The Spirit of Prophecy, Vol. III (Battle Creek, Mich.: Steam Press of the Seventh-day Adventist Publishing Association, 1878) pp. 203, 204
145. E. G. White, Manuscript 94, 1897. Cited by 5 BC, 1114
146. (The Anchor, 1997)
147. Collegiate Quarterly, March 26, 1999
148. (The Trinity Debate - Part One)
149. Dialogue Magazine, Vol. 2 No.11 November, 1991
150. Patriarchs and Prophets, p.15 Review And Herald Publishing Association, 1958
151. 8 Testimonies For The Church 263-65 (also see Ed 132, Ministry Of Healing 418-19)
152. 7 Manuscript Release 299 (see also Evangelism 616)
153. Manuscript Release #760, p 27 (Manuscript #145, 12-27-1905)
154. Notebook Leaflets 124

155. (J. B. F. March 12, 1857, Review & Herald, vol.9, no. 19, page 146, par. 20-25)
156. 6 SDA Bible Commentary 1075
157. Series B#7 p 62 (also Evangelism 615, In Heavenly Places 336)
158. Sermons and Talks, p 367-68 (7 Manuscript Release 267)
159. Series B#7 p 51 (also Evangelism 617)
160. Series B#7 p 62.
161. 5 Review And Herald Articles 143 col 3 (Reflecting Christ 178)
162. 6 Manuscript Release 167 (Manuscript #130, 10-27-1902)
163. 1 Manuscript Release 118 (Manuscript #67, 7-6-1907) (also 1 SDA Bible Commentary 1120, AG.150)
164. 5 Review And Herald Articles 341 col 1
165. Manuscript #11, 1901 (also 7 SDA Bible Commentary 908, 4 Sign Of The Times 186 col 1 (June 19, 1901)
166. 6 SDA Bible Commentary 1074 (also Faith I Live By 146)
167. 6 Manuscript Release 27 (Manuscript #78, 1905)
168. Atlantic Union Conference Record 10-7-1907
169. Evangelism 307-08 (Letter 129, 1903) (Also Our High Calling 157)
170. 5 Review And Herald Articles 45 col 1
171. 6 Manuscript Release 389 (Manuscript #45, 5-14-1904)
172. 6 Manuscript Release 29 (Sermon given March 10, 1908)
173. Sermon given Oct 20, 1906 (See Manuscript Release #307 p 2, 4, 7 Manuscript Release 267-68)
174. Camp-meeting Sermon June 27, 1907 (See Manuscript Release #135, p 4)

175. Sermon given April 3, 1901 in the early morning meeting at the 1901 General Conference Session (see 1901 General Conference Bulletin, p 36-37, Lift Him Up 109)
176. Talk given April 14, 1901 at the 1901 General Conference Session (see 1901 General Conference Bulletin, p 215)
177. 5 Review And Herald Articles 533 col 2
178. Pacific Union Record 7-2-1908
179. 5 SDA Bible Commentary 1110 (Manuscript #92, 1901)
180. 4 Sign Of The Times 282 col 1 (March 11, 1903)
181. 5 Review And Herald Articles 142 col 3
182. 6 Manuscript Release 26 (Letter 53, 1-26-1904) (also 4 Sign Of The Times 399 col 1 (Aug 16, 1905, Reflecting Christ 107)
183. 4 Manuscript Release 368-69 (Letter 53, 1-26-1904) (also 4 Sign Of The Times Articles 399 col 1 (Aug 16, 1905)
184. 7 SDA Bible Commentary 959 (also Sons And Daughters Of God 351)
185. Southern Watchman 2-23-1904 (also 4 Sign Of The Times Articles 512, In Heavenly Places 176)
186. 6 Manuscript Release 166 (Manuscript #118, 10-6-1902)
187. 19 Manuscript Release 235
188. Notebook Leaflets 12
189. (Letter of W. C. White to H. W. Carr, April 30, 1935)
190. (S.D.A. Bible Student's Source Book, pp. 298, 299)
191. (Review & Herald, November 8, 1898)
192. (March 20, 1856, Review & Herald, vol. 7, no. 25, page 199)

193. [Portions of a letter written by J. S. Washburn in 1939. This letter was liked by a conference president so much that he distributed it to 32 of his ministers.]
194. (Adventist Review, January 6, 1994, pp. 10, 11)
195. Adventist Review, October 31, 1996, p.12- Gordon Jenson
196. Respected Bible Scholar, Raoul Dederen - Andrews University

b) CONCERNING.THE FATHER

1. Review and Herald, Aug. 5, 1852, p.52.
2. (James White, January 4, 1881, Review & Herald)
3. Review and Herald, Jan. 27, 1874 p.52
4. Review and Herald, Aug. 29, 1878
5. Bible Questions and Answers Concerning Man, pp. 3-4
6. Christ and His Righteousness, p. 19

c) CONCERNING.THE SON

1. Review and Herald, Jan. 4, 1881
2. Review and Herald, Nov. 29, (1877), p. 172
3. The Day Star, Jan. 24, 1846
4. Review and Herald, Dec. 11, 1855, p.85
5. Review and Herald, Sept. 7, 1869
6. The Captain Of Our Salvation, 1886, p. 17
7. Signs of the Times, April 8, 1889 p. 214
8. Christ And His Righteousness, 1890, p. 9
9. Ibid. p. 12
10. Ibid. p. 19
11. Ibid. p. 21, 22
12. Review and Herald, April 14, 1896, p. 232

13. Review and Herald, Aug. 1, 1899 (Lessons on Faith, p. 154.)
14. (A. T. Jones, General Conference Bulletin 1895, page 448)
15. Review and Herald, Nov. 14, 1854
16. (J. M. Stephenson, November 21, 1854, Review & Herald, vol. 6, no. 15, page 114, paragraph 1-6)
17. Review and Herald, July 6, 1869
18. Review and Herald, Oct. 12, 1869, p. 123
19. Thoughts on the Book of Daniel and the Revelation 1882, p. 430
20. Looking Unto Jesus, 1898, p. 10
21. (Uriah Smith, 1898, Looking Unto Jesus, pages 23, 24)
22. The Autobiography of Elder Joseph Bates, 1868, pp. 204, 205
23. Review and Herald, Nov.10, 1859
24. (G. W. Amadon, September 24, 1861, Review & Herald, vol. 18, pages 136, par. 1-10)
25. Lift Him Up, p. 235, par 3 Chapter Title: Lift Him Up as the Crucified One 1903
26. The Desire of Ages, p. 336, par 1 Chapter Title: "Peace, Be Still"; p.313 1898 & 1940 edition
27. 4 Sign Of The Times 141 col. 3 (see also Evangelism 615)
28. Evangelism 615
29. Desire Of Ages 530
30. 2 Review And Herald Articles 151 col. 2 & 3 (also 5 SDA Bible Commentary 1126-27)
31. 5 Review And Herald Articles 227 col. 2 (also 1SM 247)

d) CONCERNING.THE HOLY SPIRIT

1. Review and Herald, Sept. 13, 1898, p. 690

2. Signs of the Times, June 2, 1898
3. Questions And Answers Vol.11, 1919, 1938 editions, p.3739. In the 1945 edition p.33-35
4. Questions And Answers Gathered From The Question Corner Department Of The Signs Of The Times, Pacific Press, 1911, p.18182
5. M.C. Wilcox, Signs of the Times, Feb. 26, 1908
6. Christ And His Righteousness, 1892, p.23
7. Signs of the Times, Oct. 26, 1891, p.342
8. Review and Herald, Oct. 28, 1890
9. The Spirit Of God; Its Offices And Manifestations, 1877
10. The Coming King, page 33
11. Desire of Ages, 669-70
12. 3 Review & Herald Articles 229 col. 2 (Feb 12, 1895)
13. 2 Review & Herald Articles 617 col. 3 (Nov 29, 1892)
14. 2 Manuscript Releases 32 (Letter 89b, 3-22-1897)
15. (Review and Herald, December 3, 1908)
16. (Manuscript 41, 1897 quoted in The Seventh-day Adventist Bible Commentary, vol. 6, p. 1112)
17. (This Day with God, p. 257)
18. (Desire of Ages, p. 805)
19. 12 Manuscript Release 260-61 (Manuscript 41, 1897)
20. Desire Of Ages, 245
21. Desire Of Ages, 277
22. Letter 124, 1897 (see also AH 350)
23. 4 Sign Of The Times 503 col. 1 (March 8, 1910)

e) **ELLEN WHITE'S ARIAN VIEWS**

1. (Spirit of Prophecy, I, p.17-18)

f) MOVING TO DEITY OF CHRIST AND THE SUPPOSED TRINITY

1. (Manuscript 101, 1897)
2. (The Adventist Heritage, Vol. 4, No. 2, 1977)

g) THE QUESTIONS ON DOCTRINAL DENIAL

1. (Eternity, September 1956 - emphasis is in original)
2. (Ibid.)
3. (Ibid.)
4. (Questions on Doctrine, pp. 354, 355 - emphasis in original)
5. (Eternity, Sept. 1956)
6. (Questions on Doctrine, p. 381 - emphasis in the original)

h) PRESENT POSITION

1. (Letter of W. Richard Lesher to Walter Martin, April 29, 1983)
2. (The Kingdom of the Cult, p. 410)
3. (Seventh-day Adventists Believe ..., p. 5)
4. (Seventh-day Adventists Believe ..., p. 313)
5. (Ibid., p. 365)
6. (Ibid., p. 110)
7. (Questions on Doctrine, p. 9)
8. (Seventh-day Adventists Believe ..., p. 4)
9. (Seventh-day Adventist Church Manual, p. 43 - 1981 edition)
10. (Ibid., p. 381 - emphasis in original)
11. http://www.adventistreview.org/2002-1524/story3.html

12. Proclamation Magazine, Volume 5, Issue 2, March/ April 2004 Stephen D. Pitcher

5) ELLEN G. WHITE'S ABERRANT VIEWS OF JESUS AND GOD

1. The Great Controversy, The Origin of Evil Chapter 29, p. 493
2. Patriarchs and Prophets, Why Is Sin Permitted Chapter 1, p. 34
3. Ibid., p.35
4. Ibid., p.36
5. Ibid., p.37
6. (Spirit of Prophecy, vol. 1, pp. 17, 18)
7. Ibid., p.761
8. Desire of Ages, p.210
9. (Spirit of Prophecy, vol. 2, p. 67)
10. The Desire of Ages, page 435, par 2 Chapter Title: Who Is the Greatest?; page 420-421, par 3 in 1940 edition

a) JESUS, AS AN ANGEL

1. The Signs of the Times, September 16, 1880, par 9 Article Title: The Great Rebellion; or, the Conflict Ended
2. The Spirit of Prophecy Volume One, p. 348, par 1 Chapter Title: Joshua; Spiritual Gifts. Volume 4A, p. 61, par 4 Chapter Title: Joshua

c) JESUS' SINFUL FALLEN HUMAN NATURE

1. (Review & Herald, Nov. 29, 1877)

d) WHO IS IN THE 'FULNESS OF DEITY BODILY?

1. (Evangelism, p. 614; The Faith I Live By, p.39; Testimonies...warning p.62; Bible Training School, Mar 1, 1906,).

e) IS ELLEN G.WHITE & THE SEVENTH-DAY ADVENTISTS GUILTY OF THE TRITHEISM HERESY?

1. (CW 45)
2. (EW 45)
3. (CW 47)
4. (Counsels to Writers and Editors, p. 47)
5. The Foundation Of Our Faith, Allen Stump
6. SDA Bible Commentary, vol. 1, p. 215
7. Evangelism, p. 615. Sabbath School Network 1998
8. Open Face, No.18 Dec 2000 David Clayton
9. 100 And More Mysteries About The Trinity, Lloyd G.Martin

6) IS JESUS MICHAEL THE ARCHANGEL AS THE SDA TEACH?

1. Desire of Ages p. 99 & 379; Spiritual Gifts, Va, p.158; and Prophets & Kings, p. 572
2. (manuscript 150, SDA Commentary V, p. 1129)
3. (Test VIII, p. 268)
4. (manuscript 59)
5. (manuscript 129; Commentary VII, p.971)
6. (Ibid., p.798)
7. (manuscript 15, 1897)

8. (1919 Bible Conference, p.62)
9. (Jude 9, Spiritual Gifts, IV, p. 158)
10. (Daniel 10:13, Prophets & Kings, p.572)
11. (Desire of Ages, p.99)
12. (Ibid. 379)
13. SDA Commentary vol. III, p.972
14. (Ibid., 973)

7) DID JESUS HAVE A SINFUL FALLEN HUMAN NATURE?

1. SDA Believe, p. 49
2. (Ibid., p. 1128)

8) WILL THE REAL JESUS PLEASE STAND UP?

1. (Manuscript 140, SDA Commentary V, p. 1129)
2. (SDA Commentary VII, 971- 978; manuscript 15, 1897; manuscript 59)
3. (Great Controversy p.266, 306, 329; 1888 edition)
4. (Early Writings, p. 36).
5. (Spiritual Gifts I, pp. 158-160)
6. A Word to the Little Flock, p. 12, par 4
7. A Word to the Little Flock, p. 12, par 5 Ellen G. White: The Early Years Volume 1 - 1827-1862, p. 125, par 6 Chapter Title: Entering Married

9) FINALLY BRETHREN ...

1. Christ's Object Lessons, p. 263, par 3 Chapter Title: A Great Gulf Fixed
2. Special Testimony to Battle Creek Church, p. 32, par 1; Testimonies to Ministers and Gospel Workers, p. 134, par 1 Chapter Title: God's High Standard ;

The Faith I Live By, p. 179, par 5 Chapter Title: Here And Hereafter
3. This Day with God, p. 87, par 1 Chapter Title: Choosing and Doing
4. Manuscript 104, Sept. 28, 1897, "Condemned by the Jews." The Upward Look, p. 285, par 5 Chapter Title: Two Spirits in the World
5. The Signs of the Times, February 24, 1904, par. 7, Article Title: The Narrow Way "Freely Ye Have Received, Freely Give."; The Upward Look, p. 379, par 5 Chapter Title: Stewards of God's Grace
6. Christian Temperance and Bible Hygiene, p. 15, par 3 Chapter Title: Our Reasonable Service; The Signs of the Times, August 10, 1915, par 12 Article Title: Satan and Our Appetites
7. Bible Echo and Signs of the Times, October 15, 1900, par 10, Article Title: Ye Are Not Your Own; The Youth's Instructor, November 8, 1900, par. 10 Article Title: Ye Are Not Your Own
8. Advent Review and Sabbath Herald, September 28, 1897, par. 4 Article Title: Preach the Word
9. The Signs of the Times, April 11, 1895, par. 4 Article Title: Revelation of God through Christ
10. The Signs of the Times, February 13, 1896, par. 4 Article Title: The Test of Loyalty
11. Manuscript Releases Volume Eleven, p. 341, par. 1 Chapter Title: Attending and Acting in Theatrical Performances
12. Manuscript Releases Volume Twenty-one, p. 402, par. 2 Chapter Title: Call to a Higher Standard
13. Sermons and Talks Volume One, p. 250, par. 3 Chapter Title: Seeking Heavenly Treasures
14. The Ellen G. White 1888 Materials, p. 814, par. 1 Chapter Title: Danger of False Ideas on Justification by Faith

15. Advent Review and Sabbath Herald, May 7, 1901, par. 1 Article Title: The Great Standard of Righteousness
16. Second Advent Review and Sabbath Herald, March 28, 1882, par. 2 Article Title: Where Are We Drifting?
17. Book of Martyrs, Book 6, Chapter 37
18. Seventh-day Adventism Renounced by D M Canright (1914)
19. The Faith I Live By, page 185, par. 4 Chapter Title: Here And Hereafter ® S.D.A. Bible Commentary Vol. 6, page 1093, par. 2 Chapter Title: 1 Corinthians

APPENDIX

3) THE PERSON AND DEITY OF THE HOLY SPIRIT

1. Notes on Galatians, by Hogg and Vine, p. 193
2. Vine's Expository Dictionary of Biblical Words) (Copyright (C) 1985, Thomas Nelson Publishers

5) THE BIBLICAL VIEW OF MAN'S NATURE

1. Vine's Expository Dictionary, p.73

KEY TO ABBREVIATIONS OF E.G. WHITE WRITINGS

AA .... Acts of the Apostles.
AG .... God's Amazing Grace.
AUCR .... Atlantic Union Conference Record.

1-7BC.	SDA Bible Commentary, Vol. 1-7.
CH	Counsels on Health.
COL	Christ's Object Lessons.
CT	Counsels to Parents and Teachers.
DA	Desire of Ages.
Ed	Education.
Ev.	Evangelism.
FLB	Faith I Live By.
GCB	General Conference Bulletin.
IHP	In Heavenly Places.
LHU	Lift Him Up.
LP	Sketches from the Life of Paul.
MB	Mount of Blessings.
MH	Ministry of Healing.
MLT	My Life Today.
MM	Medical Ministry.
1-21MR	Manuscript Releases, vol 1-21.
MYP	Messages to Young People.
NL	Notebook Leaflets.
OHC	Our High Calling.
PK	Prophets and Kings.
PUR	Pacific Union Record.
RC	Reflecting Christ.
1-6RH	Review and Herald Articles, vol 1-6.
SC	Steps to Christ.
SD	Sons and Daughters of God.

1-3SM .... Selected Messages, book 1-3.
1-4SP .... Spirit of Prophecy, vol 1-4.
1-4ST .... Signs of the Times Articles, vol 1-4.
1-9T .... Testimonies for the Church, vol 1-9.
TDG .... This Day With God.
TM .... Testimonies to Ministers.
UL .... Upward Look.

BIBLIOGRAPHY

a. GENERAL BOOKS AND PAMPHLETS

8 Testimonies For The Church (also see Ed 132, Ministry Of Healing

100 And More Mysteries About The Trinity, Lloyd G. Martin

Adventist Review, March 1977

A. J. Dennis, "One God," The Signs of the Times, V (May 22, 1879),

Answers to Objections by F. D. Nichol

Antiquities, book 11

A. T. Jones, 1901, Ecclesiastical Empire

A.T. Jones, General Conference-Bulletin 1893

A. T. Jones, General Conference Bulletin, 1895.

A. T. Jones, "Holy Spirit the Presence of Christ," The General Conference Bulletin, I (February 25, 1895

A. T. Jones, Review, February 18, 1896.

A. T. Jones, The Consecrated Way to Christian Perfection (Mountain View, Cal.: Pacific Press Publishing Co., 1905),

A. T. Jones (ed.), "The Faith of Jesus," Review and Herald, LXXVII (December 18, 1900)

A. T. Jones (ed.), "The Faith of Jesus," Review and Herald, LXXVII (December 25, 1900)

A. T. Jones, 1891, The Two Republics

A. T. Robinson, "One God and One Mediator," Review and Herald, CVI (October 31, 1929

Atonement In the Light of Nature and Revelation

A. W. Semmens, Bible Echo, April 15, 1892.

Bible Doctrine of the Trinity," The Bible Students' Library, No. 90, (March, 1892), 3-14. (Reprint from New York Independent, November 14, 1889)

Bible Questions and Answers Concerning Man

Bible Readings for the Home 1915 edition

Bible Readings for the Home 1944 edition

Bible Readings (Washington, D.C. Review and Herald Publishing Association, 1949

Book of Enoch

"Both Sides," Review and Herald, XIX (March 4, 1862)

Catholic Belief

Christian Temperance and Bible Hygiene

Clear Word Bible (1994),

Correspondents," Review and Herald, LXXIII (June 9, 1896)

C. P. Bollman, "The Spirit of God," The Signs of the Times, XV (November 4, 1889

D. M. Canright, "Jesus Christ the Son of God," Review and Herald, III (June 18, 1867)

D. M. Canright, "The Holy Spirit not a Person, but an Influence Proceeding from God," The Signs of the Times, IV (July 25, 1878),

D. M. Canright, "The Personality of God," Review and Herald, III (August 29, 1878),

Donald Grey Barnhouse, "Are Seventh-day Adventists Christians? A New Look at Seventh-day Adventists, Eternity magazine. September. 1956

D. T. Bordeau, "We May Partake of the Fullness of the Father and the Son," Review and Herald, LXVII (November 18, 1890)

D. W. Hull, "Bible Doctrine of Divinity," Review and Herald (November 10, 1859

D. W. Hull, "Bible Doctrine of the Divinity of Christ," Review and Herald, XIV (November 17, 1859)

Earnest W. Cox. "The Immaculate Christ," Ministry, December, 1957

E. J. Waggoner, Christ and His Righteousness (Oakland, Cal.: Pacific Press Publishing Co., 1890)

E. J. Waggoner, Confession of Faith ([n.p.], 1916)

E. J. Waggoner. General Conference Bulletin, 1891

E. J. Waggoner, General Conference Bulletin, 1897.

E. J. Waggoner. Series No.4. Lincoln. Nebraska, 1897

E. Farnsworth, Signs, May 6, 1897.

E. Goodrich, "No Spirit," Review and Herald, XIX (January 28, 1862)

Evangelism, p. 615. Sabbath School Network 1998

Eternity Magazine, September 1956 Donald Grey Barnhouse

Face, No.18 Dec 2000 David Clayton

Frances D. Nichol, Answers to Objections, Review and Herald, 1952

"Fundamental Beliefs of Seventh-day Adventists," Seventh-day Adventist Yearbook, (Washington, D. C.: Review and Herald Publishing Association, 1931)

G. C. Tenney, editorial, Bible Echo, April 15, 1889

G. C. Tenney, "The Comforter," Review and Herald, LX (October 30, 1883)

Gesenius' Hebrew Chaldee Lexicon of the OT

In Heavenly Places

James White, August 5, 1852, Review & Herald, vol. 3, no. 7

James White, December 11, 1855, Review & Herald, vol. 7, no. 11

James White, February 7, 1856, Review & Herald, vol. 7, no. 19

James White, Sketches of the Christian Life and Public Labours of William Miller (Battle Creek, Mich.: Steam Press of the Seventh-day Adventist Publishing Association, 1875)

J. E. Swift, "Our Companion," Review and Herald, LX (July 3, 1883)

"J. H. Waggoner's Position On The Atonement" (Paper supplied by L. E. Froom, General Conference of Seventh-day Adventists, (Mimeographed).

J. H. Waggoner, The Atonement (Oakland, Cal.: Pacific Press, 1884)

J. H. Waggoner, The Glad Tidings (Oakland, Cal.: Pacific Press Publishing Co., 1900)

J. M. Hopkins, "Grieve Not The Spirit," Review and Herald, LX (July 3, 1883)

J.M. Stephenson, "The Atonement," Review and Herald, VI (November 14, 1854),

J. N. Loughborough, "Questions for Bro. Loughborough," Review and Herald, XVIII (November 5, 1861),

J. N. Loughborough, "The Spirit of God," Review and Herald, LXXV (September 20, 1898)

Joseph Bates, The Autobiography of Elder Joseph Bates (Battle Creek, Mich.: Steam Press of the Seventh-day Adventist Publishing Association, 1868)

J. S. Washburn, "The Trinity." (Paper filed in Office of the Dean, Andrews University, Theological Seminary (Mimeographed)

Kingdom of the Cults, Dr. Walter Martin

L.E. Froom, Movement of Destiny
Letter in The Day-Star, IX – January 24, 1846
Life of E.G. White, Dudly Canright
Light Bearers to the Remnant
Llewellen Wilcox, Signs of the Times, March, 1927
Looking Unto Jesus, 1898 Uriah Smith
M. C. Wilcox, "The Divine Unity," The Signs of the Times, XXIV (December 22, 1898)
M. C. Wilcox, "The Spirit—Impersonal and Personal," The Signs of the Times, XXIV (August 18, 1898)
Medical Ministry
Ministry, September 1956
Morse, "How Many Eternal Thrones," Review and Herald LXIII (October 12, 1886),
Nelson's Illustrated Bible Dictionary) (Copyright (C) 1986, Thomas Nelson Publishers)
Notes on Galatians, by Hogg and Vine
Norman Gulley, ': Jesus Our Example," Review February 1, 1990
N.R. Gulley, Christ Our Substitute
Oriental Watchman
Our High Calling
Ralph Larson, Documentary Fraud, FF-26. now in Doctrinal History Tract book
R. F. Cottrell, November 19, 1857, Review & Herald, vol. 11, no. 2
Roy A Anderson, "God With Us." Ministry. April, 1957
Roy A Anderson, "Human. Not Carnal." Ministry magazine, September 1956
Seventh-day Adventism Renounced by D M Canright (1914)
Seventh-day Adventists Answer Questions On Doctrine. Washington, D. C.: Review and Herald Publishing Association, 1957. This work makes a clear distinction between the Arianism of the early

Adventists and the extreme positions taken by Socinians.

Smith, Uriah. Daniel and the Revelation. Nashville, Tenn.: Southern Publishing Association, 1941. Part of the Arianism excluded and part retained.

S. H. Haskell Bible Echo, March 15, 1889.

S. N. Haskell, Signs, January 17, 1900.

Sons And Daughters Of God

Stephen Haskell, Bible Echo, February 15, 1892.

Stephen Haskell, Signs, April 2, 1896.

Strong's Exhaustive Concordance Dictionary

Thayer's Greek-English Lexicon of the NT

The Arian or Anti-Trinitarian Views Presented in Seventh-day Adventist Literature and the Ellen G. White Answer, Erwin R. Gane, M.Div., M. Th

The Autobiography of Elder Joseph Bates, 1868

The Captain Of Our Salvation, 1886 C.W. Stone

The Christian Life and Public Labours of William Miller, James White

The Coming King, James Edward White

The Faith I Live By

The Foundation Of Our Faith, Allen Stump

"The Great God," Review and Herald, LXIII (May 11, 1886),

The Indian Christian, Jan 1927

The Spirit Of God; Its Offices And Manifestations, 1877 J.H. Waggoner

The Trinity Debate - Part One, V.R. Christensen

The Truth about Seventh-day Adventism, Dr. Walter Martin

The Upward Look

This Day with God, James Edward White

Thoughts on Baptism, 1878.

Tobit (LXX)

T. R. Williamson, "The Holy Spirit—Is It a Person?" Review and Herald, LXVIII (October 13, 1891)

Uriah Smith, Daniel and the Revelation (Nashville, Tenn.: Southern Publishing Association, 1941

Uriah Smith, "In the Question Chair," Review and Herald, LXVII (October 28, 1890)

Uriah Smith, "In the Question Chair," Review and Herald, LXVIII (November 10, 1891)

Uriah Smith, Looking Unto Jesus (Battle Creek, Mich.: Review and Herald Publishing Co., 1989)

Uriah Smith, Looking Unto Jesus, (Battle Creek, Mich.: Review and Herald Publishing Company, 1898),

"Uriah Smith's Restricted View Of The Atonement" (Paper supplied by L. E. Froom, General Conference of Seventh-day Adventists, (Mimeographed).

Uriah Smith, "The Spirit of God," Review and Herald, XIII (February 17, 1859)

Uriah Smith, "The Spirit of Prophecy and Our Relation To It," The General Conference Bulletin, IV (March 18, 1891)

Uriah Smith, Thoughts Critical and Practical on the Book of Daniel and the Revelation (Battle Creek, Mich.: Review and Herald Publishing Association, 1882),

Uriah Smith, Thoughts Critical and Practical on the Book of Revelation (Battle Creek, Mich.: Steam Press of the Seventh-day Adventist Publishing Association, 1865

Uriah Smith, Thoughts on the Book of Daniel and the Revelation (Battle Creek, Mich.: Review and Herald Publishing Association, 1882)

Uriah Smith, (Washington, D. C.: Review and Herald Publishing Association, 1944

Vine's Expository Dictionary of Biblical Words) (Copyright (C) 1985, Thomas Nelson Publishers)
Walter Martin, quoted in L.E. Froom, Movement of Destiny
William Branson, General Conference president, Drama of the Ages printed by Southern Publishing Association in 1950
W. W. Prescott, Bible Echo, January 6, 1896.
W.W. Prescott, Sermon October 31, 1895; printed in Bible Echo, January 6, 13, 1896.
W. W. Prescott's sermon was printed in the January 6 and 13, 1896, issues of the Bible Echo (SDA's Australian journal).

b. GENERAL PERIODICAL ARTICLES

1919 Bible Conference
A Word to the Little Flock, facsimile
Andrews University, Respected Bible Scholar, Raoul Dederen
Advent Review and Sabbath Herald, May 7, 1901
Adventist Review, January 6, 1994
Adventist Review, October 31, 1996, - Gordon Jenson
Advent Review and Sabbath Herald, September 28, 1897
Atlantic Union Conference Record 10-7-1907
Bible Echo and Signs of the Times, October 15, 1900
Christ's Object Lessons
Collegiate Quarterly, March 26, 1999
Counsels to Writers and Editors
Dialogue Magazine, Vol. 2 No.11 November, 1991
Evangelism, Sabbath School Network 1998
International Sabbath School Quarterly. "Baptism and Temptation of Jesus," Senior

Division, No.56, Second Quarter, 1909, Pacific Press)

International Sabbath School Quarterly, "God Manifested in the Flesh" (Senior Division, No.72, Second Quarter, Oakland: Pacific Press Publishing Association, 1913)

International Sabbath School Quarterly, "The Flesh and the Spirit" (Senior Division, No. 75. First Quarter, 1914, Pacific Press)

International Sabbath School Quarterly, "The Godly Life" (Senior Division, No. 112, Second Quarter, 1923, Pacific Press),

International Sabbath School Quarterly, "The Incarnation and the Priesthood" (Senior Division, No. 71, First Quarter. 1913. Pacific Press)

International Sabbath School Quarterly, "The Last Adam" (Senior Division. No.105. Third Quarter. 1921. Pacific Press)

International Sabbath School Quarterly. "The Purpose of the Incarnation" (Senior Division. No.103. First Quarter. 1921

International Sabbath School Quarterly, "The Spirit of Sacrifice" a special testimony (Senior Division, No. 41, Third Quarter, 1905, Oakland: Pacific Press Publishing Association)

Issues

Letter of W. C. White to H. W. Carr, April 30, 1935

Letter of W. Richard Lesher to Walter Martin, April 29, 1983

Notebook Leaflets

Pacific Union Record 7-2-1908

Portions of a letter written by J. S. Washburn in 1939. This letter was liked by a conference president so much that he distributed it to 32 of his ministers.

Proclamation Magazine, Volume 5, Issue 2, March/April 2004 Stephen D. Pitcher
Questions And Answers Gathered From The Question Corner Department Of The Signs Of The Times, Pacific Press, 1911
Questions And Answers Vol.11, 1919, 1938, 1945 editions
Questions on Doctrine
Questions of Doctrine Annotated Edition by George R Knight
Review And Herald Articles Reflecting Christ
Review and Herald, Aug. 5, 1852
Review and Herald, Feb. 28, 1854, The Sunday God
Review and Herald, Nov. 14, 1854
Review and Herald, Dec. 11, 1855
Review & Herald, vol. 7, no. 25 March 20, 1856
Review & Herald, vol.9, no. 19 J. B. F. March 12, 1857
Review and Herald, Nov.10, 1859
Review & Herald, vol. 18 G. W. Amadon, September 24, 1861
Review and Herald, Nov. 5, 1861
Review & Herald, November 10, 1863, vol. 22
Review and Herald, June 1, 1869
Review and Herald, July 6, 1869
Review and Herald, Sept. 7, 1869
Review and Herald, Oct. 12, 1869 John Matteson
Review and Herald, Jan. 27, 1874
Review and Herald, Nov. 29, (1877)
Review and Herald, Aug. 29, 1878
Review & Herald, January 4, 1881, James White
Review and Herald, June 17, 1884. (A. T. Jones, 1891, The Two Republics
Review, Feb 10, 1885 & Dec 15, 1896
Review and Herald, Oct. 28, 1890
Review & Herald Articles (Nov 29, 1892)

Review & Herald Articles (Feb 12, 1895)
Review and Herald, April 14, 1896 W.W. Prescott
Review and Herald, Sept. 13, 1898
Review & Herald, November 8, 1898
Review and Herald, Aug. 1, 1899 Lessons on Faith
Review and Herald, December 3, 1908
S.D.A. Bible Student's Source Book
Second Advent Review and Sabbath Herald, March 28, 1882
Sermons and Talks
Sermon given April 3, 1901 in the early morning meeting at the 1901 General Conference Session (see 1901 General Conference Bulletin)
Seventh-day Adventists Believe
Seventh-day Adventist Church Manual, 1981 edition
Signs of the Times, September 16, 1880
Signs of the Times, April 8, 1889
Signs of the Times, Oct. 26, 1891
Signs of the Times, April 11, 1895
Signs of the Times, February 13, 1896
Signs of the Times, June 2, 1898
Sign Of The Times (March 11, 1903)
Signs of the Times, February 24, 1904
Sign Of The Times Articles (Aug 16, 1905)
Signs of the Times, Feb. 26, 1908 M.C. Wilcox
Sign Of The Times (March 8, 1910) James Edward White
Signs of the Times, August 10, 1915
Signs of the Times, March 1927
Southern Watchman -1904
Special Testimony to Battle Creek Church
Spiritual Gifts IV
Talk given April 14, 1901 at the 1901 General Conference Session (see 1901 General Conference Bulletin)
Testimonies to Ministers and Gospel Workers

The Adventist Heritage, Vol. 4, No. 2, 1977
The Anchor, 1997
The Faith I Live
The Youth's Instructor, November 8, 1900

a. ELLEN G. WHITE BOOKS

_____. Daniel and the Revelation. Washington, D. C.: Review and Herald Publishing Association, 1944. All Arian teachings excluded.

_____. Patriarchs and Prophets. Mountain View, California: Pacific Press Publishing Association, 1890. Contains valuable references to the God of the Old Testament. Contains valuable references to the God of the Old Testament.

_____. Selected Messages. 2 books, Washington, D. C.: Review and Herald Publishing Association, 1958. A collection of previously unpublished materials including much on the nature of Christ.

_____. Testimonies for the Church. 9 volumes. Mountain View, California: Pacific Press Publishing Association, 1855 - 1909. Contains invaluable instruction for the Church including declarations on many doctrinal matters.

_____. The Acts of the Apostles. Mountain View, California: Pacific Press Publishing Association, 1911. The record of the spread of Christianity from Jerusalem to Rome. Contains certain statements on the nature of God.

_____. The Desire of Ages. Mountain View, California: Pacific Press Publishing Association, 1898 & 1948 editions. A masterpiece as a depiction of Christ during the incarnation.

_____. The Great Controversy. Mountain View, California: Pacific Press Publishing Association,

1888. A comprehensive presentation of the Seventh-day Adventist view of history.

_____. The Ministry of Healing. Mountain View, California: Pacific Press Publishing Association, 1905. Contains a number of enlightening statements on the nature of God.

_____. The Spirit of Prophecy. 4 volumes. Battle Creek, Michigan: Steam Press of the Seventh-day Adventist Publishing Association, 1870-1884. An invaluable indication of official S.D.A. opinion on the nature of God and the atonement.

d. ELLEN G. WHITE PERIODICAL ARTICLES

Ellen G. White 1888 Materials
Ellen G. White, Letter 280, 1904,
Ellen G. White: The Early Years Volume 1 - 1827-1862
Letters 25, 32, 83, and 84, 1895
Letter 53, 1-26-1904
Letter 124, 1897
Lift Him Up, Chapter Title: Lift Him Up as the Crucified One 1903
Manuscript Releases Volume Eleven
Manuscript Releases Volume Twenty-One
Manuscripts #15, 1897
Manuscripts #'s 19, 23, 47 and 52, 1895
Manuscript Release #26
Manuscript Release #27 (Manuscript #78, 1905)
Manuscript Release #29 (Sermon given March 10, 1908)
Manuscript Releases #32 (Letter 89b, 3-22-1897)
Manuscript #41, 1897 quoted in The Seventh-day Adventist Bible Commentary, volume 6
Manuscript #59
Manuscript #92, 1901

Manuscript #94, 1897, E. G. White
Manuscript #101, 1897
Manuscript #104, Sept. 28, 1897
Manuscript Release #118 (Manuscript #67, 7-6-1907)
Manuscript #129
Manuscript #140
Manuscript #150
Manuscript Release #166 (Manuscript #118, 10-6-1902)
Manuscript Release #167 (Manuscript #130, -1902)
Manuscript Release #135 Camp-meeting Sermon June 27, 1907
Manuscript Release #235
Manuscript Release #260-61 (Manuscript 41, 1897)
Manuscript Release #267
Manuscript Release #299
Manuscript Release #307 (Manuscript Release 267-68) Sermon given Oct 20, 1906
Manuscript Release #389 (Manuscript #45, 5-14-1904)
Manuscript Release #760, (Manuscript #145, 1905)

e. ENCYCLOPEDIA ARTICLES

Jewish Encyclopedia
The Day Star, Jan. 24, 1846

f. YEARBOOKS

1889 Yearbook

g. COMMENTARIES

SDA Bible Commentary Volume 1
The Seventh-day Adventist Bible Commentary, ed. Francis D. Nichol, V (1956),

h. UNPUBLISHED MATERIALS

John Martin alt.religion.christian.adventist Newsgroup Article John@UponRequest.com

i. INTERNET WEBSITES

http://www.whiteestate.org
http://www.egwtext.whiteestate.org/published-writings.html

LaVergne, TN USA
21 February 2011
217373LV00002B/22/A